American Insurgents

American Insurgents

Richard Seymour

A Brief History of American Anti-Imperialism

Haymarket Books
Chicago, Illinois

Published in 2012 by Haymarket Books
PO Box 180165
Chicago, IL 60618
www.haymarketbooks.org
773–583–7884

ISBN: 978-1-60846-141-7

Trade distribution:
In the US, Consortium Book Sales and Distribution, www.cbsd.com
In Canada, Publishers Group Canada, www.pgcbooks.ca
In the UK, Turnaround Publisher Services, www.turnaround-uk.com
In Australia, Palgrave Macmillan, www.palgravemacmillan.com.au
All other countries, Publishers Group Worldwide, www.pgw.com

Cover design by Josh On. Cover image of antiwar protesters
at an ROTC ceremony at Ohio State University in 1970.
Associated Press Photo.

Published with the generous support of Lannan Foundation
and the Wallace Global Fund.

Printed in the United States by union labor on FSC certified paper stock.

Library of Congress cataloging-in-publication data is available.

10 9 8 7 6 5 4 3 2 1

SUSTAINABLE FORESTRY INITIATIVE

Certified Sourcing
www.sfiprogram.org
SFI-01234

Contents

To Marie, with all my love

Preface

It is yet another Civilized Power, with its banner of the Prince of Peace in one hand and its loot-basket and its butcher-knife in the other.

—Mark Twain

Empire, Naked and Unbound

That the United States is an empire is no longer a matter of controversy. Until 2001, America's awesome global dominion had been referenced only in coy euphemisms—"leadership," "diplomacy," "dominance," or, if you were a particularly brazen Realpolitiker, "hegemony." American statesmen would respond with a mixture of bemusement, indignation, and faux-naiveté to the idea that the United States was an empire. *What, us? You misspeak. We lead, we provide an example, we may even exercise a certain power due to our unique gifts. But we are not imperialists, by no means.* And perhaps in official disavowals, there was the spirit of a saying attributed to Jimmy Hoffa: Being powerful is like being a lady. If you have to say you are, you probably ain't.

But the World Trade Center attacks changed this, just as they changed everything else. Journalists, academics, intellectuals, and even on the down-low politicians suddenly found that they rather liked the idea that America was an empire. The liberal journalist and former leader of the Canadian Liberal Party Michael Ignatieff provided the moral warrant for this turn, arguing that the United States was already an "Empire Lite" and should embrace its imperial responsibilities with more vim, in the name of "humanitarian empire."[2] From the Tory right, the Scottish historian Niall Ferguson celebrated both the British Empire and its American successor.[3] The neoconservative commentator Max Boot of the *Wall Street Journal* drew similar sustenance from the nineteenth-century imperialist tradition to argue for a benevolent American imperium.[4] Former *New York Times* editor James Atlas bemoaned the prospect of the "collapse" of "our great American empire" and urged conflict with terrorism to avert that nadir.[5]

It wasn't just 9/11 and its intimations of weakness and mortal vulnerability that produced this sudden fervor. Things had recently been going very wrong. There had been a sharp decline in corporate profitability, leading to the bursting of the stock market bubble and a recession. A series of corporate scandals, and a stolen election, had undermined the legitimacy of the dominant institutions. The neoliberal "globalization" project was meeting new challenges as each new round of trade talks stalled.

And now there was a moment in which one could openly declare for empire, and it would be intelligible and perhaps even on the right side of history, or the right side of a paycheck. Thus, in the febrile atmosphere of the "war on terror," the language of imperialism emerged from the margins of radical critique or neoconservative veneration into mainstream academic journals, newspapers, and magazines. This opened up critical possibilities, and it became feasible, with some scrupulous hedging, to mention that the United States was engaging in a little more than leadership, and a little less than diplomacy. In the large antiwar movements, of course, it is a different matter. "US imperialism" has been an established object of analysis, as well as a term of abuse, at least since the Vietnam War—and, as I aim to show here, well before even that cataclysm.

This is a history largely concerning actors who, barring some exceptional periods of tumult, exercised little power. They didn't usually win their immediate battles—in fact, they often lost catastrophically—though they made it possible for others to win theirs. The effects of their struggles were usually cumulative and gradual, and their standing in American history is often barely registered in the vast literature. And few would think of trying to explain their collective efforts in terms of a tradition of anti-imperialism. The telling of this recondite history may be justified by furnishing present-day anti-imperialists with the lessons of past experience. Yet readers encountering tales of women's peace groups, military defectors, Central American solidarity movements, segregationists opposed to the Spanish-American War, African American communists, and Native American resistance will wonder what could possibly unite them all. So I have some explaining to do. What is anti-imperialism, if it can be this capacious?

To track down the anti-imperialists of American history, and find out what, if anything, connects the minutemen of the eighteenth century with the GI refuseniks of today, it will be necessary to define, early on, precisely what is meant by imperialism here. The lazy tendency to speak of imperialism as if it were reducible to its colonial forms will not wash, as colonialism did not constitute the full range of imperialist practices even at the zenith of colonial rule in the late nineteenth and early twentieth centuries. So we must be clear in what sense it is relevant to speak of American imperialism outside of its relatively limited experiment in formal colonialism.

This is no simple matter. If you subscribe to "Realism" in international relations, imperialism is just what states do—states are power-maximizing entities that operate in conditions of international anarchy, and thus the rich and powerful states do what they can, while the weak do what they must. This account rests on bleak

Hobbesian precepts about human behavior and political authority, in which the latter arises because of the need to control the natural human propensity to expropriate, cheat, and murder one another. The state emerges to suppress conflict and, paradoxically, secure liberty in doing so. But in the international system, something like the "state of nature," anarchy, still prevails. In this system, predation and submission are the rule, and states adopt whatever strategies they can—power-balancing, for example—to ensure that they will not be the prey of some other state. Global violence and conquest, in this view, is unavoidable. To call it imperialism is at best a tautology, and at worst adds a pejorative layer to sober analysis. I reject this account on various grounds, largely in that it mystifies the real basis for state conduct by eliding the fundamental differences between a myriad of different kinds of states and their basis in different modes of production, and thus works to naturalize and universalize predatory behavior.[6] It is worth pointing out that this school is gaining a surprising following on the liberal left, some of whom greatly esteem the writings of realists such as John Mearsheimer.

The obverse tendency to treat imperialism as a particular policy, which characterized the arguments of the Anti-Imperialist League at the turn of the twentieth century (see chapter 2), is also of little use here. Such an approach cannot explain the consistency with which multifarious actors working within the dominant states have pursued imperialist strategies. A long-standing rebuke to the league has been that it failed to generate or take on board any systematic theory of imperialism based on geo-economic competition of the kind that was becoming popular at its zenith. This can be overstated, and the narrow political liberalism which undergirded the league's approach to imperialism did provide some powerful resources with which to critique the colonial project in the Philippines. And there were features of the political environment that made such an approach plausible. It made a certain amount of sense, for example, when there were actually political and business elites willing to mobilize against imperialism, to speak of it as a policy. Nonetheless, this is an aberrant case.

This book will largely refrain from pausing mid-narrative to scrutinize the theoretical scenery, but it assumes a broadly Marxist approach. Marxist analyses of imperialism inspired by Lenin and Bukharin have tended to focus on a particular period beginning in the late nineteenth century when competition between European nation-states fueled an accelerated grab for colonial territory. This treats imperialism as a phase of capitalism marked by the concentration of capital, the growing prominence of finance capital, and the merging of monopoly capital with the state. Thus, nation-states, in alliance with capital, compete to divide the world among them, the better to secure markets and exploitable resources. The highly conjunctural analysis of Lenin and Bukharin has both empirical and theoretical flaws. However, the method suggested by this analysis helps us to narrow down what is specific about imperialism, so that we don't lapse into treating it as either "just what states do" or as just a policy.[7]

By imperialism, I will refer not to the tributary empires of the ancient and medieval world, nor to colonial policies as such, but to capitalist imperialism, which is the only variety that is relevant to the period covered. The United States emerged out of a capitalist empire, that of England in the New World, and arrived on the world scene as a revolutionary capitalist state. This has profound consequences for what then unfolded. In the feudal period, the chief means that a noble had of expanding his surplus was by acquiring more territory (and the peasants who worked the land) to extract more tribute. In capitalism, territorial acquisition has its role in nation-building, in providing the space in which capital accumulation can efficiently take place—particularly if the capitalism in question is still in an agrarian phase of development—but it is not the *chief* means of increasing surplus. Rather, capitalists increase their surplus (profits) in competition with others by constantly investing in improvements to the means of production. They also compete with one another for access to the labor markets and primary resources through which they make their product, and for market share, through which they realize their investment. This is important: capital as such is an abstraction: there are only multiple units of capital, businesses, corporations, small enterprises, and so on. These units are profoundly differentiated, but they tend to cluster in certain territories, thus giving rise to localized systems of governance and producing a homogenization of language and currency. At the same time, as capitals expand, they seek new markets, new raw materials, and new pools of labor.

Thus, there is a tendency for the owners of capital, the capitalist classes, to be constituted locally (in the national state) while also being globally oriented. In a dual process, capitalism is both nationalized and internationalized at the same time. Insofar as national states provide the key strategic bases from which to make fundamental organizational decisions about capitalism's running, capitalist classes will seek to hegemonize the state apparatus through: lobbying and patronage; the circulation of personnel within the state administration (think of the Goldman Sachs and Google executives who have been through the revolving door linking Washington to private industry); class-conscious political activism (the relationship between the Koch Brothers and the Tea Party is one example of this); and the automatic "voting" that investors can engage in if they fundamentally disapprove of a government, by withdrawing investment, reducing growth, and thus creating a fiscal and political crisis for the administration in question. These nationally constituted capitalist classes come, at a certain point in development, into competition with other capitalist classes for access to the same resources, the same markets, and the same sources of revenue extraction. It is when that competition comes to be organized through the state that military conflict and predation become part of the system's logic.

When industry replaced land as the basis for capitalist production, moreover, it made possible the eventual arrival of a new geography of empire. While the phase of classical imperialism (roughly, from 1870–1945) saw states compete significantly for territorial control, the possibility of superseding territorial empire was already latent. Instead of competing for colonies, the imperialist states could compete for the control of markets in labor, capital, and commodities within a well-ordered global hierarchy of states. It was this geographical revolution, a move "beyond geography," which made it possible for the United States to forge an empire based upon the ability to deploy overwhelming military power to maintain a system of friendly states that would permit US access to their markets and resources.[8]

Who, then, counts as an anti-imperialist? Anti-imperialism as an ideology within the colonial and imperialist societies has its roots in the Enlightenment thought of the latter half of the eighteenth century. Until that time, writers such as Bartolomé de las Casas had decried colonial abuses, but not imperialism as such. Then, as an international antislavery movement took off and revolution shook first colonial America, then France, a series of Enlightenment thinkers began to challenge imperialism on a number of moral, economic, and political bases. Sankar Muthu, author of *Enlightenment Against Empire*, identifies Bentham, Condorcet, Diderot, Burke, Herder, Kant, and Smith as the bearers of this Enlightenment anti-imperialism.[9] Throughout chapters 1 and 2, this strand—comprising "free trade" arguments, humanitarian sentiment, and liberal democratic ideology—is very much dominant.

The emergence of the left as a current independent of Enlightenment liberalism opened up a new basis for anti-imperialism, predicated on the critique of capitalism and on the class analyses foregrounded by Marxism of the kind outlined above. In Europe, this was expressed by some parties of the Second International and later by the parties spawned by the Russian Revolution, but it also found purchase in the social democratic left. In the United States, the First World War constituted the first major test for the socialist left on the question of empire. As we will see in chapter 2, the socialist and populist left formed only a minor current of the anti-imperialist front in the decisive moment of 1898. Following the First World War and the split in the Socialist Party, communists were usually the most militant vectors of anti-imperialist opinion (chapters 3 and 4). Anticommunism during the Cold War thus formed a major element in consolidating popular support for imperialism and isolating anti-imperialist forces. Throughout this period, "isolationists" on the right provided a continued ideological critique of empire based on constitutionalist arguments.

The breakdown of the anticommunist consensus in the sixties made it possible for anti-imperialism to break out of its ghetto and involve a much wider layer of forces. Feminists, antiracists, liberals, anarchists, socialists, Christians, and others formed the popular bulwark against the Vietnam War (chapter 4). Similar coalitions were later assembled to challenge the Reaganite counterrevolution in Latin America and Bush père's aggression in the Gulf. The 1990s, characterized by ludicrous end-of-history millennialism and the restoration of certain aspects of colonial ideology under the impress of "humanitarian intervention," did not see prominent anti-imperialist outings. Such sentiment was largely confined to the fringes of the radical left and libertarian right. But the "war on terror," conducted with more and more explicit references to empire-building, produced a revival in attention to imperialism coterminous with an upsurge in antiwar feelings. Throughout this history, moreover, there is an important tradition of soldiers who either refuse to fight, "frag" (kill) their commanding officers, or defect. This reached its peak in the Vietnam War, and has not since been matched despite the germinal revival of such resistance during the "war on terror."

The subject of this book is not confined to those who have explicitly identified as anti-imperialist, much less those who were consistent in opposing empire or who held a "correct" theory about empire, which would make for a far more specialized history. Rather, anti-imperialism serves here as a regulatory principle, a standard by which a variety of movements opposing war and overseas domination can be assessed—and, where appropriate, criticized. This is not to take the approach that those activists who did not live up to a certain ideal type of anti-imperialism can be pithily denounced from the comfort of posterity. Those who took the step of trying to constrain their government when it engaged in imperialist violence deserve better than that. It would be all too easy to write history as a morality fable in which the "good guys" (and gals) consistently emerge, if not triumphant, then at least prescient and justified—and everyone else is damned for their deviations. But, as we shall see, activists do not labor in circumstances that favor such omniscience. The idea here is, instead, to find out what past generations of peaceniks, antiwar rebels, and GI refuseniks learned from their struggles against the empire, how they were able to apply those lessons, and how we might profit from it.

The Revolutionary Legacy, Isolationism, and Internationalism

Anti-imperialists in the United States have long sought to mobilize the legacy of the American Revolution against imperialism. It would seem to be a logical step, given that the revolution overthrew a powerful empire's dominion. But is that legacy anything other than ambiguous on the question of empire? Resistance to British colonial rule produced some radical new possibilities, but it did not always entail hostility to the colonial principles of sovereignty and racial hierarchy. The way in which the "peculiar institution" of slavery was protected by the revolution and bound up with subsequent imperialist ventures—in the conquest of Mexico, for instance—belies any simple narrative of revolutionary anti-imperialism. Even so, we will seek to show how the emancipatory Enlightenment ideology that was embodied in the revolution was used as a resource by opponents of American imperialism, from the Anti-Imperialist League onward. Since neoconservatives and the liberal *belligerati* have sought to appropriate these ideological resources on behalf of imperialism, aspects of this question will be examined in chapter 1.

But an emphasis on the peculiarities of American history can be misleading. Anti-imperialism in the United States has always seen struggles outside the United States, from the Filipino resistance led by Emilio Aguinaldo to the arc of anticolonial insurgency in the mid-twentieth century, intimately tied to domestic conflicts. Far from being isolationist, the anti-imperialist left has usually been internationalist—as demonstrated in the solidarity shown to Haitian *cacos*, or when the Abraham Lincoln Brigades helped resist Fascist imperialism in Spain, or later when thousands of American activists rallied to the defense of Central America against the Reaganite counterrevolution. American anti-imperialism can thus hardly be comprehended without contextualizing it in international movements, from the antislavery movement to the Baku Congress, the Third International, Nkrumah's Pan-Africanism, the Bandung Conference and the Non-Aligned Movement, the Cuban Revolution and the Tricontinental Conference, the Algerian struggle and Fanon, and latterly Palestine, whose eloquent advocate Edward Said inoculated many Americans against the colonial, Orientalist assumptions underpinning imperialism. Indeed, it is when Americans have been most internationalist that their anti-imperialism has been most consistent, militant, and effective.

Moreover, far from anti-imperialism being a strictly middle-class affair, or one led by pampered college students, left-wing, working-class Americans—particularly African Americans—have usually formed, if not the vanguard, then the avant-garde of resistance to imperialism. Contemporary research on American peace movements finds that class is an important factor in motivating antiwar activism, more so for those earning less than $40,000 a year than for those earning more. The experience of racist and sexist oppression is also central in galvanizing activists.[10] This would tend to corroborate the findings of studies of the anti–Vietnam War movement, which was (in defiance of the caricature of "rich college fucks" using their privilege to subvert America, as Daniel Patrick Moynihan characterized radicals at the time) largely working class and disproportionately African American.[11]

This is not to minimize the importance of the conservative, bourgeois anti-interventionism whose prominent advocates today include Andrew Bacevich, Ron Paul, and Justin Raimondo. The website *Antiwar.com* has been a valuable resource for opponents of empire, providing an analysis from the right that has sometimes been more consistent in its opposition to war than the soft left. They defend a tradition that they sometimes call the "Old Right," based on the principles of Jeffersonian democracy, evincing a suspicion of foreign "entanglements." They maintain that the republican principles on which America was founded are threatened by the accumulation of executive power entailed by constant warfare. And, not completely without justice, they trace this tradition back to the "founding fathers," the Anti-Imperialist League, and the "isolationists" of the mid-twentieth century. This tendency, particularly in its libertarian variants, also tends to espouse free-market "Austrian" economics as interpreted by Friedrich Hayek and Murray Rothbard.

Yet, as I will also argue, this tradition relies for its coherence and respectability on a degree of revisionism. Moreover, it is at best an inadequate basis for anti-imperialism. Often compromised by hewing to racist and inegalitarian principles, its anti-imperialism has been neither reliable nor internally consistent. Pat Buchanan, a classic Old Right figure who positions himself as a non-interventionist, was a member of the Nixon White House, a supporter of the Vietnam War, and later a co-architect of Reagan's aggression in Central America, who steered the administration's propaganda toward unequivocal endorsements of the white supremacist regime in South Africa.

Even the more classically non-interventionist Ron Paul has tended to argue that the United States is if anything overly benevolent rather than imperialist. During the Cold War, he repeated the most exaggerated claims of anticommunist propaganda and alleged that the main problem was that the United States funded its communist opponents, then sent troops or money to neutralize the people it had funded. In the context of the invasion of Grenada, he argued that "anti-communist military action" could be legitimate if undertaken after consultation with Congress but also that the United States should start by ceasing aid to the Eastern Bloc, which he alleged was the source of communist funding and weapons in the country. From Paul's perspective, the United States was consistently too soft on communism, such that even apartheid South Africa, with all of its "flaws," was denounced more forthrightly in the United States than "the murdering Communists." The basis for such an analysis was a belief that the United States was being pulled away from national sovereignty and toward "internationalism," toward a "one-world government." This explained the contrivance of politicians in subsidizing opponents to wage war with. This frankly baroque conspiracy theory continues to underpin Paul's analysis today.[12]

But if a bias toward domestic ideological sources of anti-imperialism is misleading, so it does not help to reduce anti-imperialism to external sources. The Cold War era was rife with this sort of paranoia, interpreting anti-imperialism as simply a pro-USSR reflex. Long after the McCarthyite years, US antiwar activists were still targeted by state bodies as if they were foreign agents or dupes for terrorists or the Evil Empire—a case in point being the harassment of the Central American solidarity campaign, CISPES, described in chapter 5. It is true that in the early years of the Cold War, antiwar activism was concentrated among a small number of embattled communist activists and others in their orbit. Yet to reduce this stance to the influence of the "long arm of Moscow," as some accounts implicitly do, is a boring, reductionist cliché from the canons of counter-subversive literature. The anti-imperialism of the American left in the Cold War was informed largely by rational self-interest and analysis. The anti-imperialist left was overwhelmingly that section of the left most rooted in the working class, particularly the African American working class, and its relationship to empire flowed from the way in which leftists theorized their experience of exploitation and oppression. Their arguments were not always correct, and misplaced sympathy for the Soviet Union arguably undermined their efficacy. But they were not just ciphers of Moscow, Manchurian candidates responding robotically to trigger words.

To correctly apprehend Cold War anti-imperialism, it will be necessary to sketch out the complex relationship between and among America's domestic class and racial struggles, anticommunism, and the anticolonial struggles in which the United States was frequently intervening. Since the Wilson era at least, the segregated South had been the most pro-war, nationalistic constituency in the United States. Contrary to the idea of southern reactionaries cleaving to isolationism, Washington's shift to empire at the turn of the century had united the emerging Jim Crow order with the American Empire—the latter reproducing the former in several frontier zones, such as Haiti, Panama, and the Middle East. As a consequence, struggles against segregation had anti-imperialism as a logical corollary—from civil rights to Vietnam was not a huge or counterintuitive leap.

But what was also pioneered in the Wilson era was the virulent, moralistic, and repressive anticommunism that treated opponents of war and radicals of all stripes as potential foreign agents. This came with a pungent dose of racist chauvinism. The Lusk Commission, set up to investigate the wave of working-class radicalism sweeping America, concluded that socialism was a "German-Jewish" system of thought (a damning indictment after the frenzied anti-German hatred propagated during America's entry into "the Great War"), while Secretary of State Robert Lansing fancied that Bolshevism proved the validity of the tsarist forgery *The Protocols of the Elders of Zion*. J. Edgar Hoover, running the Justice Department's Bureau of Investigation, the forerunner of the FBI set up to crack down on sedition, argued that African American leaders were becoming a leading element in the "Bolsheviki" bulwark, standing against "established rules of law and order." The white supremacist, nativist precepts that organized American elites' perceptions of the domestic and international order necessarily permeated their understanding of radical challenges to that order.

This is partly why the civil rights struggle was so closely interwoven with resistance to the Vietnam War. Imperial ideology also furnished one of the means by which sections of the working class were (often forcibly, on pain of blacklisting and disgrace) integrated into the system. The breakdown of the Cold War consensus and the rise of anti-imperialist critique were thus also a liberation for the American working class. It is no coincidence that Reaganite imperial revanchism came alongside an attack on organized labor and on the gains of African Americans in the civil rights era. This interrelationship belies the libertarian ideologeme in which imperialism is a "socialistic" venture, entangling Americans in a "welfare-warfare" state.

In the post–Cold War era, the left experienced a near-ecumenical collapse. The period of Clintonite expansion saw much of the left rally behind imperialism, leaving critics a marginalized minority. But Bush's gamble in invading Iraq has opened up new opportunities. The concluding chapter will therefore look at the rise of the antiwar movements under Bush, their problems and accomplishments, the surprising emergence of substantial anti-Zionist opinion in the United States, the tremendous example shown by refusenik soldiers who display impressive class consciousness, and the prospects for mobilizing resistance under Barack Obama's administration.

Unhappy Returns

This book, a history of American anti-imperialism, partially complements the analysis of my first book, *The Liberal Defence of Murder* (Verso, 2008). My debut was a genealogy of liberal imperialism, published after more than a decade in which liberal imperialism in various guises—from "cosmopolitan law" to "humanitarian intervention"—had comprised the mainstream of thinking on the international order. It is fair to say that the intensity with which such ideas were popularly held abated in the interim, though their advocates remain influential. The bloody wars in Afghanistan and Iraq have long lost whatever humanitarian veneer they once had.

However, as I write, there is a concerted effort to revive the nostrums of human rights imperialism in reference to Libya—this amid a regional revolution that is rattling and disposing of American client dictatorships with remarkable haste. If US defense planners initially seemed reluctant to commit to any major ground operations with their forces already overstretched, the need to assemble some sort of policy response to the Middle East revolutions seems to have persuaded them to coordinate and lead the air strikes on Libyan targets. They have formed an alliance with the former regime elements among the Libyan insurgency (a matter I discuss in more detail in the epilogue) with the presumable intention of avoiding the necessity of a ground invasion.

Yet it is not entirely implausible that the United States will once more find itself at home in someone else's country. If it does so, its justification will be liberal and humanitarian. It will cite America's unique leadership responsibilities, its duty to the oppressed, and its enlightened self-interest in promoting democracy—as Obama, Sarkozy, and Cameron have already done, proclaiming their mission a defensive shield against looming massacres of the innocent. Past generations of American anti-imperialists, however, have already encountered empire in its liberal, missionary capacity and found it wanting. They have found that however unsavory and downright murderous America's targets are, few dictators can match imperialists in humanitarian garb for downright viciousness. And it is their experiences that we will have to learn from if our efforts are not to consistently founder on unchallenged assumptions and unlearned lessons.

A note on the title: An important aspect of this story is the settler-colonial origins of the United States and its expansionist drive to occupy as much of the Americas as possible. It is an aspect of its global power that the term *American* has come to refer to the citizens of the United States—as in the "American Dream," *American Psycho*, *The Quiet American*, and, of course, *American Pie*—rather than the indigenous peoples of the Americas or the citizens of both North and South American states. Though aware of these implications, I have settled on *American Insurgents*, as the alternatives were either too clunky or, as in the architect Frank Lloyd Wright's term *Usonian*, too obscure.

Chapter One

Revolution and Anti-Imperialism: The Internal Foes of Empire

I would not care if, tomorrow, I should hear of the death of every man who engaged in that bloody war in Mexico, and that every man had met the fate he went there to perpetrate upon unoffending Mexicans.
—Frederick Douglass, 1849

A Republic or an Empire?

The American Revolution began as a crisis in the British Empire—a crisis, first, of administration, then of legitimacy, and at last of authority. It was a crisis in an era in which capitalism was already the dominant mode of production in the Anglophone world, and in which nation-states were becoming the dominant form of territorial organization. The British Empire was the vector through which capitalism and its philosophical justifications had been implanted in the New World, and it was as capitalists—southern slavers, northern merchants and producers—influenced by its attendant liberal ideology that the colonists embarked on a process of revolution and nation-building.[1]

At first blush, it seems astonishing that they did so. In the mid-eighteenth century, America was still a colonial backwater. The

1

metropole, Great Britain, was ascending to world dominance, but colonial America lacked the urban centers, riches, cultural development, and elaborate political system that characterized its master. Yet, by the 1770s, many of the colonists were ready to believe that they had unique virtues that endowed them with the means to create a radical, republican future.[2]

This undertaking was prompted when the British Empire began a period of internal reorganization following the Seven-Year War ending in 1763, in which Britain had defeated Bourbon France and gained territories in North America as a result. The imposition of various direct taxes was of significance less because of the revenue being extracted than because, as Robin Blackburn puts it, "it was based on unilateral metropolitan fiat."[3] The wealth of colonial America had grown stupendously, and many of its denizens were aggravated by the arbitrary power of the crown, which held up commerce and sacrificed efficiency to royal prerogative. Lacking representation in Parliament, by 1772 they began to form committees of correspondence, which were the seeds of later forms of self-government known as Provisional Conferences. The continued arrogant assertions of the crown, known as the Intolerable Acts, radicalized the colonists. By 1775, the crown was at war with the colonies and the following year the colonists formally declared their independence with a strident assertion of their natural and legal rights, drawing on the political philosophy of the liberal Enlightenment. This remarkable self-assurance included, however, a powerful dose of imperial pretension.

The literature of dissident colonists considering the question of independence from Britain spoke of, in the phrase of the revolutionary James Wilson, "an independent Empire" or, in the words of George Washington, a "fledgling," "rising empire," which would soon "have some weight in the scale of Empires." Ebenezer Baldwin sermonized that "these Colonies" could be "the Foundation of a great and mighty Empire."[4] When Baldwin spoke, he contrasted the "Empire forming in British America" to those "other great Empires" forged by "uniting different nations under one government by Conquest." America was different, comprising a "single People used to the Enjoyment of both Civil and religious Liberty." It was a nation, one that would grow up under the "friendly Auspices of Liberty."[5] It was, as Gordon Wood phrased it, an "Empire of Liberty."[6]

Yet the "Auspices of Liberty" could acquire a decidedly threatening hue for those obstructing their expansion. And expansion, necessarily entailing constant military aggression, was a constitutive component of the American project of nationhood. The westward drive that followed the revolution—the Louisiana Purchase, the War of 1812, the "Indian removals," the Mexican-American War, the filibustering to the south, the early military adventurism in East Asia, and the bid after 1898 for a global empire—all hark back to this early expansionism. The source of this expansionism can be located in the social formations making up the postrevolutionary American polity. Specifically, as mentioned, there were three dominant groups: southern slaveholding plantation farmers; northern industry; and northern mercantile capital. It is a matter of some contention whether antebellum slavery in the United States was actually capitalist, but less so that its method of growth required the continual expansion of the number of slave laborers, and the concurrent expansion of territory allotted to plantations— tendencies intensified by soil exhaustion. This is chiefly why the South was the most aggressively expansionist component of the Union. The existence of a large and expanding slave bloc inhibited industrialization and posed challenges to the dominance of industrial capital in the North, thus leading to competition between the respective sectors for territory, a logic that persisted through the Civil War. At the same time, between these blocs was a large mass of petty commodity producers, who sought freedom in the land to the west and thus constituted another drive to expansion.[7]

This is not to claim that each of these territorial aggrandizements was inevitable. As this book aims to show, empire was contested at every step, and each episode of imperial metastasis was embedded in distinct political, cultural, geographical, and economic logics. But the motors to expansion were *structural*. Moreover, the legitimizing discourses of expansion and empire derived directly from America's ambiguous revolutionary legacy and the national mythologies that arose from it.

It was upon this ambiguity that the future of America as both a republic and an empire turned. Both imperialists and anti-imperialists in the future would appeal to the revolutionary legacy to validate their perspectives.[8] At the center of that ambiguity was the question of slavery and racist oppression. If, for some, the revolution was a quest to begin a wholly new kind of society founded on republican principles, its success would have been impossible without the support of the slaveholding South, which saw revolution as a preemptive strike in defense of slavery against the antislavery movement taking root in the English working class. In the new republic, the slave South dominated the national state, the military, and the judiciary. It was in the South that Jeffersonian republicanism flourished. And the South was in general the most expansionist, aggressive component of the new nation, the site of the most violent waves of ethnic cleansing, and the source of much filibustering south of the border.[9]

Aside from slavery, American nationalism was founded in part on the principle of "clearing" so-called Indian Country and annexing it. Benjamin Franklin, who used terms like "nation" and "empire" as synonyms, had warned the British as early as 1751 that a "prince" who "acquires new territory, if he finds it vacant, or removes the Natives to give his own People Room" should be considered the father of his own nation. During the revolution itself, Native Americans, black slaves, and many poor workers sided with the British—not for love of king and country, but often from hatred of the "patriot" landowners or out of fear of what an "independent empire" would mean for them. Native Americans, who had already suffered the ravages of war and disease as a result of colonization, had been attempting to form independent nations to defend themselves against the European interlopers. As a result, their initial attitude to revolutionary war was one of studied neutrality, resistant to being drawn into a war that did not concern their interests. By the end of the war, however, the majority of Native Americans had been enlisted to fight on the English side in a series of ad hoc treaties promising the protection of their territorial rights. The British crown had, for the sake of stability in the colonies, long attempted to restrict the westward movement of European colonists, and was now using these "savages" to impede the freedom of the colonists. This grievance was duly cited in the Declaration of Independence.[10]

Though rebelling against an empire, the revolutionaries were not necessarily in rebellion against the principles of empire. The aim in deposing British rule was to build markets and develop the emerging economy—to create an independent center of capital accumulation. But this required the ongoing exploitation of slaves and the continued extermination of Native Americans. The auspices of liberty were not for everyone. Yet the point was, and is, that they *could* be. The same Enlightenment ideology that had been formative of many of the revolutionaries was also the original source of anti-imperialism and antiracism. The tension between the officially democratic ideology of the United States and the reality of racial tyranny—which some have called "Herrenvolk democracy"—would play a key role in future American wars.[11]

The War of 1812, Indian Revolts, and Slave Rebellions

Was the War of 1812 an imperialist war? The war between the United States and the British Empire was ostensibly caused by the British imposing blockades on American trade with France, with which Britain was at war. On the face of it, then, it was a war for "free trade," rooted in maritime competition with the former colonial master. The British, it was charged, were engaged in the harassment of neutral American shipping in the Atlantic. In light of such abuses, it could be seen as a Second War of Independence, protecting America's national rights from colonial abridgement. Yet, it is no secret that the maritime states of the Union, which had the greatest interest in quelling any such abuses, were the least ready for war with Britain. Connecticut, Rhode Island, New York, Massachusetts, and Delaware were overwhelmingly opposed to the war. The southern and western states overwhelmingly favored it. The material benefit sought, perhaps, was less the rights of sailors than the cession of Canada and the Floridas to protect the South and prevent external powers from using Spanish Florida to incite slave rebellions. The war was thus an exercise in territorial expansion.

Senior American statesmen and military personnel have long sought to dominate Canada, which they thought could easily be taken. For example, General Andrew Jackson, fresh from Indian hunting, had told James Madison that with a militia of twenty-five hundred he could bring back Quebec. It was not a question of seeking an alliance with the populations of those territories and inviting them to join the United States. Their views were largely irrelevant. It was a question of conquest.[12]

The war met with stiff opposition from congressmen on moral, constitutional, and commercial grounds. Massachusetts congressman Daniel Webster argued that the use of the draft showed that Americans would not enlist to fight for the conquest of Canada, or could not be paid by an exhausted treasury if they did, and that its imposition was a violation of the Constitution. The secretary of war, he maintained, was demanding a tyrannical principle, that the federal government should have a right in peace or war to force people to part them from their families and impress them into the regular army. This was the "fabric of despotism," an arbitrary and limitless power from which Americans had expended blood and treasure to be free.

John Randolph, a Virginian who feared the contraction of states' rights, charged that the war was a retreat from the Jeffersonian republicanism that he assumed the Republican Party stood for, concentrating power too strongly in the executive. The Republican Party was based largely on slaveholders, small agrarian producers espousing a (racialized) democratic ideology, in contrast to Federalism, which was built on prerevolutionary Toryism and based on the northeastern business class and bankers. While the latter had been created specifically around the idea of forging a national bank and paying off the debts incurred during the revolutionary war, the former opposed such centralization of authority. Yet opposition to the war was most strongly expressed among Federalists. Republicans, particularly in the South, overwhelmingly supported the war. John Calhoun, the South Carolina Republican later known as an arch-slaver, made something of a debut as a young politician in rallying to the defense of the war. Samuel Taggart, a Federalist from Massachusetts, argued that war was both unjust and unwise. It was an "offensive" war, entailing "the invasion of foreign territory, to which no one pretends we have any right, unless one to be acquired by conquest." He argued for the freeing up of commerce to solve the nation's difficulties and keep it in prosperity, and that war would threaten such liberty. He also doubted that the war would be as easy as many anticipated.[13]

This opposition was radicalized throughout the war and led at one point to a sustained antiwar event, the Hartford Convention lasting from December 1813 to January 1814, at which delegations largely comprised of Federalists went so far as to raise the prospect of secession and expelling western states from the Union. The Hartford Convention sought to revise the Constitution, so that states deprived of federal funding could withhold taxes from the federal government and spend it on their own defenses. This meant keeping a separate army, which may well have led to separate sovereignty.

The immediate cause of this was that the British had succeeded in imposing a blockade on the East Coast, and the Federalists were infuriated by the impact on commerce and profits, especially as President Madison refused to fund the costs of their defense because of their refusal to submit their militias to executive control. The Napoleonic wars had represented an unprecedented opportunity for US maritime traders to become very rich—representing a neutral power, they could supply foodstuffs and other goods to all sides. This was a make-or-break moment for the Federalists. Their political fortunes had long been in decline. As a party largely representing elites, they had too narrow a base to command electoral pluralities as the party system was consolidated. A brief revival for the Federalists in the first two years of the war showed that some franchised opinion was deeply worried by the war, particularly in the northeast. The conclusion of the war would ultimately finish off the Federalists as a serious force in American politics.[14]

The dissidence of the "responsible class" of bourgeois white males was naturally centered on the protection of the civil liberties that they enjoyed as privileges with respect to their racial "inferiors," on the freedom of trade and commerce from which they could reap what Taggart called "golden harvests," and—for Republican opponents—on the protection of states' rights, which ensured that slavery would be maintained. It is also true, and not insignificant, that the supporters of war argued that success would shore up the nation's fragile republican institutions rather than enfeebling them, by dealing a decisive blow for their international standing. Jefferson's own argument was that the health of republican institutions depended in part on the expansion of territory to be cultivated, as this would ensure the continued dominance of industrious commercial farmers.[15] Nonetheless, the moral element of their critique, that the United States should not engage in conquest and that its armies should be mobilized solely in defense, were what raised it above a purely sectional, self-interested argument. Were such principles adhered to, the United States would have committed far fewer injustices and slaughtered many fewer people. And even the "whites only" version of political and civil liberty contains within it an emancipatory kernel that is capable of expanding to include the hitherto excluded. Anti-imperialists of later ages consistently articulated more or less radical variants of these same principles.

Still, opposition also came in far more unsettling forms for the US authorities. An important context for 1812 was the continued hostilities with Native Americans, as the frontier was pushed ever forward. If expansionism and colonization were, as we have said, constitutive of the American nation-building project they could not but lead to constant hostilities with Indian tribes. Indeed, before the War of 1812, conflict between westward-moving US whites and Native Americans had been a regular occurrence—as in the Old Northwest War, which saw white colonists expand into present-day Ohio and Indiana against the resistance of the Miami and Indiana peoples. So it was implausible for the US authorities to blame the British for manipulating the Indians and provoking their hostility. While the British had made alliances with Indians during the Revolutionary War and again since 1807, they were not the source of that conflict. The year 1807 had been the occasion for the Chesapeake Affair, in which British vessels, conducting operations against the French in Chesapeake Bay as one of the fronts in the Napoleonic wars, attacked and boarded an American frigate named the *Chesapeake*, looking for British sailors who had deserted. President Jefferson's reaction was one of outrage, and his secretary of state James Madison approached the British to demand, among other things, that the act be officially disavowed and that British warships be withdrawn and permanently excluded from US territorial waters. This brought war with the British closer than it had been for decades and spurred the British authorities in Canada to once again attempt an alliance with the Indians.[16]

There had already been an effort in 1805 by two Shawnee brothers, Tecumseh and Tenkswatawa, to build an Indian confederation as the basis for resistance to US expansionism. Tenkswatawa, considered a prophet, was the progenitor of a spiritual revivalism that was intended to sustain pan-Indian unity. Tecumseh was the statesman and orator. Through their combined efforts, they were seeking to construct a form of anticolonial nationalism. This can be seen in Tecumseh's speeches, wherein he prevailed upon "brave Choctaws and Chickasaws" to "assist in the just cause of liberating our race from the grasp of our faithless invaders and heartless oppressors. . . . Let us form one body, one heart, and defend to the last warrior our homes, our liberty, and the graves of our fathers. . . . Haste to the relief of our common cause, as by consanguinity of blood you are bound."[17] And again, stressing the egalitarian premise of the Indian nation: "The way, and the only way, to check and stop this evil, is for all the Redmen to unite in claiming a common and equal right in the land, as it was at first and should be yet, for it was never divided, but belongs to all for the use of each. That no part has a right to sell, even to each other, much less to strangers—those who want all and will not do with less."[18]

Operating from the Northwest (territory covered by the modern states of Ohio, Indiana, Illinois, Michigan, and Wisconsin), the brothers sought to build support across the West and later the South, and did so quite effectively, largely through the efforts of the charismatic Tecumseh. Tecumseh's tactical brilliance did as much to inspire support as his reputedly enthralling orations. Peter Lamphere describes how "he didn't always need massive forces. At one point, in the Battle of Brownstown, Tecumseh led a force of twenty-four warriors to ambush and turn around an American column of 150 soldiers, who had set out from Detroit to meet a supply train. Tecumseh's political brilliance helped to expand his military victories. After Brownstown, he sent a runner to the nearby Pottawatomie warriors in Illinois who, emboldened by the Native victory, captured Fort Dearborn at present-day Chicago."[19]

A "combination of Indian tribes" was a fearful prospect for the expansionist governor of the Indiana Territory, William Henry Harrison, who eventually, in 1811, obtained government support to build an army of regulars and militia to go on the offensive. Across the frontier, Indian attacks kept coming, and the US press continued to describe them as a front in a British act of aggression.[20]

So when war broke out, it was logical that white American settlers would be looking over their shoulders for an attack from Indian quarters. There was a fear among white Americans that, among others, the Six Nations of the Iroquois Confederacy, whom government officials had attempted to persuade to remain neutral, would begin attacks on the frontiers and borders. In reality, most Iroquois remained neutral. However, there was an ongoing war with Tecumseh's confederacy, which fed as a direct tributary into the war with Britain. Thousands of Native Americans joined the British side, while more than a hundred Choctaws, Cherokees, and Creeks (Muscogees) sided with the United States. As a consequence, the war of expansion acquired a decidedly colonial hue in which white Americans took the chance afforded by war to advance the policies of extermination and clearances that had long characterized the frontier. Tecumseh himself was killed in 1813, and the uprising he led melted away after his death.[21]

Another front in the war was opened by the injustice of slavery. As the British attacked the Chesapeake coastline, the abscondment of slaves suddenly became an issue. The astonishment of white Americans at the desertion of their slaves shows how complacent was their faith in the institution of slavery. As the Haitian revolution had shown, war could precipitate slave rebellions, overthrow the masters, and burn the plantations down. The War of

1812 had come just near the culmination of the Napoleonic wars, which had fatally weakened regional slave regimes.[22]

Chesapeake slaves, anxious for their freedom, were glad to exploit the rivalry between these two white behemoths. And the British, and white Americans to their chagrin, found that slaves were ready to welcome the invaders and join their forces. Escaping from captivity, they could often be found working for the British as laborers, spies, or messengers. They would help lead missions to expropriate and terrorize their former masters. One captured crew of slaves who had fled a plantation were, it transpired, seeking arms from the British so that they might independently visit revenge on the white Americans who had enslaved them. Others led the British crews back to the plantation house where they had been locked up and requested a weapon in order to cut the master's throat.

The British were shocked, though they had only to recall that during the War of Independence, too, slaves had been willing to seek refuge and fight on their side. At any rate, they did not hesitate to take advantage of it. It made military sense, and British society was still being convulsed by a mass antislavery movement that, by the time the War of 1812 broke out, had already secured the Abolition of Slavery Act in 1807. At one point, as a military tactic, the British promised all deserting slaves the choice of fighting with the Royal Navy or living as free citizens in one of the British territories in the Americas.

This sudden hemorrhage of property, and the boost to British forces that it provided, caused serious consternation among the local bourgeoisie, who had not favored war. And it also deprived the US forces of additional recruits, since southern slaveholders were unwilling to dispatch militia forces for fear of their fate at the hands of both the British and escaped slaves. White citizens were compelled to form counter-subversive brigades, outfits to spy on and prevent the defection of slaves. In the end, thousands of slaves were able to defect—not enough to prevent the prewar economic structure from being conserved once the war was over, but sufficient to seriously impede the war effort.[23] African Americans were ever after perceived as a potential fifth column, allies of the enemy—not entirely without reason, as many African Americans did sympathize with America's opponents and would go on to become the vanguard of anti-imperialism in the United States.

The war concluded with the exhaustion of both main parties to the war, though the Treaty of Ghent, deftly negotiated by US diplomats, allowed both to claim victory. Undoubtedly, part of the reason for the failure to secure victory, much less the easy victory they anticipated, was that the scale of misgivings about the war ensured that the regular army could not be built up to its authorized size—fifty thousand volunteers were sought, only ten thousand signed up. The New Englanders would not supply troops for an invasion of Canada, preferring to defend their own borders and possibly even negotiate a separate peace with Britain. But the conclusion of the war was good enough for the Republican administration to retain its credibility, and the Federalists to lose theirs. It also had the effect of breaking the power of oppositional Indians in the Northwest and Southwest. It made the modern Deep South possible, taking what is now Mississippi and Alabama out of the control of indigenous people. The slaveocracy had been protected and augmented, ready for further rounds of expansion. The indigenes were left increasingly vulnerable to a nation still intent on territorial metastasis. Since the northern behemoth could not be absorbed, and the only permanent territorial gain in the war was a part of Spanish West Florida taken from a neutral power, the logical next step was to go west.[24]

The following sections deal with two aspects of American expansionism in turn: the continuation of the genocidal war against Native Americans and the Mexican-American War. Both were, in different ways, essential to the development of American nationhood. Eliminating serious Native American opposition to expansion facilitated the further spread of the slaveocracy, as did the annexation of much of Mexico. But the resolution of these wars also brought antagonisms between the North and South to a head, sharpening divisions over the status of labor—free or slave—that emerged in the buildup to the Civil War. They helped define the contest of the 1860s, which determined the future of American capitalism.

Jacksonian Democracy and Its Discontents

Andrew Jackson is remembered in popular and schoolchildren's histories as a "people's president," a rough Ulster Scot son of the frontier who fought in the revolution, earned scars refusing to polish British boots when captured, extended the franchise to (some) working-class American males, evangelized for the laboring majority, and championed social reform as well as laissez-faire capitalism. He was the Democrat from the backwoods of the West who provoked fanatical devotion among East Coast intellectuals such as Nathaniel Hawthorne, Walt Whitman, and James Fenimore Cooper and inspired a near-Marxist fervor for social justice, a leveling instinct owing to precapitalist republican ideology, in his protégés.

This version of Jackson was popularized by the historian and Cold War liberal Arthur M. Schlesinger, whose contribution to the canonization of Jackson can hardly be overstated. In his earlier writing, he completely neglected those less savory aspects of Jackson's politics such as his commitment to white male supremacy and savage anti-Indian policies. Even in later acknowledgments, in which Schlesinger confessed that the problems of black Americans, women, and Native Americans were "out of mind" in his original Pulitzer Prize–winning treatment, he urged readers not to condemn Jackson "out of hand."[25] Such apologetics aside, it is obvious why Jackson should appeal to Schlesinger. Jackson was a cofounder, with Martin van Buren, of the modern Democratic Party, a party whose traditions Schlesinger wished to defend. And Schlesinger was a "New Deal" liberal and in his way every bit as much a devotee of "Manifest Destiny" as Jackson himself; the combination of pragmatic social reform and imperialism was the foundation on which Cold War liberalism was erected.

Our Andrew Jackson will have to do without the dignifying redactions and excuses of posterity. In addition to "Jacksonian democracy," we will have to consider Jacksonian expansionism. This included a ruthlessly genocidal colonial policy that was in essence a continuation of a long war of conquest initiated by European farmers and which had provided the material basis for the republic to emerge. We will also have to consider the justice of his opponents. These included not only the Native Americans of the Cherokee, Chickasaw, Chippewa, Choctaw, Creek, Iowa, Menominee, Miami, Osage, Ottawa, Peoria, Potawatomi, Sac and Fox, Saginaw, Seminole, Seneca, Shawnee, Winnebago, and Wyandot nations. They also included Christians who considered the Indians to be children of Israel, as well as abolitionists who opposed his attempts to protect and expand the slaveocracy. And we will have to consider the role of slavery both in "Jacksonian democracy" and in Jackson's expansive conception of America.[26]

Jackson, before he was elected president in 1828, had distinguished himself as a soldier in the War of 1812 and the first Seminole wars. A typical southern slaveholder, Jackson was also an assiduous defender of slavery before and during his presidency. He had been partially motivated in his war with the Seminoles in 1818 by the desire to deprive runaway slaves of the sanctuary that the Seminoles provided. There are those who argue that his primary motive in these affairs was not racism but anti-British suspicion, fearing the British use of Indian rebellions to destroy the still-young American nation. This motivation cannot be discounted, but such accounts also depend heavily on strategies of minimization, which contextualize Jackson's racist contempt for Indians in his personal amity with some Indian chiefs (some of his best friends were Indians) and his express hope that some Indians could be subject to racial uplift with the aid of some judicious terror by American forces.[27] In reality, he took office fully equipped with an interest and belief in white supremacy, and this decisively shaped both his social reforms and his war policies.

Jackson's Indian removal policy was at the heart of his administration's program: "No other subject was of greater importance than this," Jackson's secretary of state and successor as president, Martin van Buren, recalled. "General Jackson staked the success of his administration upon this measure."[28] The rationale for this was that while the majority of Indians no longer posed a serious obstacle to the expansion of white America, those in the South and Southwest still could. As historian John Ashworth writes:

> The new president wished to secure large and valuable tracts of land presently held by Cherokees, Creeks, Choctaws, Chickasaws and Seminoles in the states of Alabama, Mississippi, Georgia, North Carolina and Tennessee. These "Civilized Tribes" were not nomadic but had formed settled communities resembling in many respects those of white Americans. However, the pattern of land tenure differed sharply from that of white America: land was held in common rather than by individual owners and could thus not be commodified in what for Americans was the normal way. This together with basic racial prejudice disposed large numbers of southerners and southwesterners to desire the complete removal of the Indians.[29]

As such, the removals made Jackson enormously popular, particularly in his southern strongholds.

It is important to clarify why Indian removal was so important to the Democratic Party in this era. Central to "Jacksonian democracy" were the agrarian interests that the Democratic Party defended. The democratic ideology that the party expressed placed central emphasis on the role of the farmer in the economy, society, and polity: not just farmers as such, certainly not slaves, and not tenant farmers; the ideal farmer was the freeholder, the font of Republican spirit. If Jackson's Indian removal policy was an attempt to meet Southern land hunger, it was also part of a hegemonic strategy.

Ashworth reviews the components of Democratic dominance, drawing attention to: the insistence on limited government, which reduced the threat of antislavery sentiment from outside the South; the emphasis on agriculture in discourse, which permitted slaveholders to reach into areas of the South where non-slave-labor farms dominated; the emphasis on racial differences, which disabled abolitionism and cemented loyalty to slaveholders' governments in the South; the appeal to egalitarian individualism (among whites), which was genuinely appealing to white Americans across sectional divides; and the emphasis on moral autonomy regarding slavery, which allowed individuals to choose whether or not to own slaves, thus disabling opposition to slavery. Through these means, the Democrats consolidated a "historical bloc"—in Gramscian terminology, an alliance of class forces politically organized around a set of hegemonic ideas directing and cohering its constituent elements—led by slaveholders.[30]

The policy was instantiated chiefly in two cases. First, in the policies executed under the Indian Removal Act of 1830, which offered congressional approval not for the forcible removals and treaty abrogations actually conducted by the executive, but for "voluntary" removal. And secondly, in support for Georgia's attempts to expel the Cherokees, to which end both the president and the Georgian legislature ignored a Supreme Court ruling outlawing states' efforts to redraw the boundaries of Indian land. This was another early basis for "states' rights" politics in the United States. For Georgian elites, a defining issue since Georgia had ratified the US Constitution in 1788 had been the struggle to evict the Creeks and Cherokees. But a particular urgency had been added to the struggle by the discovery of gold on Cherokee lands in 1829. The rush of white settlers and speculators into the territory was encouraged by the state, which took the cue to order the seizure of all tribal lands. Support for the removal policy came chiefly from southern politicians, including Democrats like Congressman John Bell and Senator Hugh Lawson White.[31]

There had long been Lockean justifications for driving the Indians off the land on which they lived, hunted, and recreated, based on the idea that "improvement" of the land through mixing one's labor with it was a divinely ordained mandate and the basis for property rights. This was devised in such a way as to ensure that only European colonists could exercise such rights. Jackson himself gave utterance to these principles. "Humanity has often wept" over the fate of Native Americans, he reflected, but their extermination "has never for a moment been arrested, and one by one many powerful tribes have disappeared from the earth. . . . Nor is there anything in this which, on a comprehensive view of the general interests of the human race, is to be regretted." After all, "what good man would prefer a country covered with forests and ranged by a few thousand savages to our extensive Republic, studded with cities, towns, and prosperous farms, embellished with the improvements which art can devise or industry execute?"[32] John Quincy Adams, Jackson's political opponent, was also committed to this conceit: "What is the right of the huntsman to the forest of a thousand miles over which he has accidentally ranged in quest of prey? . . . Shall the fields and valleys, which a beneficent God has formed to teem with the life of innumerable multitudes, be condemned to everlasting barrenness?"[33] Senator James Wayne of Georgia invoked the Swiss philosopher Emerich de Vattel, in some ways as influential in the formation of property rights theory as Locke, to prove that possession by those who cultivated land trumped any claims made by nomads.[34]

In opposition to Jackson's colonial policy were the Indians themselves—the "Five Civilized Tribes," Cherokees, Chickasaws, Choctaws, Creeks, and Seminoles, who lived as autonomous nations in the South and Southwest—the Christian missionaries who frequently lived alongside them, early feminist activists, abolitionists, and members of the incipient Whig Party in the North. The issue also aroused unprecedented opposition among some white

Americans, in large part due to shock at the severity of Jackson's policy. It had been widely believed that Indian policy was generally beneficent, but suddenly and with naked avarice the Indians were being subjected to brutal clearances to free up millions of acres of land for the slaveocracy. The perceived beneficence of policy under James Monroe and John Quincy Adams was based on misapprehension—the policy of successive administrations had been to facilitate or force the westward removal of Indians, by whatever means were most effective. Nonetheless, the difference between Adams and Jackson could be seen as the difference between a poison and a pistol—the more paramount threat naturally arouses the more urgent response.[35]

Petition campaigns were launched on a massive scale. Catharine Beecher, a famous writer on education and women and the sister of the abolitionist Harriet Beecher Stowe, allied with Lydia Sigourney to instigate the first national women's petition campaign to stop the removals. Beecher launched a new journal, the *Ladies' Circular*, to communicate feminist opposition to the Indian removal policy. This campaign was an extremely trying one for Beecher, causing her to suffer a breakdown, and she was later known for advocating domesticity for women and wrote to women who formed abolitionist societies to beg them not to do so, as the method of agitation could only arouse hostility.[36] Other women campaigners included abolitionist-feminists such as Angelina Grimké, later Beecher's foil in debate, and Lydia Maria Child, whose pioneering *History of the Condition of Women* was an early shot across the bow at sexist oppression. In general, abolitionists, concentrated in New England and the East Coast, originating from Protestant sects, missions, colleges, and humanitarian organizations, threw themselves into the defense of Native Americans.[37]

Working alongside Child and the Grimké sisters were Elijah and Owen Lovejoy, Beriah Green, Benjamin Lundy, Theodore Weld, and William Lloyd Garrison. All of them were in some way to be central to the abolitionist movement. Garrison, a son of working-class immigrants, was a cofounder and key figure in the American Anti-Slavery Society along with Frederick Douglass and others. He worked within a Quaker tradition of social reform. In addition to leading the most radical sectors of antislavery opinion and campaigning for women's suffrage, he was known for his advocacy for Native Americans. This advocacy turned on the question of racial oppression. As he put it in the *Liberator*, "Those who apologize for African oppression are, in a great degree, answerable for the unjust treatment of the Indians. . . . It is this wicked distinction of color in our land . . . that has robbed red men of their rights." Elsewhere, he added, "from the Indian to the Negro, the transition was easy and natural. . . . The suffering of the Negro flowed from the same bitter fountain."[38] Garrison's radicalism was limited. Though he was unlike most abolitionists in that he was of working-class stock, he was no friend of organized labor, resisted the use of the term "wage slavery" to describe the condition of waged labor, and was hostile to Jacobinism. Nonetheless, he took his support for capitalism and "free labor" to its most radical conclusions within the American polity of the time.

Christian opposition was central, articulating different lines of critique. Samuel Worcester, an activist, preacher, and missionary, worked for the American Board of Foreign Missions when he had his first sustained exposure to the Cherokee Nation, during which time he assisted in the launching of the bilingual *Cherokee Phoenix* newspaper after the Cherokee silversmith Sequoya devised a Cherokee syllabary so that the language could be written. Worcester's agitation, undertaken in collaboration with Native Americans, was based on the defense of sovereign rights claimed by the Cherokees as a nation. For this defense, he defied arrest and was sentenced to four years of hard labor by the Georgia authorities. It was his advocacy before the Supreme Court in *Worcester v. Georgia* which led to an 1832 decision confirming that the Cherokee were a sovereign people and that no state could infringe their sovereignty—a hollow victory, as President Jackson and the Georgia legislature simply ignored the decision.[39]

Other Christian advocates included the Whig senator Theodore Frelinghuysen, who served, like Worcester, on the American Board of Foreign Missions and delivered a famous six-hour speech opposing Indian removals. Frelinghuysen maintained that the Indians were the Providential legatees of God's title to this land; natural law dictated that it belonged to them, and no coherent principle could deprive them of it without their consent.[40] The young George Cheever, who would go on to become a pastor and a leading antislavery advocate, scorned the idea that questions of justice should be settled by considerations of profit and loss.[41] Others held that Native Americans were the descendants of the lost tribes of Israel.[42]

It is true that many of the missionaries had looked forward, like Jefferson, Washington, and Calhoun, to the day when Indians could be "civilized"—made into industrious farmers rather than hunters, Christians rather than spiritualists, Americans rather than Indians. However, their approach, often based on moral individualism, depended not on coercion but on transformative encounters with Christian believers. And it happened that the "civilization" policy, though racist in conception and implementation, had unintended consequences in that it contributed to the creation of a literate stratum within the Native American population which grew adept at resisting the War Department and the expansionists. It was indeed partly because of some successes in impeding expansion that Jackson and his allies argued that the aspiration to integrate Indians as American citizens was sentimental cant and embarked on more openly violent removals.[43]

Above all, the missionaries often provided the vital link between the Native Americans, whose strategy included mobilizing American opposition on their behalf, and influential Americans.

Throughout this story, such figures will constantly appear, as will the agency of the targets of US imperialism in bringing information and arguments about their struggles to the attention of strategically significant constituencies. The Cherokee, for example, lacking a military edge, attempted to forestall expansion and removals through calculated legal interventions. They collaborated with missionaries to achieve this end, and hired former US attorney general William Wirt to argue their position before the Supreme Court, most notably in *Cherokee Nation v. Georgia*—which the court threw out on grounds of lack of jurisdiction—before finding Samuel Worcester to successfully argue their case in *Worcester v. Georgia.*[44]

The Cherokees, unable to mount a military resistance, sought to make their case through their newspaper, through missionary conduits, and through the courts. But the sympathy they did succeed in generating came largely in the Northeast, not in Georgia or Alabama, where the empire-builders of the South continued their expulsions without mercy—inflicting suffering comparable with that of the Middle Passage. When *Worcester v. Georgia* was decided in favor of the Cherokee, President Jackson simply mocked the ruling. "[Justice] John Marshall has made his decision," he remarked, "now let him enforce it." The US authorities simply took an influential Cherokee into captivity, shut down the tribal printing press, and "negotiated" a treaty compelling the Cherokee to move west.[45] The subsequent forced removals were, writes historian David Stannard, "nothing less than a death march—a Presidentially ordained death march that, in terms of the mortality rate directly attributable to it, was almost as destructive as the Bataan Death March of 1942, one of the most notorious Japanese atrocities in all of the Second World War."[46]

The Creeks mounted an insurgency in 1836 but were defeated, and fifteen thousand of them were driven out of Alabama on pain of death. It was the Seminole in Florida who undertook the most active military resistance. The nation embarked on the second of its lengthy wars with the United States, lasting from 1835 to 1842. This was to be the costliest of all Indian wars for the United States, beginning with a devastating military defeat for US forces that is still referred to as the "Dade Massacre." Again, the issue of slavery was central to the wars, as at least a quarter and probably more of the Seminole nation were wholly or partially black—the tribe offered sanctuary to runaway slaves, eight hundred of whom joined the Seminole side in Florida. Southern elites, mindful of the Nat Turner rebellion that had stunned the region in 1831, were determined to obliterate such means of escape. This again provided some of the basis for moral opposition to the war from the US side, including among soldiers, many of whom sympathized with the Seminole. Despite this, the war ended on favorable terms for the United States.[47]

The Sac and Fox nations in Illinois and Wisconsin fought for fifteen weeks in the Black Hawk War of 1832, and were devastated by the militias and army. The extraordinary surrender speech by the captured Black Hawk expresses the rage and grief that defeat brought:

> You have taken me prisoner with all my warriors. I am much grieved, for I expected, if I did not defeat you, to hold out much longer, and give you more trouble before I surrendered. . . . Black Hawk is an Indian. He has done nothing for which an Indian ought to be ashamed. He has fought for his countrymen, the squaws and papooses, against white men, who came, year after year, to cheat them and take away their lands. You know the cause of our making war. It is known to all white men. They ought to be ashamed of it. The white men despise the Indians, and drive them from their homes. But the Indians are not deceitful. The white men speak bad of the Indian, and look at him spitefully. But the Indian does not tell lies; Indians do not steal. An Indian who is as bad as the white men could not live in our nation; he would be put to death, and eat [sic] up by the wolves. . . . Farewell, my nation. Black Hawk tried to save you, and avenge your wrongs. He drank the blood of some of the whites. He has been taken prisoner, and his plans are stopped. He can do no more. He is near his end. His sun is setting, and he will rise no more. Farewell to Black Hawk.[48]

The devastating blows inflicted on Native American resistance by Jackson were still insufficient to entirely quell resistance. Each phase of expansion produced new "Indian wars." The Seminole in Florida made their final stand in the 1850s. As white settlers arrived in Oregon in the 1840s and 1850s, bringing with them a measles epidemic that wiped out half of the Cayuse Indians, resistance began with an attack on US missionaries in 1847, leading to a war that lasted some eight years. US encroachment on the territories today known as New Mexico and Arizona, following its success in the Mexican-American War, saw sustained Navajo rebellion. Sioux fought to protect their hunting grounds from colonization in the Midwest—South Dakota, Wyoming, and Minnesota—from the 1850s until the closing of the frontier. Apaches resisted being placed in reservations with Navajo in New Mexico from 1864 to 1886. The Lakota, under Chief Red Cloud, led some of the most successful attacks on US troops when the United States began to encroach on their territory in Wyoming and southern Montana, forcing the authorities to assign hunting land and territory to the Indians. The Powder River Country, most centrally at issue in the war, was closed off to whites. Chief Joseph led the Nez Perce tribe of Oregon in resistance to US government attempts to drive them out of the Washington Territory and onto a reservation in Idaho. Despite their relatively small numbers, they held off much larger groups of assailing US troops until their eventual capture. Joseph's tone, upon capture, was not defiant, but desolate and resigned:

> I am tired of fighting. Our chiefs are killed; Looking Glass is dead. . . . The old men are all dead. . . . It is cold, and we have no blankets; the little children are freezing to death. My people, some of them, have run away to the hills, and have no blankets, no food. No one knows where they are—perhaps freezing to death. I want to have time to look for my children, and see how many of them I can find. Maybe I shall find them among the dead. Hear me, my chiefs! I am tired; my heart is sick and sad. From where the sun now stands, I will fight no more forever.[49]

The frontier was closed in 1890, the territory north of present-day Mexico and south of Canada successfully colonized. The last of the defensive wars by the Indians took the form of an uprising in 1898 by Chippewa Indians in Lake Leach, Minnesota. Though the forces resisting the colonial subjection of the Indians were unsuccessful, their struggles had a profound impact on the growing abolitionist movement, which in turn would play a crucial role in opposition to the Mexican-American War. Many of those who participated in anti-removal campaigns went on to become "immediatists" in the struggle against slavery. Some had favored measures such as the colonization of parts of Africa, to which slaves could return as free people, but the experience of Indian removals persuaded them that any such solution would degenerate into violent expulsions. A challenge to the racial system, to colonial expansion, and to white male supremacy was developing and radicalizing through these struggles. The intersection of these forces, often centered on abolitionism but basically predicated on a combination of egalitarianism, human rights discourse, and individualism inspired by both religion and the Enlightenment, would frequently reappear in the coming years alongside pragmatic, property-based objections to empire. And repeatedly, activists against empire would find that the struggle against US depredations abroad would be intimately linked to injustices at home.

America's "peculiar institution" had always been a foreign policy as much as a domestic one. Its defense, maintenance, and expansion were implicated in the Revolution, the War of 1812, expansion, filibustering in Latin America, and numerous overseas intrigues. In the nineteenth century, two key wars settled its fate: the Mexican-American War and the Civil War. The latter may not seem to be directly relevant to the question of empire, except that the war was partially fought over conflicting models of expansion, and embroiled within it, as ever, were those forces that sought to constrain the empire. Abolitionism was to become, after the end of the Civil War, a key tributary of turn-of-the-century anti-imperialism. By the same token, the fate of African Americans after the end of Reconstruction, and particularly the emergence of Jim Crow, was securely entangled in the battles over the establishment of overseas colonies after the 1898 war.

"The Saxons Are Coming, Our Freedom Is Nigh!" Mexico and the War for White Supremacy

The Mexican adventure was a defining moment in American imperialism, strengthening the slaveocracy while consolidating the growing hold of Anglo-Saxon blood romance and Manifest Destiny. The telling of the story in American culture tends to focus on the myth of the Alamo, wherein one hundred courageous "Texian" settlers seeking independence entrenched themselves in a Roman Catholic mission near present-day San Antonio and held out against the forces of Mexican general Santa Anna. The American settlers were "freedom fighters," while the Mexican forces foreshadowed all the dark tyrannies of the twentieth century. Certainly this was the image depicted in the John Wayne feature film *The Alamo*—a routine example of Cold War American myth-making that contains "not a single scene" that "corresponds to a historically verifiable incident."[50]

Americans had been settling in large numbers in an area of Mexico comprising some of present-day Texas since the 1820s, following a successful war of independence waged by Mexicans against the Spanish colonial power. The Mexican government responded to this colonial enterprise by imposing a ban on slavery in 1829. If the Americans were coming, they weren't bringing slavery with them, and they were to submit to Mexican law. This was not a demand with which American settlers were interested in complying—without slaves, they would be reduced to poor farmers, and their growth would be stalled for years. Their intention was expansion and ultimately annexation. Through agitation and pressure they secured the exclusion of Texas from the antislavery statute, only for new laws restricting further immigration and particularly the further arrival of slaves to be passed in 1830.

Settlers worked to overturn the laws and, in 1833, called a conference to discuss separate statehood for Texas. Stephen F. Austin, a Virginia-born politician and businessman who had led the original colonists, waged the early battles against antislavery laws in Texas, and was considered the "father" of Texas, advocated unilaterally acting on the demand for statehood and was jailed by the Mexican authorities for it. Austin is sometimes depicted as an opponent of slavery, and it is true that at times he spoke out against it. Yet he personally owned slaves and worked hard to establish slavery in Texas. This was because he saw slavery as being essential to efficient colonization—only where slavery was potentially in conflict with the colony was he prepared to countenance its suppression.[51]

From 1835 to 1836, American settlers waged a "war of independence" in Texas. The abolitionist Benjamin Lundy, having traveled extensively in Texas, argued that there was one clear cause of this war, and that was "to re-establish the SYSTEM OF SLAVERY; to open a vast and profitable SLAVE-MARKET therein; and ultimately to annex it to the United States." José María Tornel, the liberal Mexican army general who had fought in the revolt against Spanish rule, concurred: "The land speculators of Texas have attempted to turn it into a mart of human flesh where the slaves from the south might be sold, and others from Africa introduced." Austin, for his part, was convinced that "Texas *must be* a slave country." On the eve of the revolt, settlers expressed fear that a Mexican attack was imminent, and that the Mexicans would use Indian tribes and incite slave revolts to defeat the colonists. Speakers aroused Texans to rebellion by emphasizing the threat that Mexicans would "compel you to liberate your slaves." And it is certainly the case that had Texans lost the ensuing war, they would not have been able to defend the institution of slavery upon which their wealth and power was predicated.[52] Texas thus assumed independence, declaring itself the "Lone Star" republic, as a slave state.

Underpinning this expansionism was a romantic racial Anglo-Saxonism which held that the white race could not live peaceably alongside other races as equals. The more it became apparent that American and Mexican interests were set to clash, the more racist ideology foregrounded the supposed racial weaknesses of Mexicans, which were remarkably similar to those ascribed to Native Americans. Reginald Horsman writes: "Americans, it was argued, were not to be blamed for taking the northern provinces of Mexico, for Mexicans, like Indians, were unable to make proper use of the land. The Mexicans had failed because they were a mixed, inferior race with considerable Indian and some black blood. The world would benefit if a superior race shaped the future of the Southwest." It would be misleading to say that racism alone motivated expansionism. On the contrary, expansion provided untold opportunities for profitable accumulation. Rather, Anglo-Saxonism explained why the United States, claim to certain territories always trumped that of everyone else; it molded how Americans experienced the expansionist dynamic; and it provided a cohering narrative that appeared to make military conquest and tyranny compatible with, even a logical corollary of, republican democracy.[53]

What turned this colonial project into a war with Mexico, which was ultimately compelled to part not only with Texas, but the territory now covering New Mexico, Utah, Nevada, Arizona, California, and part of Colorado, was the determination of southern Democrats, having acquired control of the executive, to press forward with expansion. James Polk, with the support of Andrew Jackson, had been selected as the Democrats' pro-annexation presidential candidate. He was duly elected on an openly expansionist platform seeking the annexation of Texas (as well as the absorption of Oregon), and was anxious for a confrontation with Mexico as soon as he occupied the executive seat. He thus carefully sought to engage Mexico in a series of calculated provocations, designed to produce a war footing. One such provocation was initiated by General Taylor, who blockaded the Rio Grande leading to the town of Matamoros, preventing supply ships from reaching the town and threatening it with starvation. Matamoros was on the southern bank of the Rio Grande and, though its status was disputed, the United States claimed the territory to the north. So when a Mexican contingent crossed the river and counterattacked to end the blockade, the president claimed that Mexico had invaded and shed American blood on American territory.[54]

The war was very popular in many quarters. Americans were accustomed to revering military figures, from Washington to Jackson, and many had served in militias—"which," one writer notes, "resembled playing at soldier more than anything else"—even where no war was under way. The fever of conflict produced pro-war demonstrations, and thousands signed up for the military—in this war, the quotas were always met. Writers lent their support to the imperial mission, and poets were inclined to put iambs and trochees at the service of war. In general, they envisioned American civilization embarking on a grand, benevolent process of "racial uplift."[55] One New York poet put these words into the mouth of a Mexican peasant seeing the cavalry arrive: "The Saxons are coming, our freedom is nigh!" Others foresaw gradual extirpation of the Mexican race through the interbreeding of white American men with Mexican women. Yet others were in a vengeful, proud, boastful mood. Walt Whitman urged that "Mexico must be thoroughly chastised," and exulted that "America knows how to crush, as well as how to expand!" What had "miserable, inefficient Mexico" to do with "the great mission of peopling the new world with a noble race?"[56]

Opponents included the young Illinois congressman and member of the Whig Party Abraham Lincoln. Though Lincoln's skillful roasting of President Polk focused more on the president's apparent equivocations and incoherence, Lincoln was one of eighty-four Whig congressmen who supported a resolution charging the president with inciting the war, unconstitutionally and illegally.[57] Some Whigs charged that war would produce a de facto military aristocracy and threaten liberty. Former president John Quincy Adams was also among those congressmen opposed to the war. Some of the Whig opposition was explicitly hostile to expansionism. Robert Toombs, a Georgian Whig, urged that Americans "put a check upon this lust of dominion. We had territory enough, Heaven knew."[58] Others still were prepared to vote against all war measures, including those that funded the war. Joshua Giddings led this faction in Washington DC, arguing that he would "take no part" in "the murder of Mexicans upon their own soil, or in robbing them of their country."[59] The thrust of the criticisms thus combined pragmatic objections, constitutionalist appeals to liberty, humanitarianism, and in some cases, outright opposition to the United States ruling over others. Yet at the root of this opposition was also the growing sectional division between a North based on industry and "free labor" and a South based on rural bondage.

It should be noted, though, that most Whigs did not allow their opposition to prevent them from ensuring that the war had every material support that it needed for successful prosecution whenever the issue arose in Congress. Only a minority of abolitionist Congressmen were prepared to vote against war measures or deprive the war of funding and material support. Lincoln made a point of highlighting just this point to underline the loyalty of the congressional critics. And though the Whigs objected to the means, the great majority had no beef with the principle of expansion.[60] It was for this reason that editorials in the *North Star*, Frederick Douglass's radical newspaper, denounced the politicians who would not risk censure through "an open and unqualified disapprobation of the war," noting that their main line of objection was their "want of information as to the aims and objects of the war."[61]

Radical opponents held that the war was worse than flawed or unconstitutional—it was an evil, in Frederick Douglass's words a "slaveholding crusade."[62] Douglass's colleague and fellow abolitionist Martin Delany, who would go on to be an advocate of Liberian colonization in order to provide the basis for a new nation for freed blacks, was similarly convinced that the war would lead to the "further degradation of nonwhites."[63] The American Anti-Slavery Society held that the war was waged "solely for the detestable and horrible purpose of extending and perpetuating American slavery throughout the vast territory of Mexico."[64] William Goodell, the abolitionist pastor who would later break away from the Anti-Slavery Society to form the constitutionalist Liberty Party, later reviewed the fraudulent nature of the supposed Mexican offenses that had justified war and concluded that what the federal government was after was "territory for the extension of slavery."[65]

The tactics endorsed by abolitionists were largely peaceable and legal. Yet there were those who were prepared to engage in active disruption. Henry David Thoreau is famous for his essay *Civil Disobedience*. In it, he charged that the main obstacle to the overthrow of slavery and a just settlement with Mexico was not the southern slavers, but "a hundred thousand merchants and farmers" in the North who were "more interested in commerce and agriculture than they are in humanity, and are not prepared to do justice to the slave and to Mexico, *cost what it may*. I quarrel not with far-off foes, but with those who, near at home, co-operate with, and do the bidding of those far away, and without whom the latter would be harmless." He particularly regretted the willingness of those who in their own opinions were antislavery and antiwar, but were unwilling to do anything: they "sit down with their hands in their pockets, and say that they know not what to do, and do nothing." Under an unjust government which ruled over slaves and waged illegal war, the duty of abolitionists was to withhold their support, cease paying taxes, and risk prison if necessary—for where a government "imprisons any unjustly, the true place for a just man is also a prison."[66]

Other radical abolitionists dared to openly hope for the defeat of US forces. William Lloyd Garrison's abolitionist newspaper the *Liberator* expressed its "hope that, if blood has had to flow, that it has been that of the Americans." They wished General Winfield Scott and the southern army he commanded "the most utter defeat and disgrace." Frederick Douglass went further still: "Why may not the oppressed say, when an oppressor is dead, either by disease or by the hand of the foeman on the battlefield, that there is one the less of his oppressors left on earth? For my part, I would not care if, tomorrow, I should hear of the death of every man who engaged in that bloody war in Mexico, and that every man had met the fate he went there to perpetrate upon unoffending Mexicans."[67]

This, you might think, is a perfectly reasonable and logical position. An army engaged in an unjust war deserves the most comprehensive defeat. The humiliation of imperialist armies is a victory in the cause of freedom. Yet, of course, such sentiments are as taboo today as they were then. The pressure on critics of war to blunt the edge of their critique by proving their patriotic credentials, to make themselves into a loyal opposition merely proving by its existence the superiority of the society that tolerates such dissent, remains considerable. For that reason, I offer the provocative, elegant honesty of Douglass and others as an example to anti-imperialists today.

As things turned out, however, the US victors were shrouded in glory, not disgrace. The Treaty of Guadalupe Hidalgo handed 1.2 million square miles of territory, more than 50 percent of Mexico, to the United States. The forces of slavery were enriched and empowered. Texas joined the Union as a slave state, and slaveholding colonists struck out into the territory of New Mexico. Southern slavers did not get everything their own way, though, as California was compelled (in the "Compromise of 1850") to outlaw slavery before it would be admitted as a state of the Union. This was one aspect of a sectional truce that conserved a sort of status quo with respect to the relative weight of North and South in the Union. These patterns in the annexed territories would be central to the civil war that struck over a decade later. Texas would join the Confederacy, the territory of New Mexico would be contested and, of the annexed territories, only California joined the Union forces.

In the intervening years, the sectional agreement between North and South was severely tested. With the Union suddenly expanded and including spatially separate territories, the railroad industry experienced a boom and became America's first billion-dollar business. The basis for railroad expansion, connecting the East and West Coasts, was the subject of hot contention. Southern Democrats wanted to run a railroad through the Kansas and Nebraska territories and organize them as slave states. This would specifically abrogate the "Missouri Compromise," another sectional truce that excluded slavery from those territories. This move scandalized many Northerners who had expected slavery to be gradually abolished, not rapidly expanded; northern Democrats were all but decimated in the 1854 Congressional elections as a result, and the Democrats' long dominance of the legislature overthrown.

The modern Republican Party was born in this moment as a liberal tributary of the Whig Party, which had crumbled under the weight of a growing nativist reaction against Irish immigrants, thus giving rise to the American Party, otherwise known as the "Know-Nothing" Party, as a serious competitor for votes in the North. The ascendancy of the liberal, antislavery Republicans in 1860, the North's drive for the westward spread of railroads and industry, and the southern drive to continue the expansion of the slaveocracy, laid the basis for further sectional strife that would explode in civil war.[68] And the same radical, abolitionist, and anti-imperialist forces that had most urgently resisted the Indian removals and the Mexican-American War found themselves embroiled in a war over the Union which they sought to transform, ultimately with some success, into a war against the most aggressively militaristic, racist, and authoritarian elements in American society.

Chapter Two

Cuba Libre, the Anti-Imperialist League, and Beyond

I am an anti-imperialist. I am opposed to having the eagle put its talons on any other land.

—**Mark Twain**

The problem of the twentieth century is the problem of the color-line—the relation of the darker to the lighter races of men in Asia and Africa, in America and the islands of the sea.
—**W. E. B. Du Bois, 1903**

If the Declaration of Independence be true, then this follows as a fact regarding which there can be no mistake: the inhabitants of the Philippine Islands are to decide for themselves what the form of government shall be under which they are to live; otherwise there is no freedom.

—**George S. Boutwell**

Cuba Libre . . .

The American frontier was officially closed in 1890, following the infamous massacre of Lakota Indians at Wounded Knee, South Dakota. According to the well-thumbed thesis by Frederick Jackson Turner, this constituted a calamitous crisis for a nation whose distinctive characteristics had been acquired in the encounter between the civilized metropolis and the uncivilized wilderness. The existence of uncultivated arable land, conquerable through regenerative violence, produced American values of rugged individualism, democracy, and progressivism, and attracted wave after wave of immigrants who would also internalize these American values.[1] The thesis is now an artifact of the historical moment it sought to describe, studied less for what it tells us about that moment than for what it tells us about the mood of its receptive audience. The same themes were articulated in different ways by other actors. Theodore Roosevelt congratulated Turner for having "put into shape a good deal of thought that has been floating around rather loosely."[2]

Roosevelt himself was the author of his own frontier myth in *The Winning of the West*, a history of race war and conquest. This conquest he ranked the "great epic feat in the history of our race," the crowning glory of a series of coterminous victories notched up by the English-speaking peoples in Australia and Canada.[3] Yet with the closing of the frontier, where could America go next? Of course, the United States reserved the right to intervene in its own "backyard." In his famous corollary to the Monroe Doctrine, which asserted US hegemony in the Americas and treated all European interference or colonization there as acts of aggression against the United States, Roosevelt maintained that the United States was entitled to intervene in and "stabilize" the economic affairs of Central American and Caribbean states that could not pay their debts. This "corollary," though mandating military invasion, was still justified on the grounds of protecting the liberty of the nations concerned, as it would forestall European intervention. "It is not true," Roosevelt averred, "that the United States feels any land hunger or entertains any projects as regards the other nations of the Western Hemisphere save such as for their welfare. . . . If a nation shows that it knows how to act with reasonable efficiency and decency in social and political matters, if it keeps order and pays its obligations, it need fear no intervention from the United States."[4] This is an eloquent synopsis of the normal US mode of operation, which involves projecting power to discipline and, if necessary, overthrow unreliable states rather than exerting direct territorial control—what the geographer Neil Smith calls a "Global Monroe Doctrine."[5]

However, at this time the United States was also considering its options for further expansion, overland or overseas. Colonialism was an increasingly attractive option for a number of reasons. This was the zenith of the classical phase of imperialism (the period of inter-imperial rivalry between 1870 and 1945), during which the colonial powers of Europe had divided the African continent between them. In this way they exercised direct political control over markets in labor, raw materials, and manufacture— and denied access to their opponents. It is not the case that direct territorial control exhausted the means used by Europe's imperialist powers. As Ronald Robinson and John Gallagher argued in a famous article, "The Imperialism of Free Trade," it was as common for empires to use informal mechanisms of control as formal domination. The British Empire had successfully turned regions formerly belonging to other colonial powers such as France or Spain into economic satellites. Imperialism was being driven by the historical expansion of capitalism. The politico-legal relations established by imperialism were there to organize that process in particular ways, but they were not an end in themselves.[6]

Yet, in the last quarter of the nineteenth century, as a truly world market came into being through accelerated communications and industrialized transport networks, the rivalries among the Great Powers of Europe intensified. Britain ceased to be the only major industrialized economy, and political power was much more widely distributed. As a consequence, the race to military supremacy escalated. Further, as a major depression hit capitalist economies from 1873, capital sought more avenues for overseas investment. In this circumstance, informal networks of control through economic integration were inadequate: they permitted too wide a margin for local states and political actors to maneuver in, playing competing powers against one another. The drive to territorial conquest became compelling.[7] And the United States, as a late-emerging power, was driven to try to compete effectively in the colonial domain.

Logically, if neither Mexico nor Canada availed, a further westward push overseas seemed the most plausible move. And the United States had been probing Asia's southeast underbelly looking for possible points of entry since the Perry expedition and the "opening" of Japan, wherein US Navy fleets obliged the Japanese shogunate to open its ports to American traders. China was also endlessly fascinating as a source of potential markets, labor, and resources to American capitalists—though immigration from China was less acceptable to West Coast business and political elites and resulted in a "Yellow Peril" frenzy that produced several exclusion acts and ultimately waves of ethnic cleansing against Chinese citizens.[8]

The Spanish-American War of 1898 was to be the occasion for America's further expansion and its first experiment in offshore colonies. The Philippines would provide a base from which to project power in Southeast Asia and open Chinese markets to the United States. The move was received warmly by Rudyard Kipling, whose poem "The White Man's Burden" was a salute and an austere warning to the United States about the thankless life of manning the global color line. US planners, for their part, spent a considerable amount of time among British colonial officials learning the techniques of imperialist governance. Initially, the war was sold in part as a humanitarian crusade to put an end to Spanish atrocities. Spain was waging a vicious counterinsurgency war to crush the revolutionary nationalists in Cuba—which, bloody as it was, did not break the resistance. The United States, long harboring a desire to annex Cuba, interposed itself as savior and creditor to the Cuban people.

Such justifications subtly, and sometimes less than subtly, drew on racial perceptions: the Spanish had long been seen as a lower caste than the Teutons and Anglo-Saxons, only fit to produce medieval tyranny, while the beneficiaries of American largesse were infantilized. A satirical cartoon from the time depicted President William McKinley tutoring a "family" of children representing Cuba, the Philippines, and Puerto Rico—all drawn with the same visual tropes usually deployed in representations of African Americans. Aside from being racist in its articulation, the humanitarian pretext did not sit so well among Cubans who watched as the US Army, augmented by Theodore Roosevelt's martial cult of "Rough Riders," marched in and stole a victory that was due Cubans themselves.[9]

But it was the Philippines, ceded by Spain as a result of its defeat in the war, which the United States selected for its primary colonial testing ground. The "humanitarian" war shortly became a bloody counterinsurgency even more ruinous than Spanish rule had been. And it was this colonial policy that was the precipitant of the Anti-Imperialist League, a broad coalition of groups ranging from Bourbon Democrats and liberal Republicans to labor leaders and leftists opposing American involvement in empire. Cities across the United States hosted their own chapters and protest meetings in the hundreds. A surfeit of literature was produced and disseminated.

Nothing bearing the name "Anti-Imperialist" has enjoyed equivalent prominence in US history. The list of names involved with the league included the liberal philosopher John Dewey, the progressive feminist Jane Addams, the novelists Mark Twain and Henry James, the Harvard psychologist William James, the railroad capitalist Charles Francis Adams, the monopolist Andrew Carnegie, and the British-born president of the American Federation of Labor, Samuel Gompers. Such a coalition surely had the potential to defeat the colonial turn—but it was not to be.

The Anti-Imperialist League

That some prominent league members were initially hopeful about the Spanish-American War is suggestive of how much American mythology had been internalized, but also how quickly that mythology could be turned from a weapon of legitimacy into a weapon of critique. Samuel Gompers initially said of the war that the United States was "rendering necessary service as a champion of freedom and the protector of a weak and struggling people." As the war got under way, he submerged any doubts he had entertained about the "hysteria" of those pressing for war, declared the cause "glorious and righteous" and even claimed that a quarter of a million trade unionists had volunteered for service.[10] Mark Twain, one of the league's mugwumps, was at first of a similar persuasion. "I thought we should act as their protector," he said, "not try to get them under our heel. . . . It was not to be a government according to our ideas, but a government that represented the feeling of the majority of the Filipinos, a government according to Filipino ideas."[11] Twain had plenty of experience of colonial societies, having traveled to Europe and South Africa and tersely skewered their shortcomings, but did not anticipate that this intervention would become the basis for colonial aggression.

However, there were those whose hatred of militarism did not allow them to trust the venture for one moment. Henry James couldn't abide the spectacle and bravado of American troops strutting about in other people's lands, and least of all could he tolerate Theodore Roosevelt, "the mere monstrous embodiment of unprecedented resounding Noise." Jane Addams was similarly repulsed by the flag-waving jingoism on display. There was also scope for business opposition, as a recovery in the fortunes of capital had recently been achieved by means of a boost in exports, and war would disrupt trade and currency stability. This is not to say that business overwhelmingly opposed war. There was a case that it would boost the trade of iron, steel, and weapons manufacturers in the short run, and open up the world to further exports in the long run. Still, significant sectors of capital were opposed to the talk of war before it broke out, and these included many banks and financial houses that feared that war would be the occasion for the revival of "silverism"—the distribution of free silver to produce inflation and reduce the cost of debt.[12]

These anti-imperialists were horrified by nothing more than the prospect of the United States of America coming to emulate the colonial powers of Europe. Winslow Warren, an early founder of the league and a vice president until it was dissolved in 1921, responded to Kipling's serenade on the "White Man's Burden" with a pamphlet reviling the "simply brutal" duty that Kipling would have Americans assume. It was all the more ominous, coming as American soldiers were "slaughtering men, women and children in the Philippines, and burning and ravaging their villages and homes because, forsooth, those poor people have been guilty of the crime of desiring to govern themselves, and aspired to a freedom which we, of all people, claim to have bought of their old oppressors."[13]

The league has been mistakenly described as an isolationist coalition. In reality, the league came about because "isolation" was impossible. The imperialists were realistic on this, at least: the United States could just continue to fortify its domestic empire, but the gluttonous needs of capital were beginning to overflow the corset of nationhood. And in a world of growing economic and political interdependency and of enduring competition and conflict over commercial and territorial interests, the question of whether the United States would use its immense resources to bid for global supremacy would inevitably be put. As Senator Albert Beveridge put it: "If any man tells you that trade depends on cheapness [of price] and not on government influence, ask him why England does not abandon South Africa, Egypt, India. . . . The conflicts of the future are to be conflicts of trade—struggles for markets—commercial wars for existence."[14] The journalist and presidential advisor Charles Conant forthrightly summarized the "economic" logic of imperialism. The overaccumulation of capital meant that it required new "outlets" for profitable investment that were no longer available within the United States. Whether these profitable outlets were found through territorial possessions, dependency relationships, or some other means was less important than the object of finding them. As he put it: "The writer is not an advocate of 'imperialism' from sentiment, but does not fear the name if it means only that the United States shall assert their right to free markets in all the old countries which are being opened up to the surplus resources of the capitalist countries and thereby given the benefits of modern civilization."[15]

The league's leading lights were well aware of the changing environment and were keenly attuned to their relation to it. Not all were internationalists; many weren't even consistent anti-imperialists, but few were simply isolationist. They forged links of solidarity with the Filipino insurgents, just as the (greatly reduced) league would form alliances with Haitian rebels in later decades. Their arguments centered on the rights and well-being of Filipinos, not just on the danger posed to the US republic by imperialist intrigue and executive power.[16]

The historian John Eperjesi argues that the Anti-Imperialist League's arguments were based on an unworldly and outmoded republicanism, oblivious to the growing profile of "economic" arguments about imperialism.[17] This is not entirely untrue, but at least some of the league's members were aware of the force of such explanations. Jane Addams, broaching the subject, maintained that "Hobson has really said it all," referring to the English radical liberal John Hobson, who argued that imperialism was driven by finance capital.[18] Others, such as the Knights of Labor organizer George McNeill, who cofounded the New England Anti-Imperialist League, expressed some form of class analysis. In his worthy riposte to Kipling's siren song to America, McNeill lambasted the "poor man's burden," which was to "work for another's profit," and the "monopolistic rings" that were every bit as powerful as feudal tyrants.[19]

If the theory and propaganda of the league appeared to be stuck in the eighteenth century, foregrounding constitutional objections and Jeffersonian wisdom about "foreign entanglements," this was in part because of its unifying properties. To put it bluntly—and this we will revisit in more detail—the social forces involved in the league were so disparate in their motivations and commitments that no other framework could have brought them together. It was a means by which, in a word, they could articulate principles behind their opposition to imperialism that would be potentially universalizable, while also taking the charge out of the accusations of disloyalty. In addition, the appeal to the revolutionary legacy was a hegemonic procedure operating on the contradictions between imperialist and democratic ideologies, which would be repeated again and again by anti-imperialists throughout the twentieth century. Though the league's propaganda largely treated imperialism as a policy rather than a constitutive process of the modern capitalist states system, which could be found wanting against the standards of the Constitution, this provided the basis for a sharp critique of colonialism. If the Constitution existed to provide equal rights for all and covered all territory legally acquired by the United States, how could unequal rights be imposed on the Philippines?[20]

There are stronger grounds on which the league might be criticized. But having said something about their discursive approach, it is worth adding that the anti-imperialists were as conservative in their tactics as in their rhetoric. The league devoted all its effort to seeking legal, peaceable transformation through public education and electoral activity. The league's leadership was in most cases impeccably bourgeois, consisting largely of professionals, politicians, and businessmen. They had no propensity toward militancy, and as a result of investing so much energy in the 1900 election, which became the testing ground of the anti-imperialist coalition, they experienced a protracted decline.

The presidential election of 1900 was to represent the major challenge for this anti-imperialist coalition. Indeed, following the war's prosecution and the ratification of the Treaty of Paris, the election became the primary focus of the league, as it sought by throwing its weight behind the Democratic candidate William Jennings Bryan to stop the arch-imperialist Republican, William McKinley. Bryan would not have been the first choice of the anti-imperialists. While the Republicans favored "sound money," the Democratic candidate was campaigning for "free silver." This was a deliberately inflationary policy that would benefit rural debtors at the expense of financial creditors largely based in the Northeast. It could also potentially devalue workers' wages, and thus could be seen as a narrowly sectional program. This was a subject that vexed many of the league's members because it would undoubtedly cost Bryan political support in New York, Massachusetts, and Connecticut. William Croffut, secretary of the Washington, DC, branch of the Anti-Imperialist League, wrote to Bryan begging him to drop this policy on those grounds.[21]

But Bryan was a child of the Midwest, a "Jacksonian Democrat" supported by the Populists and aligned with the progressivism of the era, characterized by support for trust-busting, social reform, peace, and temperance. Like many Progressives of the era, such as Woodrow Wilson under whom he served, he was also committed to white supremacy—and indeed, in his defense of Jim Crow, he could cite the inconsistency of northern Republicans who criticized segregation but would impose laws on Filipinos under which they themselves would not live. The "free silver" policy could be seen, in this light, as possibly anti-Semitic in targeting financiers regarded as a "Jewish" clique. However, circumstantial evidence seems to show that Bryan was not motivated by anti-Semitism, but merely genuinely aimed to curtail the concentration of financial power. Whatever the motive, he could not be shifted on it.[22]

A somewhat more serious failing, perhaps, was that Bryan had been among those to support the ratification of the Treaty of Paris, through which the United States assumed control of Spain's lost territories for the bargain price of $20 million. Thus, he had helped inflict the first serious defeat on the league, despite the fact that the treaty fulfilled every condition of imperialism that Bryan had anticipated. His reasoning was that only by approving the treaty would hostilities be ended. In fact, this was the least plausible outcome of ratification. By taking control of the Philippines, the United States became embroiled in a prolonged counterinsurgency war in which approximately eighteen thousand Filipinos were killed, and up to six hundred thousand died as a result of the conditions of war and the concentration camps built by US forces. Many observers had been all too well aware that a military resistance awaited the United States if it tried to usurp the freedom for which Filipino nationalists had been fighting. The league debated alternatives, possibly including impeachment proceedings against McKinley or a third party devoted to the single issue of imperialism. For his part, Twain declined to vote for either candidate, convinced that Bryan was unsafe on finance and McKinley wrong on the Philippines.[23]

Bryan's ultimate defeat demoralized the majority of the league's members, who slipped out of activism, leaving a greatly reduced core. The decision to support Bryan represented an episode in a long-standing tendency for antiwar movements in the United States to be co-opted by one of the two capitalist parties, particularly the Democratic Party. This would again pose problems in the run-up to American participation in World War I, as Woodrow Wilson's Democratic campaign was able to raise the slogan "He Kept Us Out of the War," even if he was about to lead America into the war. Throughout the twentieth century, the Democrats—despite their warlike propensities—would continue to cultivate a reputation as the party of "peace." As we will see, this has had profoundly demobilizing effects on antiwar movements. It is worth saying something here about how the Democrats relate to mass movements. As mentioned, Bryan's candidacy was supported by the Populists. In fact, just as much as the investment in Bryan's candidacy demobilized the Anti-Imperialist League, so Bryan's annexation of much of the Populist agenda for the Democratic platform was a kiss of death to the Populist movement, which subsequently lost much of its appeal as an autonomous, dissident movement. It is this habit of co-opting and neutralizing oppositional movements that has led some to characterize the Democratic Party as "the graveyard of social movements." In Gramscian terms, we could characterize its mode of operation as "transformism." That is, it absorbs elements of popular dissent, neutralizes their oppositional force, and incorporates them into a politics of the pro-capitalist center. This became a core Democratic practice, particularly after the "New Deal" consolidated the Democrats' support among working-class constituencies.[24]

The emergence of hard evidence of US atrocities in the Philippines, which were brought to the attention of the Senate Committee on the Philippines in the winter of 1902, reinvigorated the Anti-Imperialist League. The army had constructed concentration camps and destroyed crops to starve the population into submission, policies that were remarkably similar to those used by the Spanish colonial authorities in Cuba, which had supposedly scandalized American statesmen. Some of the inspiration for this policy came from the British Empire and its war on the Boers of South Africa. Winston Churchill had proselytized for its use while on a speaking tour of the United States, and two months later the first American camps were being constructed in the Philippines.[25]

Twain was in his element when wearing his spleen on his sleeve over this issue, satirizing talk of "collateral damage": "Thirty thousand [US soldiers] killed a million [Filipinos]. It seems a pity that the historian let that get out; it is really a most embarrassing circumstance."[26] Dissent once more reached into the highest chambers of government. Republican senator George Frisbie rose in the

Senate to denounce the Washington men who had "devastated provinces . . . slain uncounted thousands of peoples . . . established reconcentration camps," and who had made the US flag "the emblem of sacrilege in Christian churches, and of the burning of human dwellings, and of the horror of the water torture." The league itself did not hesitate to document and describe "the treatment which the Filipinos have received at the hands of subjugating armies" and draw out the implications. "The truth is," it argued, that "the colonial system, if not administered with absolute barbarism, seems to have broken down all round." The idea that any government, whatever its pretensions to humane nobility, could impose its rule on another people by beneficent means had been severely tested and found wanting in the colonial frontiers.[27]

However, the anti-imperialists, for all that they channeled the shades of 1776, had been susceptible to charges of lacking patriotism, of being insufficiently supportive of the troops. This was a charge they took pains to refute. Yet, they also sought to counteract the veneration of militarism. In their 1902 annual meeting, the Republican cofounder of the league, George Boutwell, complained that "a new feature has been introduced to our public policy. The army is sacred. Nothing else is sacred," he noted, but the army had been "freed from reproach, whatever its misdoings may be."[28]

No matter how much they railed against it, however, the anti-imperialists had to find ways of coping with this new esteem in which the military was held. This efficiently disarmed some of their propaganda efforts over the atrocities of the US military. Andrew Carnegie, who had little to fear personally from public opinion, financed an investigation by Herbert Welsh into the atrocities, but later thought better of it: "We have only to dub ourselves as blackeners of the American troops," he explained, "to render ourselves impotent for all good to the people of the Philippines."

A combination of racism, patriotism, and militarism had inoculated many Americans against the charges. Perhaps many were also receptive to Theodore Roosevelt's bogus claim that American atrocities were aberrant, and that for every one of those were a hundred worse crimes by Filipino rebels. It is a style of argument that has long since entered the repertoire of all guilty men in the heat of war.[29] The momentum gradually passed, the Senate investigation ended, and the league continued its efforts in a greatly reduced capacity.

. . . and Beyond

Having outlined the league's humanitarian, internationalist, and solidaristic aspects, we must revert to a more critical mode. The league was built on an alliance between people who abhorred the subjection of human beings to racist, imperialist bondage *and* those who actually favored it. Many of its members were not consistently anti-imperialist. Some, such as Andrew Carnegie, favored annexation of other territory (Canada or Hawaii). William Jennings Bryan, the league's de facto candidate in the 1900 election, would go on to serve under Wilson through successive imperialist ventures, including America's entry into the bloodbath of World War I.

Worse, many were Southern Dixiecrats, racists who were even then still erecting the Jim Crow structure that would not be overthrown until roughly the same moment at which another great anti-imperialist movement emerged. The Dixiecrats' racism was not unconnected with their opposition to expansion, moreover, as they believed that empire would necessarily result in the Philippines becoming a territory of the United States with the same constitutional rights—adding more brown-skinned people to the population did not seem to them a fitting mode of expansion. In essence, this objection was similar to southern segregationist objections to making Hawaii a state in 1959.[30] The Dixiecrats lambasted imperialism in the language of "plunder" and "robbery," but put a malicious twist on these terms by suggesting that the "black

Republican party north" was stealing from the Philippines just as they had once stolen southerners' slaves.[31]

It is true that the dominant tenor of the organization's platform was antiracist. Many of the league's supporters had cut their teeth in antislavery activism. Some supporters, such as William Lloyd Garrison and Oswald Garrison Villard, bore the name of abolitionist forebears.[32] The platform of the league stressed the rights of Filipinos and others to self-government: "all men, of whatever race or color, are entitled to life, liberty, and the pursuit of happiness." A key early speech by cofounder Carl Schurz compared those who would argue that "we are in it, and now we must do the best that we can" with the "slavery compromisers," who accepted injustice supposedly the better to mitigate its effects. Twain, at this point in his career a long-standing antiracist, could be relied upon to mock the pretensions of a country that proclaimed to be "standing up for human rights everywhere," "the refuge of the oppressed from everywhere . . . anyone except a Chinaman."[33]

In defending the right of Filipinos to self-government, the fifteenth annual meeting of the league noted the rising arc of Jim Crow and Tammany Hall corruption in the United States to argue that Filipinos should not be denied self-government on the basis of standards that did not even apply in the United States: "While colored men are denied the suffrage in defiance of the Fifteenth Amendment, while lynchers go unwhipped of justice, while night-riders are found in Kentucky . . . while Tammany threatens New York . . . it is not for us to insist that the Filipinos must do what after centuries of experience we failed to do."[34] Yet the league in practice accommodated and even relied on the segregationists. And racism did not stop at the Mason-Dixon Line. Some of the league's leading figures were well known for their anti-immigrant views, not least the immigrant labor leader Samuel Gompers, part of whose reasoning in opposing the war was that annexation of the Philippines would lead to competition from cheap Filipino labor. Others regurgitated the southern elites' argument that Filipinos participating in the government of the United States would be a disaster. As one speech in the House of Representatives put it: "No matter whether they are fit to govern themselves or not, they are not fit to govern us."[35]

Partly as a consequence, the league did not largely reflect or incorporate the widespread opposition of African Americans to the Spanish-American War. African Americans were not prominent in the league, but black voices against the war were prominent. African American newspapers urged their readers to support the Cuban rebels, but not to fight on the side of imperialism, which blighted "the manhood of the darker races."[36] The Black Man's Burden Association in Chicago highlighted the Anglo-Saxon supremacist aspects of the war.[37] In fact, Kipling's poem produced quite a few satirical take-offs, including J. Dallas Bowser's "The Black Man's Burden," which inverted the missionary appeal of the original, urging African Americans to "Stoop with a freeman's ardor/Lift high a freeman's head,/Stand with a freeman's firmness/March with a freeman's tread."[38]

African Americans formed their own independent anti-imperialist organizations—such as the Negro National Anti-Imperial and Anti-Trust League and the Colored National Anti-Imperialistic League. Booker T. Washington wrote to the Anti-Imperialist League to profess his support.[39] African American women organizing against lynching saw their campaign as being part of the anti-imperialist movement.[40] For W. E. B. Du Bois, the aggression in the Philippines underlined the connection between imperialism and Jim Crow, demonstrating the futility of solutions to racism based on migrating from the United States: "Where in the world may we go and be safe from lying and brute force?"[41]

It is also true that many African American soldiers did serve in Cuba. Among their reasons for doing so was that the frontiers of war offered an escape route from submission to Jim Crow and constant racist denigration. On the front line, they could partake of the 'manliness' usually attributed exclusively to white males in racist discourse. Yet there is also the splendid example of African American soldiers rebelling against their commanders in a series of actions that US military officials characterized as an "insurgency." Aside from the dozens of African Americans who deserted, whose names have not been preserved in mainstream histories, there was the case of David Fagen, a corporal who decided to join Emilio Aguinaldo's revolutionary army. Fagen very quickly found himself a trusted and effective ally of the Filipino national movement, a captain of his own unit who fought against the troops whose imperial mission he was supposed to be supporting. His tactical successes saw him promoted within the guerrillas to the rank of captain and won him notoriety among US forces. In addition to Fagen, there was the "Unknown Soldier" whose body was found after a battle in which the Filipino guerrillas were given "the necessary castigation," the "cold steel," in the words of Colonel Frederick Funston. Funston's memoirs describe how "among the dead we were surprised to find a very large and coal-black negro. As this was many months before any of our colored troops had been brought to the islands, the man could not have been a deserter from them, but was probably some vagabond seaman who had run away from a merchant-vessel in Manila Bay." Of those who deserted the US Army, the names of seven who joined the Filipino guerrillas are known. Part of the motivation for this rebellion was the experience of racism both in the armed forces and in US society more widely. A contemporary journalist observed that "the negro soldiers were in closer sympathy with the aims of the native population than they were with those of their white leaders and the policy of the United States." This continued the tradition of rebellions and desertions by US soldiers in imperial frontiers which, by the time of the Vietnam War, had become a serious obstacle to the war machine.[42]

If the league was overwhelmingly white, it was also largely male, with women not being allowed to serve as officers until 1904. Some of the strongest supporters of the Anti-Imperialist League and opponents of the Spanish-American War were women's groups such as the National Council of Women and the National American Woman Suffrage Association. The progressive feminist Jane Addams, who had helped found the Chicago branch of the Anti-Imperialist League in 1899, linked her peace activism with her suffragism. Part of Addams's reasoning was that empire was bringing out the most violent, destructive aspects of American society, producing a brutalization of American culture. The imperialist moment she saw was in part the result of a breakdown of the order in which America could exist in relative isolation. The fate of different peoples was becoming increasingly interwoven, and so nationalism had to give way to internationalism, patriotism to humanitarianism.[43]

However, all this notwithstanding, Erin Murphy's archive-based study of the league's activism shows how the organization was all too ready to make use of female labor, donations, and other contributions while denying women full membership. Its vocabulary was gendered, as was its activism. One could almost be forgiven for writing these anti-imperialists off as bourgeois, white men anxious to maintain the privileges of a bourgeois, white, male republic.[44]

When Mary Livermore of the Massachusetts Woman Suffrage Association spoke at a gathering of the Anti-Imperialist League in Boston in 1903, she tried to persuade the male liberals present to see the connections between their struggle and that of American women: "I have for half a century been slowly, with a company of other women, trying to obtain for women the rights which you want for the Filipinos—the right to vote, to have a voice in the representation, and to effect something. I think I have got a good deal of the Filipino spirit in my veins, which enables me to sympathize with the work you are doing for the Filipinos." In making such a connection, she was not articulating the views of the largely bourgeois white suffragists who linked their claims for citizenship with their whiteness. Nor did she succeed in shifting the league's practices.[45] As Murphy puts it: "While [the league] espoused freedom, liberty, and self-determination, they practiced patriarchal control of the resistance. While they tried to prevent the nation from committing violence against racialized imperialist subjects, they kept Black men and women at the margins."[46]

In addition, because the political coalition behind the league rested on some reactionary forces, this tended to exclude the left. The American Federation of Labor (AFL) was represented by Samuel Gompers. To its credit, the AFL had adopted a consistently anti-imperialist stance. To its discredit, this was often infused with racist hysteria about "semi-barbaric" and "servile" races flooding into America and reducing the wages and conditions of US workers. The left largely was not represented. This was not entirely the league's fault. While socialist workers and parties were opposed to the war, and most socialist organizations had maintained opposition throughout the war, their publications mostly saw the war as an attempt to divert working people from their domestic struggles. The *People*, published by Daniel DeLeon's Socialist Labor Party (SLP), argued that the war distracted "the attention of the workers from their real interests," while the *Appeal to Reason* argued that war was "a favorite method of rulers for keeping the people from redressing domestic wrongs." Opposition to war and militarism was often conditioned by workers' own experiences of being attacked by soldiers during strike actions.[47] As David Montgomery writes:

> Both the regular army and state national guards had been called out to break strikes again and again during the 1890s. Troops suppressing the Coeur d'Alene, Homestead, and Pullman strikes had attracted national attention, while the 1897 massacre of Slavic strikers at Lattimer Mines, Pennsylvania, and the 1898 confrontations at Virden and Pana, Illinois, coincided with the Federation's convention debates about war and imperialism. AFL president Samuel Gompers had declared back in 1892 that "membership in a labor organization and the militia at one and the same time is inconsistent and incompatible."[48]

Some socialist literature made occasional reference to imperi-alism as a drive for markets and raw materials, but by and large it was not animated by the McKinley-Bryan debates on imperialism.[49] When the debate took place in the AFL, the only opposition to the majority anti-imperialist position came from socialist delegates who considered the issue a contrivance of the ruling class that workers should have "nothing to do with." There was a basis for such views in that Gompers's position meant taking organized labor into an alliance with a section of business, and that aspects of his stance were predicated on a national chauvinism that, while less immediately dangerous than imperialist chauvinism, was no more acceptable to socialists. As a consequence, for example, the SLP, having organized antiwar demonstrations in 1898, declined to make it an issue in their electoral campaign.[50] Perhaps some of the reason for this is that many socialists at the time were committed to na-tionalist and racist chauvinism, seeing no conflict between this and their avowed internationalism.[51] In DeLeon's case, it was more likely due to his dogmatic approach to national liberation struggles, which he saw as a concession to bourgeois ideology, replacing one group of capitalists with another.[52] The league was convinced that something radically novel was taking place with colonization, and they were right. It was the socialist organizations who missed a trick here—and in fairness, their European comrades didn't see anything exceptional in it either. Still, it is known that the league attracted workers and radicals and, with the exception of certain labor leaders who could hardly be classified as radical, they were largely excluded from its running.[53]

Yet for all the failings of, and repugnant elements in, the league, it still had the moral advantage on its opponents. While the league cited the Declaration of Independence and championed the Filipinos' right to self-determination, Albert Beveridge argued that the declaration applied "only to people capable of self-government. How dare any man prostitute this expression of the very elect of self-governing peoples to a race of Malay children of barbarism, schooled in Spanish methods and ideas?" And he could not resist the Lockean pretext for white rule—as in China, he perceived, the "careless natives" had not properly used and developed the gifts of the earth. They were the inheritors of great mineral riches that had lain dormant due to the inhabitants' "superstition," "dishonesty," and "disorder in the habits of industry."[54]

As it turned out, the southern segregationists had much to gain from colonial expansion. Northern Republicans could hardly object to Jim Crow in the South when they were busily imposing Jim Crow in the Pacific and Caribbean. And the former were as contemptuous of the rights of the "colored people" they now governed in the Philippines, Puerto Rico, and Cuba. The turn to colonies was coterminous with a severe racial reaction in the United States, as northern liberals expressed and reinforced the same supremacist attitudes that southern conservatives did. In recognition of a shared interest, many southern senators backed the Republican McKinley, while the Republicans in turn made no attempt to stop the Jim Crow system in its tracks. Imperialism became a vector through which the racist assumptions of southern whites were nationalized. By 1908, the Republican president and Rooseveltian imperialist William Taft was reassuring southern audiences that racial equality would never be imposed by law, that the federal government had nothing to do with social equality, and that Jim Crow was entirely compatible with the Fifteenth Amendment.[55]

For this reason, the coalition that liberals were willing to forge with southern reactionaries was all the more disastrous to their cause. Rather than seek alliances with more radical forces, they sought to use the support of southern racist elites to fight political battles within the legislature. First, they tried to stop the ratification of the Treaty of Paris, ceding territorial control of Cuba and the Philippines to the United States. But of twenty-five southern senators, ten voted in favor of it, and the treaty was ratified. Similarly, their reliance on William Jennings Bryan's Democratic candidature, predicated on southern support, ultimately resulted in defeat.

While the league experienced a decline after 1900, this age also saw the beginnings of mass pacifism reflected in antiwar literature. Women's movements for peace proliferated, and the socialist challenge to capitalism and empire began to take off independently of the league. Legal approaches to antiwar activism also saw their beginnings in this era. In 1899, the First Hague Peace Conference provided the beginnings of an international legal rationale for opposing war. The result of the conference was a set of conventions "for the pacific settlement of international disputes," which came to be known as the Hague Conventions. These were far from anti-imperialist in spirit. The first convention appealed to "the solidarity which unites the members of the society of civilized nations." Yet, by indicating that arbitration through a legal apparatus should be the alternative to war, it seemed to offer anti-imperialists and peace movements a language with which to constrain the warmongers.

Some on the left, including the British Fabians, had long advocated some form of international legal framework, a United Nations of some kind, to deal with issues of war and peace. In America, the feminist and peace activist Lucia Ames Mead argued for arbitration coupled with an "international police force" as a means of dealing with international conflicts without appealing to action from self-interested national states. Such a police force could "bring stubborn nations to the World's Court with the same efficiency as the city police separate two men, glaring at each other with murderous knives unsheathed, and drag them to the Police Court." This disturbed Captain Alfred Thayer Mahan, a key advocate of empire, who maintained that the United States could not have acted according to its conscience in the Philippines if the matter had been referred to a court or arbitration.[56]

However, appeals to international law, while consistent with the legalist, parliamentarist approach that characterized the Anti-

Imperialist League at its height, contained their own dangers. International legalization began as a process within imperialism and colonialism, the logical and necessary corollary of a competitive states system, rather than as its negation. And imperialist powers have largely been responsible for the construction of the global deliberative bodies where legal arguments are resolved. For example, the United States and its imperialist allies took the lead in founding the League of Nations at the Paris Peace Conference. The United States later played the key role in the formation of the United Nations, which has more often facilitated US aggression than constrained it. In the century after the Anti-Imperialist League was founded, activists found international bodies either incapable of preventing imperial aggression (as in the case of Mussolini's invasion of Ethiopia, the US invasion of Vietnam, or the US-led invasion of Iraq) or directly complicit in it (for example, the UN's support for the United States in the Korean War, or Operation Desert Storm, or the multilateral invasion of Haiti in 2004). Marx's incomparable expression, "between equal rights, force decides," is relevant here. If law is founded on violence—is, in a sense, congealed violence—then it follows that the interpretation and application of law is largely in the gift of those with a superior capacity for violence.[57]

In the coming years, resistance to war would take on a more radical hue. The leadership of bourgeois white males would give way to broad coalitions of militant workers, feminist women, and African Americans. The methods emphasizing electoralism and lobbying would give way to strikes, mass protests, and international solidarity. In the next wave of anti-imperialist struggle, socialists would have the initiative. In the next chapter, the rise of Wilsonian "liberal internationalism" is contrasted with the concurrent rise of socialist internationalism.

Chapter Three

From Wilsonianism to Bolshevism

American Business Men in Mexico are a degraded race. They have a deep-seated contempt for the Mexicans, because they are different from themselves. They prate of our grand old democratic institutions, and then declare in the same breath that the peons ought to be driven to work for them with rifles. They boast in private of the superiority of American courage over Mexican, and then sneakingly buckle to whatever party is in power.
—John Reed, "What About Mexico?" 1914

War is the health of the State. It automatically sets in motion throughout society those irresistible forces for uniformity, for passionate co-operation with the Government in coercing into obedience the minority groups and individuals which lack the larger herd sense. The machinery of government sets and enforces the drastic penalties, the minorities are either intimidated into silence or brought slowly around by a subtle process of persuasion which may seem to them really to be converting them. Of course the ideal of perfect loyalty, perfect uniformity is never attained. . . . But in general, the nation in war-time attains a uniformity of feeling, a hierarchy of values, culminated at the undisputed apex of the State ideal, which could not

possibly be produced through any other agency than war.
—Randolph Bourne, "The State," 1918

Woodrow Wilson is invoked with reverence in certain foreign policy circles. Both liberals and neoconservatives claim a Wilsonian mandate, and Wilsonian scholars tend to make a very easy transition to policy making. He is associated with the nobler goals of statecraft: progressivism at home, liberal internationalism abroad. In foreign policy terms, he is considered an "idealist" in contrast to hard-nosed "realists," in that he maintained that it was possible to transcend force and gently civilize international affairs through appropriate multilateral institutions and legal regimes. In this sense, Wilson is seen as an heir to Kant, whose "democratic peace theory" maintained that democracies tended to be less likely to wage war with one another. The goal of US governments, then, ought to be to spread democracy where possible and build a liberal world order recognizing the self-determination of nations.[1] I will be brief with this reputation.

First, a word about the situation in which Wilson was operating. The United States had until 1898 been a strictly regional power. The colonial turn marked America's emergence as a potentially global power. In 1898, 90 percent of investments by US capital were still domestic, but overseas expansion and the control of new markets potentially offered a means to export more capital.[2] However, as Neil Smith writes: "The taking of Cuba, Puerto Rico, and the Philippines in 1898—the crumbs of the collapsed Spanish empire— were woefully insufficient to absorb the surplus capital, and the prospect of battling existing European powers, especially Britain, for new territory was hardly enticing." In addition, fighting indigenous populations and all the while maintaining customs, legislation, a civil service, and a global military presence was neither inviting nor plausible on a global scale. If the United States was to be a global power, it would have to find a way to dominate capital and trade flows without direct territorial control.[3]

Wilson's engagements with imperial politics took shape during this transitional period. His conception of a liberal global order was essentially colonial and was profoundly shaped by his native racism. His attitude to statehood and governance was based centrally on the Aryanism that would color his reception of the Ku Klux Klan and his attitude to segregation. Extolling European and American states, he noted that they derived their political habits and ideals from "the Aryan and Semitic races" with "Semitic institutions" occupying "only a secondary place" as the "main stocks of modern European forms of government are Aryan." The Aryan races had the peculiar advantage of patriarchy, whereas other races had been held back by allowing women to be in charge, and the ideal state was the father or "spiritual God-parent" of the nation.[4]

If the main stocks of best government came from the "Aryan races," it logically followed that colonialism was a sort of preparatory school for statehood. If the US state was a guardian and parent to Americans, its tutelage of other peoples who lacked a satisfactory parent could be seen as a kind of foster care. That the United States should be willing to offer its services in this regard constituted one of the core elements of Wilsonian idealism. Consequently, when the matter of American colonies in the Philippines arose, Wilson was on the side of the imperialists.

The United States had a "moral obligation" to prepare Filipinos for "the long discipline which gives people self-possession, self-master, the habit of order." Further, "we cannot give them self-government. Self-government is not a thing that can be 'given' to any people, because it is a form of character and not a form of constitution."[5] As a result, America should rule the Philippines "with a strong hand that will brook no resistance, and according to principles of right gathered from our own experience, not from theirs, which has never yet touched the vital matter that we are concerned with. . . . They are children and we are men in these deep matters of government and justice." This noble, philanthropic mission,

Wilson averred, would also have the advantage of overcoming the narrow commercial and material interests that had long breached the American national fabric along sectional lines.[6]

The liberal world order of self-determining peoples that Wilson envisaged would thus be organized around a caste of European and American states, beyond which self-determination would be subject to any curtailment that the Aryans might wish to impose.[7] As Wilson put it, the principle of the "consent of the governed" that anti-imperialists cited was inapplicable to "politically undeveloped races, which have not yet learned the rudiments of order and self-control."[8] Later, his secretary of state Robert Lansing agreed that "races, peoples or communities whose state of barbarism or ignorance" deprived them of "the capacity to choose intelligently their political affiliations" were not fit for self-government.[9] As such, "the integrity of other American nations is an incident, not an end."[10]

Lastly, Wilson's nobler aspirations for the United States were always allied to the interests of capital: thus his famous argument that as "trade ignores national boundaries," the flag of the nation must follow the manufacturer in his search for world markets. The state must batter down the doors closed to him, "even if the sovereignty of unwilling nations be outraged in the process. Colonies must be obtained or planted, in order that no useful corner of the world may be overlooked or left unused."[11] We will see how such ideas were implemented, and contested, in Wilson's interventions in Mexico, Haiti, and World War I. For it was here, with such colonial precepts ready at hand, that Wilson first defined a global role for America as a counterrevolutionary force speaking the language of revolution. And it was the growing socialist left that was to find itself in the vanguard of opposition.

Mexico, Haiti, and Counterrevolution

After the Spanish-American War, the United States would build up a catalogue of interventions into revolutionary situations. In each case, the United States would proclaim its support for the revolutionary ideas of democracy and constitutional liberty; in each case, the United States would end up on the side of reaction and tyranny. The staggering number of interventions notched up after 1898 included a joint invasion of Nicaragua with British forces in 1899, the suppression of the Chinese "Boxer Rebellion" in 1900, several interventions into Colombia and Panama the same year, interventions in the Dominican Republic in 1903 and 1904, in Cuba in 1906–07 (putting down revolutionary insurgency and imposing a stable regime), in Honduras in 1907 and 1911, in Nicaragua again in 1910 and then from 1912 to 1925.[12] Major-General Smedley Butler, a highly decorated marine who became an outspoken critic of imperialism, summarized the thrust of US policy in this period from a participant's perspective:

> I spent thirty-three years and four months in active military service as a member of this country's most agile military force, the Marine Corps. I served in all commissioned ranks from Second Lieutenant to Major-General. And during that period, I spent most of my time being a high class muscle-man for Big Business, for Wall Street and for the Bankers. In short, I was a racketeer, a gangster for capitalism.
>
> I suspected I was just part of a racket at the time. Now I am sure of it. Like all the members of the military profession, I never had a thought of my own until I left the service. My mental faculties remained in suspended animation while I obeyed the orders of higher-ups. This is typical with everyone in the military service.
>
> I helped make Mexico, especially Tampico, safe for American oil interests in 1914. I helped make Haiti and Cuba a decent place for the National City Bank boys to collect revenues in. I helped in the raping of half a dozen Central American republics for the benefits of Wall Street. The record of racketeering is long. I helped purify Nicaragua for the international banking house of Brown Brothers in 1909–1912. I brought light to the Dominican Republic for American sugar interests in 1916. In China I helped to see to it that Standard Oil went its way unmolested. . . .
>
> During those years, I had, as the boys in the back room would say, a swell racket. Looking back on it, I feel that I could have

given Al Capone a few hints. The best he could do was to operate his racket in three districts. I operated on three continents.[13]

Two examples from the Wilsonian period, interventions in Mexico and Haiti, will demonstrate how this counterrevolutionary praxis was first defined and implemented.

"Regime Change" and the American Left

The Mexican revolution of 1910–14 was made possible by a fissure within the ruling class, opened by the aging dictator Porfirio Díaz when he broached the possibility of stepping down and allowing free elections. As often happens when such insincere pledges are offered by tyrants, people chose to take him at his word, and so began a frenzied process of jockeying by elites, seeking their own candidate to advance their interests. In the countryside, and among the growing urban working class, long-standing grievances that had been repressed began to be aired. Rural elites resented their marginalization under Díaz's dictatorship, peasants were enraged by the loss of their land to "modernization" (capitalist reform designed to consolidate land ownership for the production of export crops), and workers in the mines, railroads, and textile factories had long suffered wage restraint and violent repression when they attempted to form unions or to strike. The middle class grew, the rich became superrich, but peasants and workers suffered as food prices soared.[14]

Economic crises had produced waves of struggle, food riots, and strikes in which dozens were killed by soldiers. There was a national component to this class resentment. The dictatorship was correctly perceived to be in hock to foreign investors. Díaz's modernization project, essentially aiming to use overseas investment to turn Mexico into an efficient center of capital accumulation, put the disciplinary apparatus of the state at the service of international capital.[15] Feudal systems, rather than being torn down, were integrated and adapted to the new capitalist order. For example, the hacienda continued to dominate the countryside even as land was concentrated and put to use for the production of cash crops.[16]

The national dimension of Mexican working-class struggle was noted by a visiting Socialist Party member in the era of *pax Porfiriana*: "The government continues to dole out the national resources of the country to foreign money-bags while Mexican workers grovel in filth, disease and ignorance, for lack of access to these same resources." The leaders of the revolution would later hail largely from the northern states that operated as a free trade zone for US capital. On occasion, North American forces like the Arizona Rangers—essentially, southwestern frontiersmen modeled on the Texas Rangers—were deputed by Mexican firms and regional authorities to cross the border and attack and murder striking workers. This potent mixture of class and national feeling was a source of considerable instability. Until 1910, however, elites remained cohesive enough for the regime to be viable.[17]

When the dictatorship was finally obliged to stage an election, opposition was organized around the candidacy of Francisco Madero, a centrist from the ruling class whose personal wealth financed his campaign. He won elite support by promising democratization while protecting the basic class structure.[18] He also won support from middle-class reformers who saw the Porfirian regime as a collection of "mummies that obstruct our march towards progress."[19] Repression forced working-class and leftist forces into a subterranean abeyance for the duration of the election, so Madero was able to channel popular as well as elite dissent.[20] Even so, he was prepared to compromise to the end, offering to withdraw his candidacy if he could be Díaz's vice-presidential running mate. The dictatorship turned him down, rigged the election as it had always done in the past, and claimed that Madero had only won just under two hundred votes.[21]

At this point, Madero started to consult with colleagues about the possibility of organizing a revolution. The plan was to annul the elections, declare Madero the provisional president, and prom-ise free elections. Urgent popular demands—say, for land reform—were quietly skirted. Madero would by no means harm business interests. He sought "to avoid as far as possible the disorders in-evitable in any revolutionary movement."[22] Even so, in the imme-diate term, Madero's forces succeeding in hegemonizing the revolutionary coalition that emerged, and some early successes were won under its impress.

As the revolution proceeded, however, it was successively rad-icalized and pulled to the left by the growing importance of popular forces—particularly the peasants, who formed the most radical sec-tion of the revolution. Madero had "unleashed the tiger," according to Díaz, and he could not ride it. The plantation owners were be-sieged. Wherever the Maderistas won, sharecroppers and renters seized the land. Reports warned that workers and peasants were "displaying an improper equality." Landowners were found slain by their own servants, and in some areas Indians armed themselves to dispossess the landlords. Madero's response to this was to try to di-rect popular dissent into the ballot box while building alliances with the Porfirian old guard—a fact that greatly distressed many of Madero's supporters who saw the revolution "heading towards col-lapse." As a result, new insurgencies arose, directed against the Madero government, including many of his former supporters. In the state of Morelo, the forces under Emiliano Zapata formed a Rev-olutionary Council of the State of Morelos, announcing their in-tention to turn over land, woodlands, and waters to the "villagers or citizens who have the appropriate deeds and have been dispos-sessed through the trickery of our oppressors." When Madero was deposed by General Victoriano Huerta, acting under the influence of the US ambassador, the rebellions continued and spread. Huerta's repression was so vile and bloody that even the liberal middle classes in Madero's former strongholds could not be assured of their own safety. The old guard could not be conciliated. They took up arms, calling themselves the Constitutionalists, and among them was an increasingly radicalized layer at odds with the conservative leadership of Venustiano Carranza. The revolution now involved workers, peasants, and the prosperous middle classes in different regions of the country.[23] And the US government did not intend to passively await the outcome of this process.

The United States was connected to the fate of the Mexican Revolution by several interests. First of all, there was the particular interest of capital in various timber yards, mines, and farms in which they had investments. There were the railroad investments, as US lines were extended south of the Rio Grande after 1880. Most of Mexican industry was owned by overseas investors and the greater share of US foreign direct investments were concentrated there. When the leftist army officer Francisco J. Mugica presided over the writing of Article 27 of the new constitution, he ensured that it allowed the national government to nationalize and regulate private property—including that owned by overseas investors. This was the first alarm bell for US corporations. Secondly, there was the general interest of US capitalism in a stable, business-friendly Mexico—an interest that, as we have seen, Woodrow Wilson was disposed to protect and defend. Thirdly, there was the quite contrasting interest of Latino residents of the United States, as well as the left and American workers more generally, in seeing the success of democratic and popular forces in Mexico. It worried the Texas authorities in particular that many Texans of all ethnicities were fiercely supportive of the revolution, and the Texas Rangers played a very bloody role on the border, supported by politically active elements in the business community.[24]

Developments since the zenith of the Anti-Imperialist League had changed the political environment in the United States. As the state began to embark on reforms aimed at co-opting working-class dissent, much of the skepticism that the leadership of the organized labor movement held toward empire had evaporated. It resulted in

Gompers quitting the league. The AFL ceased to agitate around the colonies, and moved very close to the Wilson administration. The AFL still had an interest in building international affiliates, but Mexican workers under the dictatorship were largely unable to join unions and, where they did, they tended not to associate with the AFL's international unions. Ideologically, many Mexican workers were closer to the syndicalist union, the Industrial Workers of the World (IWW)—known as the "Wobblies." The Wobblies, founded in 1905 with the support of socialists such as Eugene Debs, Daniel DeLeon, and William ("Big Bill") Haywood. The IWW was founded on the principle that multiracial industrial unionism open to everyone regardless of skill, gender, race, or nationality was superior to the conservative, white, male craft unionism practiced by the AFL. Through its support for Mexican immigrant workers in labor-intensive sectors of the US economy, it exerted a profound effect on the emergence of Mexican workers' radicalism.[25]

International solidarity was an imperative of the socialist left. Given US investments in Mexico, workers from the North tended to circulate among Mexican workers, bringing with them a familiarity with the American left and union movement. The Socialist Party, formed in 1901 from a merger between Daniel DeLeon's Socialist Labor Party and the Social Democratic Party of America, began to make tentative connections with Mexican leftists in 1905, particularly with the Mexican Liberal Party (known by its Spanish acronym PLM), an anarchist party that reflected many of the views of the IWW and that had long-standing involvement in building strikes in the north of Mexico, as well as organizing Mexican workers in Texas.

From its offices in California, the Socialist Party began to build solidarity with PLM activists, whose headquarters were in Los Angeles due to repression within Mexico. They set up the Mexican Revolutionists Defense League to support PLM members prosecuted by the United States over alleged plans to mount an invasion of Mexico from St. Louis. Socialist Party writer John Turner became a minor celebrity among Mexican workers due to his regular dispatches for *American Magazine, Appeal to Reason,* and others on the exploitation of Mexican workers, and his advocacy for Mexican refugees in the United States. When the revolution broke out, he was an early supporter, comparing the practices of US capital in Mexico to slavery—indeed, hacienda owners bought and sold workers just like slaves, under the pretense that these arrangements were servicing a debt—and the revolt to abolitionism. The idiom of abolitionism was neither incidental nor accidental. Just as the later struggle against civil rights would segue into antiwar activism, its vernacular mobilized in critique of imperialism, so abolitionism was an auspicious component of the American left's vocabulary in the Progressive era, a discourse that united issues as disparate as the Civil War, the Haymarket martyrs, and, indeed, the Mexican Revolution.[26]

Wilson's Debut

The 1912 presidential election, which Wilson won on a reform agenda, was also a breakthrough for the socialists. Eugene Debs, running for the Socialist Party of America, gained nearly a million votes, and 6 percent of the national total. Aside from votes for Debs, the Socialists gained congressmen, mayors, and a host of lesser positions in cities across the country. The immediate challenge was to oppose the drift toward military intervention in the Mexican Revolution.

Wilson's express fear, providing the apparent motive for intervention, was that the revolution was out of control. Madero had been losing popular support due to his failure to carry out land reforms, and the United States had supported General Victoriana Huerta in launching a conservative coup against the Madero government in February 1913. By 1914, however, Wilson was convinced that this was a mistake. An apostle of liberal capitalism, Wilson was confident that educated Mexican elites would, if they could take control of the process, build a stable state that would act as a guardian of enterprise. Thus, he explained that US political and economic elites ought to be "the first to take part in assisting" the revolution. He argued that Mexicans could be "made to be capable of self-government," and promised that the United States would never again acquire "one additional foot of territory by conquest."

Yet, if territorial annexation was out of the question, intervention was not. Wilson explained that he would "teach the South American republics to elect good men." If they insisted on rebelling against those good men, the United States reserved the right to intervene—as when Secretary of State William Jennings Bryan negotiated an agreement with President Díaz of Nicaragua, where US Marines were protecting the regime against potential uprisings, which gave the United States a perpetual right to intervene in the country's affairs. Although Wilson was concerned to ensure that the government of Mexico should have constitutional legitimacy, he had little to say about the burning agrarian question and nothing at all about the growing labor insurgencies. Indeed, the main concern of the administration and its successor was to ensure that no Mexican government embraced a policy of economic nationalism. Thus, under Wilson, the United States could appear to champion revolution without supporting a revolutionary agenda.[27]

Wilson's first attempted intervention began with the occupation of Veracruz in April 1914, just as Huerta's rule was jeopardized by the forces of the peasant revolutionary Emiliano Zapata and Venustiano Carranza, a constitutional liberal from a large landowning family. The pretext for this intervention was a petty diplomatic incident in which Mexican soldiers detained a number of US sailors due to a misunderstanding. As neither the soldiers nor the sailors spoke one another's language, the soldiers, expecting attacks from the opposition, detained them. Wilson demanded and received Congressional authority for an armed invasion of the territory. The apparent aim of the occupation was to destabilize Huerta's regime by making it impossible for him to use his base and to embolden the liberal wing of the revolution.

Yet the liberals who were supposed to benefit bitterly denounced this instance of yanqui imperialism. Carranza, who went on to assume the presidency when Huerta fled, was among the leading critics. Still, Wilson recognized the new regime when it agreed to protect overseas property, and American oil companies lavished the new president with gifts in the hope that their interests would be conserved. It worked, inasmuch as Carranza declined to engage in any substantial reforms and did not nationalize capital held by foreign investors. It was for this reason that the revolution continued, and radicalized, under the leadership of Zapata and Pancho Villa, another peasant leader.[28]

The second occasion for Wilsonian intervention arose when Villa, angry over US support for Carranza, engaged in an expedition into the United States, invading the town of Columbus, New Mexico, in January 1916 and killing seventeen US citizens. The United States responded by sending a force of six thousand people under General John Pershing to chase Villa three hundred miles into Mexico, though their quarry eluded capture. Carranza denounced the invasion, and his forces had a direct engagement with US troops in which seventeen of the latter were either killed or captured. War seemed an inevitability, especially after the Mexican government passed a new constitution in 1917 that allowed for the nationalization of Mexican resources. But Mexico was a large, populous country that would be no easy conquest. At any rate, America was already mired in a counterinsurgency in Haiti and had a Great War on the European continent to contemplate. Nonetheless, the pressure for intervention periodically returned, as in 1919 when an influential Senate subcommittee claimed that Mexico was circulating Bolshevik propaganda. Congress and the press amplified these claims, which shortly gave way to the cry "Mexico next!"[29]

US intervention divided the American left. The Socialist Party was largely against the intervention. Dan LaBotz writes:

> The Socialist Party vigorously opposed and vehemently condemned Woodrow Wilson's invasion of Veracruz. Mary E. Marcy, in an article titled "Whose War Is This?" published in June 1915, immediately after the invasion, argued that neither the Mexicans nor the Americans had anything to gain from a U.S. war. In the tradition of international socialism she argued that "If we are working men or working women, we HAVE NO COUNTRY. . . . The working men and women of ALL countries are OUR countrymen."
>
> Moreover, wrote Marcy, "American working men have no quarrel with Mexican working men. Their interests are our interests. . . . The only war in which we should engage is the working class war, which will abolish Poverty from the face of the earth!"
>
> Marcy's article was accompanied by an article by Manuel Sarabia in which, after giving a long historic background of the Revolution, he argued that "The Mexicans must be left alone to work out their own salvation."
>
> In addition to those two articles, there was a letter from "I. D.," a "U.S. Marine," written to his sister, presumably a member of the Socialist Party who had passed it on to the [International Socialist Review]. The Marine described how the invaders had killed 300 Mexicans and how one naval bombardment had hit a school and killed 100 children. "Everywhere you look you would see a dead Spick, and the street all over blood," wrote the Marine. "Sad sight to look upon." It has a familiar ring even today.[30]

Yet there was much on which fractions of the American left and labor movement, whose response to the revolution had been relatively conservative, could agree with the Wilson administration. Eugene Debs, "Mother" Jones, and Samuel Gompers had all supported Madero and the moderate capitalist currents around him, rejecting calls for peasants to seize control of the land on the grounds that it was "premature." Many socialists were, like their Second International equivalents in Europe, beholden to a "stageist" view of history—a conception of progress in which all societies must move through certain discrete stages of economic development, or modes of production. Mexico, they maintained, would have to pass through a process of bourgeois democracy before it could attain socialism. As a consequence, many were able to view US capitalist dominance in the Caribbean and Central America as historically progressive. It was in this vein that the *International Socialist Review* carried an article justifying US intervention, which it foresaw would eventually absorb the country, as a boon for Mexican development. Furthermore, when Villa's forces entered Columbus, many previously antiwar socialists suddenly favored intervention, though the Socialist Party maintained an official policy of opposition.[31]

John Reed, the distinguished socialist journalist, covered the revolution and took the side of the revolutionaries. His *Insurgent Mexico* sympathetically described firsthand the battles of the insurgents, drew invaluable thumbnail sketches of the revolutionary leaders Carranza and Villa, and is notable for the constant attention it gave to "the land question" against those who would marginalize it.[32] Early on, he foresaw the danger of US intervention posing as an ally of the revolution the better to destroy it:

> The other foreigners in Mexico usually stand firm on the side of the oppressor, but the American can be found hat in hand in the audience room of the Palace at all seasons of the year, so long as there is some hope of protecting his little investment. And it is for the benefit of these men—who admittedly make forty or fifty per cent on their money, because they say they are taking a "gambler's chance," and then squeal when they lose—that the United States has been pushed to the very brink of conquest. . . .
>
> But if we are forced over the Border—if in any way we inject ourselves into Mexican politics—it will mean the end of the Revolution. For we could never recognize a government there unsuited to the European Powers—indeed, I don't see how we can now; and a government suited to the European Powers would mean the confirmation of foreign concessions, the establishment of the "respectable" element in power, and the subsequent checking of anything like a radical distribution of lands among the peons. We could not sanction a government really elected by the peons, because they would elect a government which would give them what they have been fighting for so long.

And that means Confiscation—which the merest school-child knows to be a worse crime than the robbery of peons!

So I think that the United States Government is really headed toward the policy of "civilizing 'em with a Krag"—a process which consists in forcing upon alien races with alien temperaments our own Grand Democratic Institutions: I refer to Trust Government, Unemployment, and Wage Slavery.[33]

Ironically, however, an anti-imperialist answer to Wilsonian intervention was supplied by Woodrow Wilson himself in a 1914 interview with a journalist. "I challenge you," he said, "to cite me an instance in all the history of the world where liberty was handed down from above. Liberty is always attained by the forces working from below, underneath."[34] A revolutionary idea, this, and one all too often forgotten or ignored by the soi-disant friends of liberty.

Haiti

In July 1915, the tiny island state of Haiti, the slave republic and polestar of Black freedom, presented a much more appealing conquest than Mexico. Here, it took little effort to dissolve the legislature and impose a loyal marionette—Phillippe Sudre Dartiguenave—who would "put an end to the revolution," seize the custom houses, take over the financial institutions, impose a new constitution favorable to overseas investors, and begin to impose a new system of slavery, a form of forced labor known as *corvée*. US Marines had to fight a prolonged war against indigenous resistance, the Cacos, based in the countryside. But they succeeded in imposing the new model state that they had in mind, and erected a gendarmerie (National Guard) to protect the state once the marines ended their nineteen-year occupation.

As far as the US military was concerned, this was all as it should be. They were fathers and protectors to a people treated as minors. The Haitians, Major General Smedley Butler later testified, "were our wards . . . we were endeavoring to make for them a rich and productive property, to be turned over to them at such a time as our government saw fit." In this respect, the intervention was not that different from the occupation of Nicaragua six years earlier. These interventions built on previous subventions in South America and reflected America's naval supremacy in the Caribbean. They also expressed the long-standing attitude that the islands of that sea, as well as the territories south of the US border, were a backyard for the northern behemoth—though perhaps "backyard" doesn't quite sell it, as it is a rare backyard that functions simultaneously as plantation, mine, labor camp, and laboratory.[35]

The publicly expressed mission of the US Navy in invading Haiti was to restore order following the revolution against the pro-American dictator Jean Vilbrun Guillaume Sam. To be sure, US investments were threatened by instability, but there was also an element of competition with European powers, as British and German capital had begun to penetrate Haitian markets, their trading shops docked at Haitian ports, and a German submarine base at Haiti was mooted. Racism predictably conditioned the specific policies of US elites, for whom knowledge of Haiti was slight, and hastily battened onto the assumptions of Anglo-Saxon paternalism. Secretary of State William Jennings Bryan, who was in charge of the mission, knew so little about Haiti that he requested a report from American businessmen about the country. His reaction: "Dear me, imagine that! N*****s speaking French."[36]

The US labor movement was largely unmoved by the occupation. The AFL offered no gesture of protest, being far more consumed with arguments over the fratricide of European workers in the "Great War." The Anti-Imperialist League did raise its voice in opposition, reprehending the "Wilsonian phrases with which United States thuggery disguises its deeds." With business no longer a prominent component of the league, it ventured: "What reason can be given for our imperial policy save the desire of the ruling class to plunder and invest?" Progressives like Jane Addams echoed this criticism.

But the earliest opposition came from African Americans, whose fellowship with the Haitian republic was demonstrated in manifold campaigns intended to pressure the State Department and the executive. The Haitian Revolution, a slave rebellion that established a black republic in the Caribbean, had long been the polestar of freedom for African Americans. Frederick Douglass put it like this in 1893: "[W]e should not forget that the freedom you and I enjoy today; that the freedom that eight hundred thousand colored people enjoy in the British West Indies; the freedom that has come to the colored race the world over, is largely due to the brave stand taken by the blacks sons of Haiti ninety years ago. When they struck for freedom . . . they struck for the freedom of every black man in the world."[37]

If the Haitian Revolution was an example to black slaves, it was also a warning to their captors. Until Haiti "spoke," Douglass pointed out, "the slave trade was sanctioned by all the Christian nations of the world." Afterward, they had to calculate afresh, and the instance of a successful slave revolt impinged on Atlantic debates, not least in the British metropole.[38] In just the same way, the US assault on Haiti resonated with African Americans confronting resurgent white supremacy. W. E. B. Du Bois assailed the occupation in the NAACP publication *Crisis*. Not all African American leaders were sympathetic to the Haitians, however. Booker T. Washington estimated that they were a backward people in need of enlightened tutelage. Others were taken in by the macabre tales of "voodoo heresy" on the islands. Nevertheless, the African American press largely took an anti-imperialist stance. The *Afro-American Ledger*, for example, lamented that the United States had reduced Haitian sovereignty to a "scrap of paper," using Haiti to demonstrate the superiority of America's naval fleet.[39]

African American leaders used the 1916 presidential election, working within the Republican Party, to assail Wilson's Haiti policy. Republicans were quite content to avail themselves of this advantage. Roosevelt, who rarely saw a war he didn't like, claimed that it was incongruous that Wilson had turned Haiti into a "virtual protectorate." William Wilcox of the Republican National Committee denounced Wilson for replacing the African American ambassador to Haiti with a white man, maintaining that "Wilson preaches new freedom, but practices new bondage." Significant sections of the African American press duly rallied behind the Republican candidate. Elections were not an ideal terrain for African Americans to make their pressure felt, however, as the southern black electorate was disenfranchised, and Wilson won with the combined support of liberals, farmers, labor, and intellectuals.[40]

It was not until after World War I, after the Cacos insurgency had been harrying US Marines in the countryside for several years, that a movement in favor of Haitian independence began to consolidate. President of the NAACP James Weldon Johnson visited Haiti to write a scalding dispatch on the occupation for the *Nation*, which hosted the arguments for Haitian independence from dissidents like Ernst Gruening, a future co-architect of the "good neighbor" policy, and Oswald Garrison Villard, veteran of the Anti-Imperialist League. The Haiti–Santo Domingo Independence Society began to organize meetings denouncing the occupation. The support of US anti-imperialists was a crucial component of the struggle of Haitian opposition groups like the Union Patriotique. Unable to publicize their cause and arguments effectively under martial law, they relied on strategically well-placed Americans to carry out their publicity, to make submissions to Senate inquiries, and to argue their case in the media.[41]

Radical pacifists also played an honorable role. In the same year that Wilson invaded Haiti, the Woman's Peace Party was launched, later known as the Women's International League for Peace and Freedom (WILPF). The feminists Jane Addams and Carrie Chapman Catt called the founding meeting, involving some 3,000 white women, in Washington, DC, in January 1915. This group, mobilizing progressive, pacifist, and feminist women around opposition to war, had roots in both the Anti-Imperialist League and the women's suffrage movement and operated comfortably in a leftist milieu. For example, while not communist, it has for most of its history been hostile to anticommunism. Moreover, by opposing institutionalized violence, it was able to make connections between different struggles—against patriarchy, racial oppression, and war. Though for most of its history it remained predominantly white, it was distinguished by its commitment to attacking the bases of racist oppression, surmising that the situation of women and African Americans was not unconnected to the sources of war. In the 1920s, it emerged as one of the major defenders of Haiti, composing a report favoring "the restoration of the Independence of the Negro Republic."[42]

Much of the work came to fall on the shoulders of a left that had been suscitated by the Russian Revolution. Socialist Party members joined campaigns to restore sovereignty to Haiti, and the Communist Party USA (CPUSA), formed in 1919 and initially operating under conditions of severe repression, became central to the organization of pro-Haiti solidarity. Its "Anti-Imperialist Department" agitated through the 1920s for independence for all the Caribbean islands under US control, as well as for an end to colonialism in the Philippines. Particularly after 1925, the CPUSA worked to clarify its stance on Haiti, and by 1929 it was leading protests against "Yankee Imperialism," working through the Anti-Imperialist League and the American Negro Labor Congress, both organizations in which it played a directive role to defend Haitian rebels. This alliance was partially expedited by the fact that the anti-imperialist struggle in Haiti was also, increasingly, a class struggle, and that the Haitian opposition was moving to the left. Leading figures such as Jacques Roumain, the grandson of Tancrède Auguste, who had been president from 1912–13, were active communists. Roumain cofounded the Haitian Communist Party in 1934, the same year that US troops left Haiti, and was subject to constant imprisonment and finally exile. The socialist poet Langston Hughes was among those US activists to form a personal relationship with Roumain and advocated on his behalf following a particularly harsh sentence. Through the 1930s, left-wing antiracist struggle segued repeatedly into anti-imperialist agitation around Haiti.[43]

Wilson and the Great War

Great Britain, Italy, France, Germany, Russia, and the Austro-Hungarian Empire were the masters of Europe, Asia, and Africa. The terms of this mastery—who possessed how much of these continents—were the matter over which European statesmen and monarchs marched their subjects to war just five weeks after the assassination of Archduke Franz Ferdinand by a Bosnian Serb assassin whose goal had been to break the Austro-Hungarian Empire's control over the South Slav regions so that they could form a new nation, Yugoslavia. Europe's socialist parties pledged to counter imperialist war with class struggle. British Labour's opposition gave way to full-throated support and collaboration. The "general strike" pledged by the German SPD (Social Democratic Party) and the French socialists (SFIO) was not forthcoming—their promises by no means resembling Adonis's garden, but every bit as barren as the no-man's-land into which they pitched themselves. The United States was entangled, for its part, in competition with the United Kingdom and Germany for the resources and markets of South and Central America. Officially, America remained aloof from the war, policy makers seeing no interest in US participation and every chance to gain from Europe's downfall, but sentiment in the press tended to favor the Entente powers, of Britain, France, and Russia while President Wilson was privately partial to London.[44]

Remote from the gigantomachy, America could sustain a much wider debate about its causes. Opposition to any US involvement in the Continental holocaust united religious pacifists educated in Christian doctrines of nonviolence, socialist anti-imperialists, single-tax radicals inspired by the political economist Henry George, socialists, and anarchists. At the beginning of World War I, the Socialist Party (SP) was the single largest left-wing party in the United States. The SP's approach to the European war consisted of two differing but not necessarily opposing tendencies. One argued that the war was being pursued as an inter-imperialist rivalry among capitalist states for markets, while the other maintained that these same capitalist states were more interested in suppressing domestic working-class movements.

There was perhaps a basis for both beliefs. There was unquestionably territorial struggle over the control of Alsace-Lorraine, the Balkans, the Middle East, and Africa. And there had been wave after wave of intense class struggle, a forward march for labor as well as for the left, just as in the United States the strike waves continued, the IWW continued to grow, and the socialists made electoral advances. War temporarily convoked an axis of the state and capital, which coordinated their activities to suppress labor and contain the left. The party's antiwar "manifesto" emphasized the "economic" rather than "political" causes of the war, stressing inter-imperial rivalry above reactionary politicking by ruling classes. Wherever the accent was placed, as it was a capitalist war, it could only come at the expense of the working classes. For this reason, the SP argued that the United States should shut off all supplies to the different sides in the war, the better to end it sooner. They knew that US capitalists would try to profit from the war, as indeed they did, by selling supplies to every side.[45] They anticipated that war would drive up the costs of food and essential goods, and argued that if necessary the "sources of supplies" should be seized—thus, their slogan ran: "Starve the War and Feed America." As the party's magazine, *American Socialist*, put it:

> War in Europe can only continue if fed by America.
> To feed that war, the workers of America must starve.

> While the war lords of Europe are leading the workers to slaughter the money and food lords of America seek to profit by that slaughter by increasing the cost of food. . . .
> (1) We must starve the war by cutting off supplies; (2) We must feed our own people by seizing all sources of supplies.
> We must stop the shipping of all supplies into the war zone.
> Not a penny for loans, not an ounce of food should leave these shores to prolong this terrible shedding of blood.[46]

Organized labor cleaved to a similar analysis. The IWW, the AFL unions, the Knights of Labor, the Coast Seamen, and the Locomotive Firemen all blamed capitalism for the war. The Railway Conductors held that it was a war for "markets" and for "imperial and commercial supremacy." As such, their analysis demanded strict neutrality in the war—no side was more just, more deserving, all parties were sacrificing their working classes for profit. Yet neither labor nor the socialists could engage substantively with the failure of their brothers and sisters across the pond to oppose the war, to agitate for general strikes against it, as they had almost uniformly pledged to do. The war came too fast, it was beyond their control, and they did not have time to organize their forces. Therefore, they failed to anticipate any difficulty with their own stance in favor of a general strike should the United States join the war.[47]

Woodrow Wilson was the peace candidate in 1916. While the Republicans could opportunistically bash his imperialist conquest of Haiti, their leaders were no less hawkish, being advocates of partisanship with the Allied powers and of military "preparedness"—a euphemism implying that to plan for involvement in the charnel house was mere prudence. Republican Charles Evan Hughes was thus the Atlantic candidate to Wilson's pacific candidature. As noted previously, labor rallied its forces behind Wilson in the 1916 election on the basis of his antitrust reforms and concessions to labor. A right-wing revisionist current among the Socialists also favored a close alliance with Woodrow Wilson, and Eugene Debs decided to stay out of the race, thus leading to a poor result for the

Socialists. Shortly after the election, however, it became apparent that Wilson was preparing to lead America to war in Europe. Debs warned that this would strengthen militaristic and despotic tendencies in American society, a prescient observation notable for its incongruity with the feeling of many liberals and socialists that the war would enhance American democracy.[48]

As the war preparations became more obvious, it began to become clear that many of those who said they were antiwar would back Wilson when the time came. Samuel Gompers had told AFL delegates that he was a pacifist, but he increasingly favored "preparedness," as did a number of other labor movement figures. The rightward-moving elements of socialism and social democracy began to hint that despite all the talk about capitalism causing the war, Germany was actually to blame, and that America's proper place was in an alliance with the Entente powers.[49] When, on the pretext of a German attack on a US supply ship to Britain, Wilson finally seized his moment to bring the United States into the war, a layer of progressive and reforming intellectuals found themselves enlisted on the ideological front, arguing the case that war would enrich American society and democracy. Even W. E. B. Du Bois, who had argued that the war was a struggle over colonial possessions with origins in Africa, was swept along by the idea that American participation would enhance national democratic life and improve conditions for African Americans—a forlorn hope.[50]

Still, for all the gyrations of leftist intellectuals and union bureaucrats, there does not appear to have been much popular enthusiasm for war. The government sought to enlist a million soldiers, and only got seventy-three thousand volunteers before it turned to conscription. It was partly for this reason that the Wilson administration had to rely on the most sophisticated, orchestrated propaganda campaign in the history of the American state at that point, while also cracking down with, in Woodrow Wilson's words, a "firm hand of stern repression" on dissidence. Even then, tens of thou-

sands of people evaded the draft. Indeed, thousands of "slackers"—
socialists, syndicalists, anarchists, and pacifists opposed to the
war—fled to Mexico, still undergoing its revolution, to avoid being
conscripted. The Socialist Party maintained opposition in its majority to the war, and risked repression by campaigning against it.
But it operated in extremely difficult circumstances, with state officials, federal marshals, and lynch mobs interpreting dissidence as
a treasonable offense. Striking workers were subject to the most exacting punishments. Debs himself was jailed under the Espionage
Act in 1918 for speaking against the war. In the speech for which
he was jailed, he witheringly denounced the petty tyranny unleashed by the war state, the "Wall Street Junkers," and "the gentry
who are today wrapped up in the American flag" "who have their
magnifying glasses in hand, scanning the country for evidence of
disloyalty, eager to apply the brand of treason to the men who dare
to even whisper their opposition to Junker rule in the United
States." And he reminded his listeners of the class interest lurking
behind "patriotic" sentiment:

> Wars throughout history have been waged for conquest and
> plunder. In the Middle Ages when the feudal lords who inhab-
> ited the castles whose towers may still be seen along the Rhine
> concluded to enlarge their domains, to increase their power,
> their prestige and their wealth they declared war upon one an-
> other. But they themselves did not go to war any more than the
> modern feudal lords, the barons of Wall Street go to war. The
> feudal barons of the Middle Ages, the economic predecessors
> of the capitalists of our day, declared all wars. And their miser-
> able serfs fought all the battles. The poor, ignorant serfs had
> been taught to revere their masters; to believe that when their
> masters declared war upon one another, it was their patriotic
> duty to fall upon one another and to cut one another's throats
> for the profit and glory of the lords and barons who held them
> in contempt. And that is war in a nutshell. The master class has
> always declared the wars; the subject class has always fought the
> battles. The master class has had all to gain and nothing to lose,
> while the subject class has had nothing to gain and all to lose—
> especially their lives.

> They have always taught and trained you to believe it to be
> your patriotic duty to go to war and to have yourselves slaugh-
> tered at their command. But in all the history of the world you,
> the people, have never had a voice in declaring war, and strange
> as it certainly appears, no war by any nation in any age has ever
> been declared by the people.[51]

The October Revolution in Russia refreshed the American socialist movement. For Debs, Russia under a workers' state was "the
soul of the new-born world."[52] Later, he would write: "From the
crown of my head to the soles of my feet, I am a Bolshevik and
proud of it."[53] Debs understood that the very success of the revolution would drive the US authorities to even more repressive
measures, but it still filled him with optimism.[54] The vital fact was
that after years of bitter defeat in which international socialism had
succumbed to national chauvinism, the anti-imperialist left, the
"Zimmerwald left" that rejected the war, had accomplished the
most remarkable thing: the world's first socialist state. In the couple
of years that followed, American society experienced the most intense wave of political struggles, climaxing in 1919.

That extraordinary year saw the Seattle General Strike, which
was the culmination of numerous radicalizing trends, from antiwar
activism to intense and frequently leftist labor struggles, and which
was openly inspired by the Bolshevik Revolution. During the strike,
the IWW and AFL Metal Trades Council formed a Soldiers', Sailors',
and Workingmen's Council deliberately modeled on soviets—the
institutions of self-government formed by revolutionary Russian
workers.[55] As the United States sought to arm the counterrevolutionary White armies of Russia, Seattle longshoremen refused to
load arms onto a ship destined for Siberia and even attacked strike-
breakers who tried to load it.[56]

Wilson, who had based his strategy in Europe on the need to
isolate Russia, was having no radicalism from the people to whom
he was, recall, a sort of spiritual godparent. Having pioneered America's global role to combat socialism abroad, he deployed its internal

repressive apparatus to crush socialism at home, and convoked an alliance of businessmen, small proprietors, police, spies, patriotic civil society groups, and others to take the fight to the radicals. The "Palmer Raids" rounded up thousands of radicals, often immigrant workers—specifically to accentuate the "alien" nature of the creed they were resisting. And the Bureau of Investigation, the forerunner of the FBI that gave J. Edgar Hoover his first major bureaucratic office, hammered the left. If Russia hosted the world's first communist state, the United States was the world's first anticommunist state.

Bolshevism, Anti-Imperialism, and Anti-Fascism

In the years after the Russian Revolution, American communists were at the fore of anti-imperialist movements, whether allying with Haitian insurgents or mobilizing against European Fascism. Anti-imperialism, for US communists, was inseparable from the defense of socialism. One of their first tasks, after all, was to help fortify the besieged ramparts of socialism, which had been assailed by Entente intervention, de-recognition, and blockades since the revolutionary outrage—a campaign in which they enjoyed some success.[57] But it was in the 1930s that the questions of war and imperialism would challenge the CPUSA in a serious way.

Antiwar, pacifist, and "isolationist" sentiments were not uncommon in 1930s America. The legatees of World War I were determined that "never again" would such a war consume so great a fraction of humanity. Veterans who had once marched for the government were as likely now to march against it. In one extraordinary incident, the disillusionment of war veterans combined with the radicalization produced by the Depression to produce a grave crisis for Washington. The famous March of the Bonus Army, which included the renegade Major General Smedley Butler, involved ex-servicemen from World War I demanding immediate payment of the value of the service certificates they had been issued on completion of duty. Initially, the certificates had not been due for issue until 1945, but due to the dire conditions of the Depression, they demanded payment immediately. Their first marches in the spring and summer of 1932 were attacked by police. They formed a camp in Washington which was violently cleared by the US Armed Forces, under the command of General Douglas MacArthur and armed with six tanks, under Hoover's instructions. They used tear gas, and the army charged with fixed bayonets. The result was that fifty-five veterans were wounded in an attack by soldiers whom they initially believed had come to show support. Franklin Delano Roosevelt's approach was more conciliatory, allotting the bonus marchers a campsite and providing meals, but he would still not budge on the issue of the certificates. It was not until 1936, when a Democratic Congress overrode a presidential veto, that the certificates were paid.[58]

This protracted affair is emblematic of the way in which the United States in the '30s was lacerated by domestic warfare on several fronts. The CPUSA sought to lead the left and working class in all these battles. However, it was skewered by its frequently opposing commitments to, on the one hand, the utterly uncritical defense of the Soviet Union, and, on the other, its leading involvement in several critical fronts of leftist struggle. By this stage, the Soviet Union had long since ceased to be the vibrant, revolutionary nation embarking on an experiment in radical democracy. The Bolsheviks had won the civil war at the cost of decimating the working class upon which the revolution had been founded. Increasingly the party, itself moving in a perpetually authoritarian direction, substituted itself for that class. A bureaucracy arose that found itself trying to develop Russia's productive capacities in an isolated setting, and increasingly its interests were at odds with those of the workers who supposedly ruled in the new society. By 1928, this bureaucracy had launched the first of a series of "five-year plans" that decisively subordinated all remnants of working-class democracy to the development of Russian industry. Arguably, the state had come to behave as a capitalist bureaucracy, with the cult of Stalin's leadership exemplifying some of its most reactionary aspects.[59]

In defending the Soviet Union, the party had to maintain an implausible stance on the question of the show trials that shook Russia between 1936 and 1938. Worse still, and far more fatal in the long run, it had to suddenly abandon its previous commitment to antifascist work in July 1941 when the Hitler-Stalin Pact was formed. As we will see, this more than anything else alienated would-be "fellow travelers," since the CPUSA's reputation was built less on the specifics of "Marxism-Leninism" (as the shape-shifting dogma of the Soviet Union and its allies was known) than on the reputation of communist activists as sincere, dedicated fighters. The CPUSA would be known for its activism on three fronts. The first of these was the struggle against racism, which saw activists throw themselves into the defense of the Scottsboro Boys and later their own comrade, the African American communist Angelo Herndon. In this era, US communism could boast the talents of Harry Haywood, Sylvia Wood, Claude Lightfoot, and Richard Wright, as the CPUSA consciously sought to build among the most class-conscious black workers.[60] The second was the related endeavor of organizing America's working class, a task that was easier in industrial northern cities than in the segregated South, but which left the Communists with some considerable influence in the radical unions of the CIO. The third was the peace movement.

The CPUSA faced a particular challenge in reconciling peace activism with antifascism. The American League Against War and Fascism was fairly typical of the kind of "popular front" initiative that was undertaken in the 1930s. In 1933, when the league was launched, the CPUSA was still repeating the shibboleths of "third period" Stalinism, which held that socialists and social democrats were "social fascists," and that fascism and bourgeois democracy were qualitatively indistinct variants of capitalist class rule. But the practice of the communists was already in conflict with their rhetoric, as they sought to build an antifascist coalition that included religious ministers, union members, and pacifists. This was the popular front style. The league was an urgent effort to answer the challenge posed by fascist imperialism in Europe without encouraging the United States to plunge into yet another world war. This was possible because, the league maintained, "both war and fascism were organized by the same people for the same purpose—the preservation of their power and privilege." At its height, this organization claimed to incorporate almost a third of the labor movement.

Students were also joining the ranks of politicized peace activists. Half a million joined the American Youth Congress, which worked alongside the communist National Student League, the liberal National Students Federation of America, and the social democratic Socialist League for Industrial Democracy. In its campaign for peace, this movement sought to overcome the divisions between different social layers—between students and workers and between white and black students, for example.[61]

Divisions in the peace movement began to emerge over the issue of the Spanish Republic in 1936. Spanish socialists and republicans, allied in a popular front, had defeated the parties of the right in the spring elections. The old elites instantly dropped their short-lived pretense of supporting parliamentary democracy, and armed combat ensued in Madrid and other major cities between the fascist Phalange and the left. By July Generalissimo Franco, having "pacified" the revolt in the Moroccan Rif, was ready to launch a reconquest of Spain using the same techniques of counterinsurgency that he had deployed in the colonial sphere and more recently in the suppression of labor rebellions in southern Spain. Despite an official arms embargo and a policy of non-intervention, Nazi Germany and Fascist Italy began sending tens of thousands of troops, weapons, and aerial bombers to the republic to support Franco's forces. There seemed to be an unexceptionable case for intervention on the side of the antifascists.[62]

This placed a particular demand on the communist wing of the movement, which had reason to fear the success of the reactionary powers that had signed the Anti-Comintern Pact. The democracies, to which many looked for intervention on the republican side, were imperialist states, hostile to the republic and entangled in their own internecine rivalries over the division of the world's spoils. They would not intervene or, if they did, it would probably be against the republic.

The Soviet Union, on the other hand, started arming the republic in August, though it placed strict conditions on the receipt of military aid. This aid was essential. Without it, the republic would probably not have survived the first year. Yet the conditions imposed by the Soviet Union entailed demobilizing the very revolutionary process that was essential to defeating fascism. In November 1936, Moscow authorized the formation of a military brigade to bring aid to the republic from the United States. This brigade became known as the Abraham Lincoln Brigade. Communists were not alone in playing this role. Workers' movements from across Europe had already begun to extend solidarity to the republic. And the Socialist Party in the United States attempted to get its own "Eugene Debs Column" up and running, despite the stunned, heartsick objections of the pacifists among them. But communist parties in Europe and America were at the forefront of organizing aid and solidarity campaigns, as with the "Aid Spain Movement" launched in 1936 by the Communist Party of Great Britain. International brigades convoyed to Spain from fifty-three countries, with volunteers numbering at least thirty-two thousand and perhaps as many as forty thousand. Here was a form of interventionism that no one could classify as imperialist. It was, if anything, a logical extension of the anti-imperialist movement, an attempt through popular solidarity to defeat fascist imperialism before it had the chance to sink the world into another conflagration.[63]

There was an element of adventure and escape in this international insurgency. Harry Fisher describes the intermittent boredom and tension as he and his comrades waited in Paris to be called to join the loyalists, the excitement when they were finally called, and the warmth and knowing smiles of students and townspeople as they traveled south, through Perpignan, and into Spain. For some African American communists who joined the struggle, it was also a relief from the racist aggression and hostility of the United States. James Yates recalls in his memoir of his time in the brigade that while in Paris, en route to Madrid, "I found the Champs Elysees and couldn't believe that I, a poor fellow from Mississippi, was walking upon such a famous street. . . . In contrast to the response I was accustomed to receiving from people in America, Parisians smiled and greeted me in the street."[64]

The brigades could not defeat fascism, however. By the spring of 1938, the republic was recoiling, fatally wounded by the chemical and incendiary warfare of the fascist leviathan. By December, Catalonia was being devoured, and the republic was finished. If the combined forces of the left couldn't stop fascism, then it seemed logical and inevitable that war would follow, and that the working classes anxious to defeat fascism would be willing conscripts for that war. This would constitute a major defeat. For while the working classes and left largely joined and supported the war out of the need to defeat fascism, the war nonetheless took on an imperialist form.

This is a point that is unlikely to resonate with those who see World War II as unambiguously a "people's war" against fascism. Yet many of the same dynamics that underpinned World War I were present here. Chief among them were the presence of inter-imperialist rivalry for market access and world hegemony, with anticolonial wars playing an important role. The world system during the Great Depression had become increasingly disarticulated.

Britain had removed itself from the "gold standard" and imposed a system of Imperial Preference involving India and the Dominions. Germany's strategy for reintegration into the global economy along pro-US lines had been wrecked by the Depression, and the Nazis attempted to radicalize an old strategy of economic bloc-building through expansion in order to overcome the endemic weaknesses of its own economy—Lebensraum ("living space") and *Generalplan Ost* (expansion to the east) were the literal expressions of this drive. While Britain sought to defend its colonial supremacy, Nazi Germany attempted to emulate British success through the colonization of Russia. The Soviet Union, for its part, sought to bolster its position by exploiting Great Power rivalries—the Hitler-Stalin Pact was an example of such maneuvering. For the United States, such rivalries took the form of the Pacific contest with Japan over access to Chinese markets, as well as an attempt to take over global leadership from the British Empire. The colonial powers among the Allies were so keen to defend their overseas properties that until 1943 they concentrated much of their energy on protecting colonies in Africa and Asia, allowing the Soviet Union to take the brunt of Nazi attrition.[65] If the defeat of fascism was tied to such imperialist logic, it would come at tremendous cost for popular forces and result in much more bloodshed.

Some tried desperately to resist this logic. Radical and revolutionary pacifists continued to try to uphold the idea of nonviolent resistance. They cited the Gandhian idea of *satyagraha* as a moral alternative to violence. And when war came, they refused to enlist or be conscripted. Forming a minority of conscientious objectors, they endured jail and the calumny of their peers, but were thereby prevented from being politically effective.[66]

Leon Trotsky attempted to arm his supporters in the United States with a different understanding. He maintained that the war was inevitable, as was US participation, and so what was needed was a strategy for turning the imperialist war into a revolutionary war. The Trotskyists elaborated a "proletarian military policy" through which socialists could support the military defeat of Nazism without being subsumed into an imperialist war. This held that the capitalist classes had neither the desire nor the ability to fight fascism properly, and that workers had to fight within the war for their democratic aims. Thus, they agitated for trade union control of the military training of workers and the democratization of the armed forces. Trotsky argued that:

> Neither Roosevelt nor Willkie are free to decide; they must prepare the war, and when they have prepared it they will conduct it. They will say they cannot do otherwise, because of the danger from Hitler, etc., of the danger from Japan, etc. There is only one way of avoiding the war—that is the overthrow of this society. However, as we are too weak for this task, the war is inevitable. The question then, for us, is not the same as in the bourgeois salon—"let us write an article on peace, etc.," which is suitable for publications like the *Nation*. . . . We must say: "Roosevelt (or Willkie) says it is necessary to defend the country; good! Only it must be our country, not that of the 60 families and their Wall Street. The army must be under our own command; we must have our own officers, who will be loyal to us."[67]

This was, however, a position that the marginal forces of Trotskyism were unable to implement in any serious way. At any rate, outside of the United States, Trotskyists were faced with different dilemmas, such as how to survive under Nazi occupation.[68]

But the standing of the CPUSA in the peace movement was to be grievously damaged by its approach to antifascism. First, its approach to the question was determined by its loyalty to the Soviet Union. This meant that in practice the party endorsed collective security internationally, predicated on an alliance between the Soviet Union and the democratic capitalist states (this line decided by the Seventh Congress of the Comintern in 1935), and popular frontism domestically. But these commitments frequently collided. In supporting the Soviet Union, they had to contend with the strength of pacifist and "isolationist" feeling in the United States, which cut across ideologies. From the reactionary anticommunist Father Charles Coughlin to the isolationist Huey Long to the Socialist Norman Thomas, support for "neutrality" and non-intervention by the United States was widespread. Supporting war to oppose fascism was futile, said Norman Thomas, as war "means inevitable fascism at home."

Even so, the menace of fascism began to push even lifelong pacifists to reevaluate their positions. Albert Einstein, for example, maintained that the presence of such aggressive powers as Japan and Germany rendered immediate disarmament "impracticable." The CPUSA general secretary Earl Browder, speaking in 1936, argued that it was "nonsense to talk about peace except insofar as we mobilize all peace forces in the world to place obstacles in the way of these fascist forces who are preparing war." By and large, the liberal left agreed with him. The *Nation* and the *New Republic*, having initially supported non-intervention, came around to the CPUSA's view when Hitler and Mussolini were found to be supporting Franco. For the *New Republic*, the question was simple: "Are you for fascism . . . or against it?" Even well-known critics of the CPUSA such as Archibald McLeish, Lewis Mumford, and Reinhold Niebuhr agreed to work with communists in popular fronts against fascism. Indeed, such was the urgency of this front that many were prepared, when news of the Stalinist show trials—in which leading Bolsheviks were publicly put on trial over trumped up charges—hit the United States, to either suppress their criticisms or swallow the Soviet story wholesale.[69]

The party energetically sought to position itself in the mainstream in this era. Its popular front strategy included serenading capitalists on the benefits of siding with the Soviet Union. It would be bad for capitalism, Browder argued, for the United States to adopt an isolationist posture. "The United States has the strongest selfish interest in peace, without which it cannot maintain world commerce so necessary to it under the present system. . . . The United States holds in its hands the key to world peace."[70]

When the Molotov-Ribbentrop Pact was struck, however, this cultivated mainstream niche was abruptly brought to an end. The CPUSA almost instantly switched from antifascism to "anti-imperialism," without explanation. For the party, the Molotov-Ribbentrop Pact seemed to protect Russia from Nazi aggression (while allowing the Soviet Union to help itself to Finland), and that was enough to qualify it as anti-imperialist. The party muted its criticisms of Hitler and argued that the objective of war for the Allies was to replace Hitler with someone who would turn their imperialist war into a counterrevolutionary war against the USSR.

The result of this volte-face was the severance of many relations on the left, and the departure of at least 15 percent of its members between 1939 and 1940 (at least, this is the figure acknowledged by the party). As a result of this shocking betrayal of the antifascist cause, liberals began to articulate a long-standing anticommunist trope which held that fascism and communism shared identical objectives and methods. Everything the communists did was a self-interested manipulation, every "ally" was a dupe. Liberal organizations and unions began to pass "Communazi" resolutions barring both communists and fascists from their organizations. The American Civil Liberties Union (ACLU) followed suit, and the *New Republic* approved. Relations with organized labor were fraught. In November 1940, the Congress of Industrial Organizations (CIO) national convention passed a resolution banning "Nazism, Communism, and Fascism" as "foreign ideologies" with "no place in this great modern labor movement."

The CPUSA's subsequent whip-pan reverse when Russia was attacked in June 1941 led to them embracing patriotism, "Americanizing" their discourse, and cooperating with the war effort. In the short run, this offered the party a reprieve from its isolation, as US and USSR interests coincided for a time. But their return to the patriotic fold had its dark side, as it led to them embrace repression that was aimed at the left. The "Red Scare" against them was ended, and they backed a no-strike agreement signed by the AFL and CIO, breaking with their previous militancy. They expelled Japanese members during the period of internment and supported the use of the Smith Act—a tool of repression that had been crafted for use against them, and would be used against them again—against their Trotskyist rivals.[71]

It was emotionally understandable, certainly, that movements that had invested in the Soviet Union, earnestly believing it to be humankind's sole hope, would be prepared to see it protected and defended at almost any cost. Seeing their role as its defenders, they could sacrifice consistency and credibility if they needed to. But this came at considerable cost to their wider relations in the American left. The popular front left briefly revived during the US-Soviet alliance, but the distrust and betrayal that resulted from the Hitler-Stalin agreement endured and would provide some of the basis for the Cold War rift.

Chapter Four

The Cold War
and Decolonization

*No I'm not going 10,000 miles from home to help murder
and burn another poor nation simply to continue the domination of white slave masters of the darker people the world
over. . . . The real enemy of my people is here.*
> **—Muhammad Ali, 1967**

*The fact is the US Blacks have been among the vanguard of
anti-imperialism and militant political activity.*
> **—Gerald Horne**

*Vietnam, like Mississippi, is not an aberration. It is the mir-
ror of America. Vietnam IS American foreign policy.*
> **—Vietnam Day Committee**

*Richard the Third in the White House / Cowering behind
divided curtains.*
> **—Manic Street Preachers**

The post–World War II order placed the United States at an unprecedented advantage with respect to competing states. The colonial
powers that had divided the world among them, effectively freezing
the United States out of some of the world's largest markets, were in
a parlous state. Through the Marshall Plan and a series of targeted

interventions—for example, on the side of the monarchists in the Greek civil war—the United States bailed out European capitalism and at the same time conscripted the Western European powers into the NATO military alliance. A system of bipolar competition took shape between the United States, leading an alliance of antisocialist ruling classes, and the Soviet Union and its "socialist" allies and dependencies. The stakes of direct inter-imperialist conflict had been escalated by the advent of nuclear weapons, and the effect of this was to push this conflict to the margins of the world system. Regional and national struggles, particularly the anticolonial revolts that swept Africa and Asia in the postwar decades, were subsumed into this wider structure. For the United States, this often meant intervening in anticolonial revolts to prevent them from falling into the Soviet "sphere of influence," or indeed from charting an independent path. Ideally, they would be integrated into the US-led global economy, with their markets opened to investors—though, in the postwar period, investment was increasingly concentrated in the core capitalist economies rather than what came to be called the Third World.

This was also the beginning of a "golden age" of capitalism, characterized by an unprecedented period of sustained growth in the core capitalist countries. The anomalously high arms expenditures warranted by Cold War hostilities played an important role in this. Military spending was in one sense a drain on investment. But precisely because of that, it offset tendencies toward the overaccumulation of capital, thus stabilizing the system and enabling the larger economies to plan ahead. With the United States by far the dominant capitalist economy, American policy makers simply assumed that the role of reorganizing the world's economic and financial system was theirs—albeit in partnership with the United Kingdom, which remained the center of global finance. "New Deal" thinkers among the state's managers prevailed over traditional laissez-faire liberals, and the Bretton Woods architecture reflected this.[1] In this way, the United States found that it did not have to be a colonial power to be an imperial power. It could direct and control trade and capital flows in its interests.

It is a cliché to say that anti-imperialism, characterized as "isolationism," was a largely right-wing phenomenon during the early years of the Cold War. A recent history recounts: "Leftist isolationism had clearly reached its peak in the 1930s, and the majority of isolationists after the war belonged to the conservative camp."[2] There is some basis for this judgment, inasmuch as the left was almost entirely defanged on questions of war and imperialism throughout the early period of the Cold War. However, the category of "isolationism" is problematic here. Many of those on the right who opposed specific wars did so for pragmatic reasons or because of their long-standing concern with an excessively powerful executive. They were neither pacifists, opposed to all wars, nor were they anti-imperialists, opposed to US dominance. Meanwhile, leftist opponents of US aggression tended to be strongly internationalist in outlook. There were, in fact, only a few genuine isolationists opposed to the Cold War.

The "Forgotten War": Korea and the Anticommunist Consensus

Defeat of the Popular Front

1948 was a nodal point in the Cold War during which a number of tendencies crystallized, a number of decisive battles were settled, and a new order came into view. By 1948, the Cold War liberal group Americans for Democratic Action (ADA) had been formed. Kennan's "Long Telegram" and Winston Churchill's "Iron Curtain" speech had dictated the broad lineaments of Cold War doctrine. Harry Truman's loyalty programs had begun, the House Un-American Activities Committee (HUAC) had become a standing committee, and there were investigations under way into Hollywood communism. The anti-union Taft-Hartley Act had been established over the objections of organized labor. The ultimately doomed attempts to unionize the South—the CIO's effort, known as "Operation Dixie," was the more energetic of these—had been launched. Internationally, the anticolonial movement had scored a painful victory with independence for India, though it came with the bloody division of the continent thanks in part to Lord Mountbatten. Apartheid laws were being promulgated in South Africa, just as Israel was being founded on the land of expropriated Palestinians. The Republic of Korea was founded amid conditions of intense social struggle tending toward civil war. The "Berlin Blockade," in which neither the United States nor the Soviet Union acquitted itself honorably, was under way, and Russian control of the Eastern Bloc was being consolidated.

As we have seen, the anti-imperialist movements of the 1930s had based their appeal considerably on avoiding the nightmare of another world war. In any event, they could avoid neither world war nor American involvement in it, and anti-imperialism after Pearl Harbor became potentially treasonous. Moreover, the Communist contingent of the anti-imperialist left was discredited by its support for Stalinist imperialism in the form of the Molotov-Ribbentrop Pact. As the historian Robbie Lieberman explains, this meant that the cause of peace seemed to be opposed to the cause of freedom; the war meant that one could not both be an antifascist and an anti-imperialist. "The split between peace and freedom," she writes, "had serious consequences on the domestic front. It was not only Europeans who felt forced to choose between the 'peace' promoted by the Soviet Union, and the 'freedom' promised by the United States. American citizens had to make a similar choice."[3]

The 1948 presidential election was to be the last test of the "Popular Front" left, whose candidate Henry Wallace enjoyed the backing of those layers of the left and labor movement that had not been co-opted into the anticommunist front. Wallace was dyspeptic about the possibility of a US Empire, whose skeletal outlines he perceived in the rush toward hostility with Russia. It was a "wild and mad" nightmare, yet "this position of ruthless imperialism is the position which all groups blinded by hatred of Russia must ultimately defend." Wallace promised peaceful coexistence with communism at a time when most Americans believed that the Soviet Union posed a serious threat to American security and thus to freedom.[4]

Democratic strategists began planning for a Wallace candidacy in 1947, on the assumption that Wallace was being driven to a third-party bid by communist elements that wanted to "hasten the disintegration of the American economy." They held utterly to the prevailing view, promoted by even more sophisticated liberals such as George Kennan, that the Soviet Union was engaged in a conspiracy to subvert the "free world." In the formative years of the Cold War, such beliefs were expressed in Congressional and Justice Department investigations into "foreign agents" and espionage, which was alleged to have taken place at the highest levels of government. As such, the Wallace campaign was susceptible to charges of treason and disloyalty if it could be depicted as a communist front. Democratic strategy, outlined in the "Clifford memorandum," duly sought to "identify him in the public mind with the Communists."[5]

This was an effective strategy, compelling liberals and moderate socialists to make clear their objections to Wallace's "appeasement." Norman Thomas accused Wallace of condoning "human slavery under Stalin." But it was Americans for Democratic Action, an influential liberal anticommunist bloc, that landed the most damaging blows. It was a cardinal conviction of anticommunism in this era that it was impossible to cooperate with communists in a progressive cause; that "united fronts" inevitably became communist fronts; and that good liberal causes ended by being subverted for the ends of a foreign tyranny. This issue was the key one that divided the ADA liberals from the Progressives supporting Wallace. With the founding support of the grande dame of New

Deal liberals, Eleanor Roosevelt, the ADA was well placed to exploit the Progressives' weakness. Nor was it only the liberals who belabored Wallace. The radical pacifist A. J. Muste denounced Wallace, describing him as "the instrument and captive" of the CPUSA, while Dwight MacDonald argued that whether or not Wallace was an agent of Moscow, he "behaves like one."[6]

The Progressives were defeated, gaining just over 1.1 million votes, 2.4 percent of the national total and just under the share won by the Dixiecrat Strom Thurmond—though the latter gained 39 electoral college votes thanks to his support in the South, compared to none for Wallace.[7] Truman's canny election campaign produced an upset. But more than that, it may be argued, it consolidated the emergence of what can be called, following Gramsci, a Cold War "historical bloc." That is, under Truman, a union of social forces was formed in which Fordist producers integrated with the state and exercised hegemony, providing moral and ideological leadership in order to co-opt "subaltern" classes.[8] US capital had a historic mission, that of asserting American global dominance purportedly to protect freedom and democracy against its Soviet opponents, and this mission was one that could attract the support of many who might otherwise be opponents of capital. The combination of McCarthyism and the defeat of Wallace, followed in 1950 by the beginning of the Korean War, isolated and marginalized not merely the communists, who suffered the brunt of legal (and extralegal) repression, but also the radical left.

The Left and Nationalism

The causes of the Korean War are still the subject of controversy today. Yet, some of its outlines are clear. The United States and the Soviet Union, racing for influence in Southeast Asia at the tail end of World War II, took control respectively of the South and North of Korea. In both North and South Korea, there was a brewing civil war between a largely peasant population and the extant ruling class. In the South, the United States supported a coalition of businessmen and landlords headed by the right-wing nationalist Syngman Rhee. In the North, the Red Army began to construct a state modeled on the Soviet Union. Because this state offered popular reforms, and because the Red Army was respected and supported by much of the population, its level of repression did not approach that of the South. The United States, determined to have a pro-American state in the South, urged the United Nations to expedite elections in the territory—though these were boycotted by the left as well as much of the political center. The right claimed a landslide and continued the policy of violent repression of its opponents.

As the civil war wore on—with guerrilla movements, strikes, and protests besieging the dictatorship—and skirmishes took place along the thirty-eighth parallel, where the country had been divided, Stalin gave indirect support to Kim Il-sung in his decision to invade the South. Following the success of the Chinese Revolution and the withdrawal of US troops from the South, he seems to have believed that it would constitute a relatively simple strengthening of the "socialist" camp in the East. The US invasion internationalized a civil war, yet the Truman administration maintained that its intervention was simply to restore the status quo consolidated with the UN supervised elections in 1948. But its intervention did not stop at the thirty-eighth parallel. While the North Korean forces sought to reunite Korea under Kim Il-sung, the United States sought to unite Korea under the right-wing dictatorship in Seoul—and perhaps even to proceed farther, into China, and defeat Mao's revolution.[9] Yet the US government had remarkable success in persuading Americans, including most on the left, that the war was exclusively the result of Soviet aggression. In part, this was thanks to the UN mission in Korea (UNCOK) blaming the whole war on the North Korean side. But there had to be an audience receptive to such rationalizations, and Cold War fear allied with militaristic nationalism had prepped the audience in advance.

The active opposition to the Korean War within the United States was thus, for the most part, marginal. One history argues that beyond the hard left and the isolationist right, "the vast majority of Americans simply accepted the war . . . as one further consequence of global leadership in the fight against Communist aggression." In fact, amid intense anticommunist repression most of the left, even much of the hard left, diapered themselves in the stars and stripes. Supporters of the war included Norman Thomas, the Socialist Party, journals such as the *Nation* and the *Progressive*, and Henry Wallace, who disavowed his communist backers and broke with the Progressive Party. Wallace, who had only recently been a staunch critic of NATO, was suddenly as belligerent as his opponents had been. When "my nation is at war," he said, "and the United Nations sanctions that war, I am on the side of my country and the United Nations." If necessary, he continued, the United States should use atomic weapons. The Socialist Party was also nearly unanimous in its support for the war, leading a young Michael Harrington to extricate himself and join Max Shachtman's Young People's Socialist League (YPSL). The Shachtmanites were antiwar, though their opposition to the war was so deformed by Shachtman's "Stalinophobia" that they refused to call for the United States to leave Korea and supported Britain's role in the war because it had a Labour government.[10]

The Socialist Workers Party, which would play an important role in the anti–Vietnam War movement, was the major Trotskyist organization in the United States throughout much of the twentieth century, and approached the Korean War on the basis of its understanding of the Stalinist states. Cleaving to the orthodox Trotskyist conception of these societies as "degenerated workers' states," they opposed what they saw as the counterrevolutionary bloc led by Stalin, but felt that they should nonetheless offer a political defense of these states against their capitalist opponents. As such, while they criticized the Stalinists for engaging in an imperial carve-up at postwar negotiations in Yalta and Tehran, when it came to the Korean

War, they defended both North Korea and China against the United States. For them, the US intervention was a "war of aggression by US imperialism against a colonial people" whose revolutionary initiative had created the state under attack. Strategically, they raised the idea of a referendum on war. Congress had abdicated its constitutional rights with respect to war powers, they argued, and only a popular referendum could prevent the issue from being decided by an over-powerful executive. Further, since "it's always the people who do the dying and sacrificing in war," neither Truman nor his allies in Congress would fight the war, and no one was better qualified than the people to make the decision. They contended that their proposal was "a more practical method for mobilizing the mass anti-war sentiment and putting the people on guard against the warmongers' conspiracies than any other yet advanced."[11]

This may be doubted. Polling suggested that the pro-war argument was winning among the American public at the beginning of the war. In fact, as war began, 53 percent supported plans for the "total mobilization" of all civilians, and some 70 percent were prepared to pay higher taxes to support military build-up, while 45 percent were ready to drop the A-bomb on China if full-scale war broke out. Any referendum was unlikely to disclose mass antiwar sentiment. However, despite the grip of anticommunist hysteria, pro-war opinion was always far more fragile than it appeared. Support for the war's prosecution depended on its success. Setbacks in the early months meant by that January 1951, 66 percent wanted the United States to "pull out" of Korea altogether. Highlighting the dangers of the war and the undemocratic way in which it was prosecuted, the SWP attacked one of the weak links in the pro-war argument. It was certainly more promising than scholastic explanations as to the class nature of the North Korean and Chinese regimes and their necessary defense against capitalist attack.[12]

The CPUSA, which had looked forward to a postwar order based on cooperation between the United States and the Soviet

Union, was bunkered and demoralized by the Cold War. Under Earl Browder, the party had pursued a strategy of Americanization, and it did not go unnoticed that the party enjoyed greater success and public support when its goals seemed to coincide with those of the US government—hence, the patriotic "Popular Front" during World War II. But the Moscow leadership, perhaps cognizant of looming clashes over the future of Eastern Europe and Southeast Asia, signaled that Browderism had to come to an end. Earl Browder was swiftly deposed, and William Z. Foster directed the party into battle with US imperialism. This shift had an apocalyptic air, with communists at least premature in warning that the midnight of fascism was descending on America. Such arguments may have seemed more plausible to communists on the receiving end of repression under the Smith Act—though, in an ironic blowback from World War II popular frontism, the CPUSA had previously supported some of the uses of such legislation against opponents of the war. The communist-led elements of the peace movement were thus poorly placed to operate in a situation in which their ideological framing could be treated as anti-American, in which they were suspect because of the hysteria over espionage, and in which their uncritical support for the Soviet Union alienated growing numbers of Americans who took seriously the idea that the Soviet Union was the major threat to world peace.[13]

The difficulty for the party was that it was attempting to build a peace campaign while buttressing its own credentials as a party committed to the constitutional road to socialism, at just the time when Stalin's idea of "peace" looked very much like imperialism and when communist parties internationally were publicly sounding very bellicose. Maurice Thorez and Palmiro Togliatti, leaders of the French and Italian communist parties, respectively, had claimed that a Soviet invasion of Western Europe to protect against foreign aggression would be welcomed as a "liberation," a line that the CPUSA felt obliged to endorse. Further, it came just as their own putsch against Browder signaled their reconstitution as a party committed to "Marxism-Leninism." While they were hardly a threat to the US government, it was all too easy to depict them as a conspiracy; while they continued to operate on the tenets of popular frontism, the departure of Browder seemed to signal a rejection of that approach, making it easier to isolate them within the left.[14]

Through international organizations like the pro-Soviet World Peace Council (WPC), however, the CPUSA could be nourished on antiwar opinion outside the United States. The WPC was a global giant of the peace movement, embodying seventy-five national committees and a hundred and fifty thousand local groups. It blamed the United States exclusively for the war, demanded "the withdrawal of all foreign armies from Korea," and called for an international commission to investigate the crimes committed therein.[15] Though there was intellectual opposition from some nonaligned leftists such as I. F. Stone, only a handful of activists and intellectuals risked censure and even prison by actually agitating against the war. The poet George Oppen, then a communist, briefly launched a petition campaign against the war, only to flee to Mexico for fear of being brought before HUAC and risking imprisonment.[16]

African American leftists were among the most inclined to publicly oppose the war. W. E. B. Du Bois, then heading the NAACP, forthrightly attacked the war, arguing that it was only being undertaken to perpetuate the war economy and prevent the system from entering into crisis. While the NAACP board voted to support US efforts to "halt Communist aggression in Korea," Du Bois charged that the Cold War was America's strategy for asserting its global dominance after its attempt to supplant Britain as the major colonial power had failed: "We must have war," he argued. "[In] no other way can we keep our workers employed and maintain huge profits by spending seventy thousand million dollars a year for war preparation and adding to the vast debt of over 200 thousand millions."[17] The Korean War, he said, was cultivating tyrannical crackdowns on liberty as peace campaigners were arrested—he himself was later indicted under the Foreign Agents Registration Act along with four colleagues in the Peace Information Center, which he had founded to propagate the case for peace. Du Bois suggested that those who wished to keep their liberty were in effect compelled to declare that they favored war with Korea, hated Russia, and hated socialism and communism, were prepared to wage war anywhere anytime to defeat it, and would report neighbors who were not so inclined.

To support peace efforts, he spoke at rallies calling for arbitration and organized a statement titled "A Protest and a Plea," signed by several African American leaders, to protest the war. His efforts were effective enough to gain the attention of Secretary of State Dean Acheson, who wrote to rebuke the Peace Information Center, the host of one of his rallies. HUAC issued a strident attack on the peace campaign, arguing that it was intended to "confuse and divide the American people" in the interests of their enemies.[18]

Alongside the communists were the radical pacifists. The War Resisters League, now drawing on the *satyagraha* (soul force) strategy of nonviolent resistance developed by Gandhi, refused to support either side in the war. Although their propaganda tended to accept that Russia had initiated the conflict, innocent of the extent to which it derived from a domestic civil war, they nonetheless affirmed that violence in response was unacceptable and urged that mediation be undertaken immediately, nominating the Indian prime minister Jawaharlal Nehru for the purpose. They particularly lamented that the Korean conflict had transformed the United Nations into "an agency of war on the side of the United States" and urged people to drop their primary allegiance to their own states and declare themselves world citizens. This internationalism was reflected in actions by leading activists, mainly those who had collaborated as conscientious objectors during World War II, including agitation within Europe and even within the Soviet Union itself to urge nonviolent resistance to militarism. It was, again, not an ideal position to win support within the United States itself.[19]

On the right, the criticisms of the war chiefly consisted of the argument that it could not be won. Furthermore, the administration had selected the wrong opponent—it should be taking on the Chinese.[20] General Douglas MacArthur, a swooning admirer of China's former Nationalist ruler Chiang Kai-shek, argued that the war should not be fought simply to restore the status quo. The future of humanity was in Asia, and the United States had the unique opportunity to stamp its authority on the continent. When Chinese forces entered North Korea to repel the US invasion, MacArthur advocated extending the war to various means of attack on the People's Republic of China, including perhaps the use of nuclear weapons. He held that the "Oriental psychology" was such that they "respect and follow aggressive, resolute and dynamic leadership." When MacArthur was dismissed for repeated indiscipline, Senator Joseph McCarthy charged that this was the result of communist intrigue rather than the will of Truman, president "in name only."[21]

The old "isolationist" right had its say as well. George Morgenstern of the *Chicago Tribune* polemicized against US imperialism, recounting the "evangelical" excuses for the Spanish-American War and Wilson's intervention in World War I and describing the Korean venture as a "holy war." This style of critique fits with the general tendency for the "Old Right," as they fashioned themselves, to criticize imperialism as an irrational and dangerous exuberance, as fanatical rather than self-interested and rational. Joseph P. Kennedy, a businessman, politician, and anticommunist nationalist whose anti-Semitism was notorious, opined that though he hated communism as much as anyone, it was not America's business to dictate what happened halfway across the globe.[22] The journalist Garret Garrett, sticking to the rhetoric of "republic versus empire," which had motivated much of the Anti-Imperialist League's output, maintained that the United States had ceased to be a constitutional republic and that Truman's war constituted a usurpation of congressional authority. The language of the war, he claimed, of defending civilization from Russian barbarity and upholding Western morality, was the language of empire.[23]

It wasn't just the radical left and the "isolationist" right that had doubts about the war. A swathe of newspapers, from the *Wall Street Journal* to the *Christian Science Monitor*, called for a negotiated settlement in the early months of the war. This was not based on principled criticism. Rather, commentators felt that the government had miscalculated, that it was showing bad leadership, and that the United States was on the verge of a terrible defeat. It was a mood that, at different times, was shared even among sections of the bipartisan pro-war coalition in Congress.[24]

Such divisions among elites would usually augur well for the prospects of antiwar mobilization. However, the widely shared anticommunist consensus and the repression that anyone suspected of radicalism or "treason" could face demobilized much potential support. Organized labor, for example, was largely absent from antiwar demonstrations. With the left on the retreat in these unions and the right using anticommunist nationalism to bash radicals, the union bureaucracies were being successfully co-opted into the United States' Cold War front. As a result, not only did organized labor register no protest over the war, but its leaders openly called for aggressive mobilization. William Green, then president of the AFL, called for "all-out preparedness for any eventuality," including the total mobilization of labor. The unions were close to the Truman administration, the leadership conciliatory and willing to constrain rank-and-file militancy. They were staunch supporters of anticommunist "containment," and in the early months of war had formed the United Labor Policy Committee to galvanize support for the administration's war preparations. One of their first announcements was to say that they would support a wage freeze. This is not to say that conflicts didn't emerge. The administration chose the abrasive president of General Electric to head its mobilization effort, and his tendency to steamroll labor opinion led to friction and even contributed to the revival of militancy. But the alliance between the labor bureaucracy and the empire state was deeper than just a set of agreements and corporatist wartime instruments. It would emerge in the 1960s that union leaders had been participating in a covert alliance with the CIA and the State Department to promote the government's goals abroad. This included the AFL-CIO and its international affiliates being used by the agency to attack communists in the European and Latin American labor movements. Sidney Lens, an activist and historian of the "Old Left," drew attention to the AFL-CIO's participation in the American Institute for Free Labor Development in Latin America.[25] This collaboration with imperial policy was to have profound effects on the emergence of the antiwar coalition over Vietnam.

The Korean War was opposed by a majority of Americans by the time of its conclusion in 1953. As mentioned above, support for the war was always more fragile than the bellicose public atmosphere at times suggested. Media coverage, heavily censored, fed the public "good news" angles at strategically important moments and sustained support at times when it was endangered. The sudden lurches in the public mood, from majority support for withdrawal to belligerence over prisoners of war, showed the public's receptivity to this propaganda. Yet by the time of the 1952 presidential election, with casualties mounting and discontent over its prosecution being expressed in Congress, 56 percent of the public had decided that the war was not worth fighting. Eisenhower capitalized on this discontent in his campaign, and it is said to have had a decisive effect in turning opinion in his favor. A major point of discontent with the war was the view that the Truman administration was waging a futile war to reverse a communist invasion that it had not done enough to prevent in the first place. Eisenhower tactfully suggested that the country couldn't rely on the administration "to repair what it failed to prevent." As a result of his stance, expressing dissent well within the anticommunist mainstream, he picked up the support of independent voters and moderate Democrats, sufficient to give him an impressive 55.1 percent of the vote.[26] This continued the pattern, which persists to this day, for Republicans and Democrats to criticize one another's wars, channeling popular discontent into their own campaigns where it is disarmed, while preserving the ideological underpinnings of US imperialism.

By the time public opinion had decisively shifted against the war, however, the government had succeeded in ravaging the Korean peninsula and fundamentally reconstructing the American polity without generating a significant antiwar campaign. Dissidents were too easily hounded or simply frightened into silence, and operated in fragmented isolation. For anti-imperialism to become the basis of a mass movement again, it would be necessary for the Cold War certainties to break down, for the anticommunist consensus to erode, and for a New Left to emerge where the CPUSA, ruined by repression and almost finished off by the Khrushchev disclosures and the invasion of Hungary, had stood.

This took place to a considerable extent courtesy of the civil rights struggle, which radicalized millions of Americans and raised some doubts about the virtues of American nationalism. The African American left had long been the constituency least susceptible to anticommunism—barring certain exceptions such as the conservative George Schuyler and the ex-communist Richard Wright—and nationalism. If anything, there was a long history of African American "sympathy for the devil," from pro-German attitudes during World War I to pro-Japanese sentiment among African American intellectuals before and during World War II. On top of this, bonds of solidarity connected communities in Harlem to anticolonial activists in India, Kenya, and the Caribbean. In the period from 1941 to 1945, the NAACP was a self-described "anti-imperialist" organization, aligning with leftist anticolonial movements in Africa and beyond. Even when McCarthyism applied its mortifying grip to black political movements, the fate of the colonies and ex-colonies continued to be of paramount interest to African Americans during the Cold War.[27]

Red-Hunters and White Supremacists: African Americans, the Cold War, and the Color Line

Cold War anticommunism had, as we have seen, its liberal and social democratic variants. Yet anticommunism has an elective affinity with reactionary, nativist, and racist ideology. Ever since the Russian Revolution, US elites have interpreted communism as a phenomenon alien to Anglo-Saxon culture. Anticommunism and racism combined in a relatively uncomplicated way in the period prior to the Cold War. Repressive laws wielded against radicalism, such as the Sedition Act (1918), were directed against "foreign agitators." Institutions like the Lusk Commission (1919) brought to bear American "race-thinking" to the problem of socialism. As Joel Kovel writes: "The Lusk Commission, established in NY state in March 1919 to look into seditious activities, argued that there was 'not a single system of Anglo-Saxon socialism, nor a single system of Latin race socialism.'" The only scientific system of socialism was "of German-Jewish origin.'" This was a charge that had a particular resonance in the backwash of bestializing propaganda about Germany in the "Great War." J. Edgar Hoover argued that African American leaders were peculiarly susceptible to the communist message.[28]

The early anticommunist networks promoted nativist and racist ideology as an explanation for radicalism and a justification for its repression, and this came from the top of the American state. Secretary of State Robert Lansing, George Simons, and elements of military intelligence all credited the fraudulent thesis of the *Protocols of the Elders of Zion* in response to Bolshevism.[29] Race theorist Lothrop Stoddard, in "The Rising Tide of Color against White World-Supremacy," charged that the Bolsheviks were race traitors seeking "the proletarianization of the world."[30] Thus, nativism in the Wilsonian register, xenophobia, anti-Semitism, and Jim Crow all combined to briefly cohere an antisocialist power bloc comprised of business groups such as chambers of commerce, civil society organizations like the American Legion and the Minute Men, and state bodies.

The ensuing period did little to undermine the view of Bolshevism as a racial conspiracy, with the Moscow Congress of the Communist International supporting self-determination for the Black Belt in 1928. To this was added CPUSA support for the Scottsboro Boys after March 1931, the prosecution of black CP organizer Angelo Herndon in Atlanta for "inciting insurrection," and ongoing communist agitation against the white oligarchies of the Deep South. The lack of union progress in the 1930s against the southern business class did not prevent communists from gaining among the most disaffected workers in southern industries like textiles. Overall, CPUSA efforts contributed to an increase in black union membership from 150,000 in 1933 to 1.25 million by the end of the war. And throughout the '30s, biracial unions were formed, even in some southern cities. Black members of the CPUSA made up 7.2 percent of the total in 1931, and 14 percent in 1946. So anticommunism, particularly in the South, meant the preservation of Jim Crow and vice versa. [31]

After 1945, the relationship became more complex. America assumed a hegemonic position among an alliance of (mainly European) capitalist classes opposed to socialism. In a way, the rise of anticolonial struggles, often influenced by communism, would have fit neatly into traditional racial perceptions. Yet, if the United States often sought to shore up the colonial powers, for example by supporting the French in Indochina, and was very reluctant to abbreviate the privileges of its southern elites, its interest in not losing support among newly independent states demanded a more complex response. The United States had to offer a persuasive and attractive image of democracy, which was incompatible with caste rule. As Richard Nixon put it following a visit to the newly independent state of Ghana in 1957, "We cannot talk equality to the peoples of Africa and Asia and practice inequality in the United States." In *Cold War Civil Rights*, Mary Dudziak summarizes the thrust of this logic: the world in which America wished to operate was in some senses like a panopticon. Egregious abuses would be witnessed by world opinion, which would in turn apply pressure. Dudziak maintains that the US government was deeply reluctant to implement changes to the racial order and did so only on the basis of global hegemonic considerations.[32]

There were other pressures. World War II had nominally been a "democratic" war against racist tyranny. Yet, as Ronald Takaki writes,

> The "Arsenal of Democracy" was not democratic: defense jobs were not open to all regardless of race. The war against Nazi Germany was fought with a Jim Crow army. During the fight against Hitler's ideology of Aryan supremacy, ethnic enmities exploded in race riots in cities like Los Angeles and Detroit. The president who led the fight for freedom also signed Executive Order 9066 for the evacuation and internment of 120,000 Japanese Americans without due process of law.

It was struggles by ordinary African Americans in this context that forced the US government to embark on the first major attack on Jim Crow, particularly with Roosevelt's executive order ending segregation in the armed forces passed to avoid the embarrassing spectacle of more than a hundred thousand African Americans descending on the White House in protest against official racism.[33] By 1945, moreover, the changes in the economy of the black working class and the emergence of a black middle-class and political leadership meant that neither party could afford to ignore black votes.[34]

This meant that global empire-building could potentially divide the Cold War power bloc. The South had to fight for its version of the national interest. Thus, while southern industry and state authorities were by far the most committed and militarily aggressive component of the Cold War anticommunist bloc, they deeply resented policies designed to win the Cold War with "soft power." Georgian senator Richard Russell was happy to vote for large military appropriations, for example, but resented the use of federal troops south of the Mason-Dixon Line to enforce civil desegregation. He argued, in so many words, that soldiers should be fighting Reds, not the South, which was a bastion of Americanism. Furthermore, "If communists support racial integration, what greater proof could there be of its immorality?" White supremacists had plenty to draw on in the American lexicon. The republican, "states' rights" ideology of Jefferson, Madison, and Calhoun availed itself in the battle against imposed desegregation, while the language of antitotalitarianism could be mobilized in opposition to the federal government.[35]

Above all, however, the defenders of segregation against the civil rights left invoked the Red Peril. If McCarthy said there were communists in the federal government, how hard was it to believe that the civil rights movement was the result of communist agitation? If global communism was, as all elements in the political establishment agreed, bent on a conspiracy of subversion and sabotage determined to overthrow "Western civilization," what was paranoid or disproportionate about attention to Martin Luther King Jr.'s communist associations, or Senate investigations into the activities of civil rights groups? Why shouldn't HUAC have something to say about the Congress of Racial Equality? Was not the Civil Rights Congress, which embarrassingly charged the United States with genocide against African Americans when it was representing itself as the vanguard of global democracy, actually a communist front? At any rate, much of the information used to discredit the foes of white supremacy was coming directly from Hoover and the

FBI, who were engaging in extralegal spying and repression programs aimed against radicals. The Deep South could defend its ascriptive hierarchy using precisely the same hegemonic language and institutions that its occasional critics had already deployed. Moreover, this intersected with international concerns that were shared in Washington. If southern politicians deemed decolonization a danger due to the unfitness of former colonial subjects for self-government, so Washington feared "premature independence" on the same grounds—and its policies in Vietnam, the Congo, and Latin America reflected this commitment.[36]

Manning Marable describes how Cold War anticommunism set back the African American civil rights struggle:

> The democratic upsurge of black people which characterized the late 1950s could have happened a decade earlier. . . . Most of the important Supreme Court decisions that aided civil rights proponents had been passed some years before. . . . Yet the sit-ins, the non-violent street demonstrations, did not yet occur; the façade of white supremacy was crumbling, yet for almost ten years there was no overt and mass movement which challenged racism in the streets. . . . The impact of the Cold War, the anti-communist purges and near-totalitarian social environment, had a devastating impact upon the cause of blacks' civil rights and civil liberties.[37]

The repression of communism deprived African Americans of some of their most militant allies. It is important not to paint too rosy a picture of this relationship. CPUSA support for no-strike pledges in World War II had inspired resentment in many black militants, as it seemed that the party was placing the needs of the Soviet Union above those of black workers, while more middle-class layers of African Americans had always shunned the communists. But the Cold War accentuated and added to these divisions, as African American leaders sought to dissociate themselves from Marxism—espousal of which, in some states, could lead to imprisonment or the death penalty. Just as the labor movement was de-radicalized, so were mainstream civil rights organizations such as the NAACP. As a result, they eschewed the sorts of militant tactics that would prove so successful from the late 1950s on. For example, when the Congress for Racial Equality (CORE) embarked on "Journeys of Reconciliation" (the precursors to the 1960s Freedom Rides) to test desegregation on southern buses, the NAACP leadership energetically opposed the move. Thurgood Marshall warned that "a disobedience movement on the part of Negroes and their white allies, if employed in the South, would result in wholesale slaughter with no good achieved." CORE, for its part, was profoundly disabled by its fear of red-baiting. It did everything possible to distance itself from communism, and announced that it would not work with "communist-controlled" groups. The result was that CORE saw its growth slowed to a near standstill and its organization reduced to a shell.[38]

The civil rights movement, when it did emerge, was intimately tied to anticolonial struggles, and its radicalization in the sixties owed much to their success. The example of India's independence struggles exerted a profound effect on African American struggles. Martin Luther King Jr. adopted Gandhi's doctrine of nonviolent resistance for the US civil rights movement. "To other countries I may go as a tourist," he said upon visiting Delhi, "but to India I come as a pilgrim." About the specific methods of Gandhi, he cited the example of the Montgomery Bus Boycott: "We have found them to be effective and sustaining—they work!"[39]

In 1960, the same year that sit-ins and Freedom Rides began, a host of independent African states came into being: Congo, Benin, Togo, Cameroon, Somalia, Niger, Mauritius, Burkina Faso, Ivory Coast, Chad, the Central African Republic, Gabon, Senegal, and Mali. The emerging "New Left" paid attention. The famous Port Huron Statement of Students for a Democratic Society in 1962 celebrated the "revolutionary feelings of many Asian, African and Latin American peoples" and the "social sense of organicism characteristic of these upsurges" against which American apathy stood in "embarrassing contrast."[40] In 1963 the Organization of African Unity was formed to represent the interests of the newly independent states, a move which would inspire Malcolm X to cofound the Organization of Afro-American Unity the following year. "It was our intention," Malcolm said on its founding, "to try and find out what it was our African brothers were doing to get results." After all, a mere decade before, "our people were colonized. They were suffering all forms of colonization, oppression, exploitation, degradation, humiliation, discrimination, and every other kind of -*ation*. And in a short time, they have gained more independence, more recognition, more respect as human beings than you and I have. And you and I live in a country which is supposed to be the citadel of education, freedom, justice, democracy, and all of those other pretty-sounding words."[41]

In 1966, the first conference of the Organization of Solidarity with the People of Asia, Africa and Latin America was held in Cuba. Involving left-wing activists from three continents, it sought to forge alliances not between states but between anti-imperialist movements.[42] The entry of the Third World onto the stage as a serious and radical political entity reinforced radicalizing trends in the United States itself and disrupted the master narrative of the Cold War, in which there was only one fight that mattered, that between totalitarianism and democracy. The civil rights movement, even when it accommodated itself to the strictures of McCarthyism, ended up challenging a particular idea of Americanism based on support for aggression ("containment") overseas and repression ("security") domestically.[43] It educated new cadres in the tactics of disruption and civil disobedience, and made all the difference between the insipid acquiescence of much of the left during the Korean War and the rowdy, insurgent, disobliging fury of the New Left during the Vietnam War.

Vietnam, the End of Colonialism, and the Breakdown of the Anticommunist Consensus

The United States had defended its fiefdom in South Korea, but following the collapse of the Kuomintang in China in 1949, the successes of the Viet Minh (an anticolonial coalition formed in 1941 to free Vietnam from French rule and resist Japanese aggression) could not but appall policy makers. The Truman administration sought early on to determine the outlines of a postwar settlement in Vietnam. Ideally, they wanted a nationalist figure who was also anticommunist to rule the country, but were prepared to work with the chosen client of the French colonial power, Bao Dai. Until 1954 the United States sent aid totaling $3.6 billion to the French military to counter Chinese and USSR support for Ho Chi Minh's North Vietnamese republic.[44] By 1954 the United States had also successfully helped its client state in the Philippines defeat the Huk Rebellion—another leftist insurgency based in the peasantry—by sponsoring a combined counterinsurgency and land reform program.[45]

In the same year, Leo Huberman and Paul Sweezy composed an early warning to Americans about the coming catastrophe of US intervention in Vietnam. The article, written for *Monthly Review* following the Geneva Conference at which Vietnam was divided along the nineteenth parallel, asked how it could be that Americans who opposed colonial domination were about to be dragged into a course of aggression toward Indochina. "Are we going to take the position," they asked, "that anti-Communism justifies anything, including colonialism, interference in the affairs of other countries, and aggression?"[46] While Huberman and Sweezy might have known that the answer was yes, they could not have known that this aggression would include serious consideration of a nuclear attack on Vietnam and the ongoing use of America's nuclear superiority to cow opponents.[47]

As the French withdrew, the United States shifted its weight behind Ngo Dinh Diem as a reliable anticommunist dictator. Elections were broached at the Geneva Convention, but everyone from the president to those in the CIA knew that the Viet Minh would win. Instead, Diem was encouraged to build up his repressive apparatus, killing thousands and jailing more than a hundred and fifty thousand people.[48] The Kennedy administration was belligerent and operating on the assumptions of Cold War orthodoxy, which held that communism would spread like the fall of so many dominos if one country were allowed to topple, and that the only remedy for this was the credible application of US power. It therefore dedicated itself to the development of an effective counterinsurgency program.[49] One expression of this was the Strategic Hamlet Program, which forced Vietnamese peasants into militarized compounds to deprive the guerrillas of a base. This was not markedly different from the policy of using concentration camps in the Philippines. In less than two years, sixteen thousand such "hamlets" appeared across South Vietnam. And the escalation continued, justified by racism in both the mandarin and demotic registers, with the "modernization theory" of Walt Whitman Rostow providing the former and the "mere gook rule" supplying the latter. The Gulf of Tonkin incident, in which North Vietnamese forces were provoked into an attack on the USS *Maddox*, provided the pretext for aerial attacks and a buildup of US troops eventually reaching half a million. The aim at this point was simply to avoid humiliation. The price, at a total of three million deaths across Vietnam, Laos, and Cambodia, may well have seemed worth it.[50] But the anti–Vietnam War movement set out to make it cost the prosecutors of the war something that they cared about: their right to govern.

From Civil Rights to Civil Disobedience

Some of the earliest activists in the antiwar movement were veterans of the civil rights movement. Opposition to the war was concentrated especially among nonwhites, though they were underrepresented in demonstrations called by students, liberals, and pacifist organizations. This was in part due to the heavy price people of color paid. One high-profile case of African Americans being punished for antiwar stances was Julian Bond, whom the Georgia legislature illegally refused to seat due to his opposition to the war. Similarly, Muhammad Ali was stripped of his boxing title and threatened with jail. Ali's response to this shameful bullying was characteristically ebullient: "Damn the money. Damn the heavyweight championship. I will die before I sell out my people for the white man's money. The wealth of America and the friendship of all the people who support the war would be nothing if I'm not content internally and if I'm not in accord with the will of Allah."[51] On the attempt to draft him into the war, he offered this defiant riposte:

> Why should they ask me to put on a uniform and go 10,000 miles from home and drop bombs and bullets on Brown people in Vietnam while so-called Negro people in Louisville are treated like dogs and denied simple human rights? No I'm not going 10,000 miles from home to help murder and burn another poor nation simply to continue the domination of white slave masters of the darker people the world over. This is the day when such evils must come to an end. I have been warned that to take such a stand would cost me millions of dollars. But I have said it once and I will say it again. The real enemy of my people is here. I will not disgrace my religion, my people or myself by becoming a tool to enslave those who are fighting for their own justice, freedom and equality. If I thought the war was going to bring freedom and equality to 22 million of my people they wouldn't have to draft me, I'd join tomorrow. I have nothing to lose by standing up for my beliefs. So I'll go to jail, so what? We've been in jail for 400 years.[52]

More grievously, however, grassroots activists were in particular danger of violent assault. The Chicano Moratorium in Los Angeles, representing Mexican American antiwar protest, was attacked by policemen with guns and clubs during a protest in 1970, leaving three protesters and one journalist dead.[53]

Nonetheless, civil rights activists and leaders were essential to the success of the antiwar movement, and the connections between a racist system and a racist war were quickly drawn by its articulate spokespeople. Stokely Carmichael of the Student Nonviolent Coordinating Committee (SNCC) argued that the use of conscription in this war involved "white people sending black people to make war on yellow people in order to defend the land they stole from red people."[54] In July 1965 the Mississippi Freedom Democratic Party, organized in Mississippi the previous year with the assistance of SNCC to challenge the all-white southern Democratic Party, issued a leaflet against black participation in the war: "No one has a right to ask us to risk our lives and kill other Colored people in Santo Domingo and Vietnam so that the White American can get richer." In January 1966, SNCC adopted a position against the war: "We believe the United States government has been deceptive in the claims of concern for the freedom of the Vietnamese people, just as the government has been deceptive in claiming concern for the freedom of the colored people in such countries as the Dominican Republic, the Congo, South Africa, Rhodesia and in the United States itself."

Martin Luther King Jr., against the advice of allies in the civil rights struggle, finally spoke out in 1967, belaboring "the greatest purveyor of violence in the world today—my own government." In a carefully targeted intervention, he pointed out that black soldiers were dying in numbers disproportionate to their representation in the general population, ostensibly to "guarantee liberties in Southeast Asia which they had not found in Southwest Georgia and East Harlem."[55] In April 1968, in the week following King's assassination, 125 towns and cities went into rebellion.

This had a tremendous impact on the availability of black troops, and worried generals sick. It also stressed where the real battle for freedom for African Americans was taking place. The slow, legal overthrow of Jim Crow had done little as yet to ameliorate the economic conditions of working-class blacks, especially as war brought conscription and inflation to the ghettos. Rebellions broke out in the ghettos in 1964 and, as noted, Malcolm X, following the tradition in which the Nation of Islam stressed the colonized identity of black people, linked the black liberation struggle to that of the national liberation movements. The "long, hot summers" of inner-city rebellion began thus. The Pentagon was sickened, too, when it learned of the growing convergence between the Black Power and antiwar movements.[56]

Antiwar activists made use of some of the same tactical repertoire as CORE and SNCC. Many leaders of the New Left, for example in Students for a Democratic Society (SDS), emerged directly from the civil rights movement. Until the sixties, SDS was the Student League for Industrial Democracy (SLID), the campus wing of the League for Industrial Democracy, a genteel social democratic organization representing the left wing of liberalism. After it was re-launched as SDS, civil rights work formed the core of its activities, and Tom Hayden was sent to Atlanta to work in the civil rights movement, coordinating SDS's efforts in this respect with its first president Al Haber. In the fight against Jim Crow, activists built on the example of Rosa Parks by consciously breaking segregation statutes. Coordinating their efforts, black and white protesters would simultaneously breach "whites only" and "colored only" zones. They learned the hard way, through sit-ins and Freedom Rides, that the authorities were unlikely to listen to persuasion. Having been beaten by police, had colleagues murdered by the Klan, and been stoned by members of the public, they were battle-hardened and ready with a set of disruptive tactics in which they assumed personal danger. Perhaps as importantly, having seen the way in which Democrats defended segregation and the southern racist establishment, they learned that the Democratic Party was not their friend in struggle.[57]

Once the movement began, these tactics of disruption and civil disobedience spread very quickly. One immediate form of civil disobedience available to protesters was to refuse to be conscripts. The first public burning of draft cards took place in midsummer 1965. A "freedom draft card" distributed that year read: "I refuse to destroy a country by fighting for a government with no claim to represent the people. I believe that the US must support movements abroad for revolutionary social change, and I am fully against their suppression by military force." In August, members of the Vietnam Day Committee in Northern California attempted to block troop trains by lying on the tracks. In the same month, 350 people were arrested for civil disobedience in Washington, DC. By 1971, civil disobedience was so widespread that the number arrested for such offenses at the May march in Washington—some fourteen thousand—would have been a good-sized march in 1965. However, civil disobedience wasn't a tactic everyone was happy with. Some socialists felt that the movement's goals were best met through mass antiwar demonstrations, and that the lapse into civil disobedience was adventurist. Nonetheless, some forms of civil disobedience were shown to be effective. Certainly one tactic that the administration hated was draft resistance at a time when the demand for soldiers was soaring.[58]

For those who abjured violence toward others, there was self-immolation. In March 1965, Alice Herz set herself ablaze in Detroit. In November, Norman Morrison, a Quaker, burned himself to death outside the Pentagon with Defense Secretary Robert McNamara watching. A week later, Roger Allen Laporte immolated himself outside the UN building in New York. Two years later, Florence Beaumont repeated the act outside a federal building in Los Angeles. The symbolic significance of Americans burning themselves as the Vietnamese were being scorched to death was not lost on McNamara.[59]

Radicalization and the Breakdown of the Consensus

The peace movement eventually embraced a total of up to six million Americans, with an estimated twenty-five million sympathizers.

For much of the time they were in a minority, but they tapped into latent and growing doubts among the public. The first large-scale national action against the war was electoral activity in 1964 in support of Lyndon Baines Johnson, who promised not to send US troops to Vietnam. Less than three weeks after his inauguration, in February 1965, Johnson started the bombing of North Vietnam. In late March that year, the first teach-ins began. Teach-ins were logical, since the dominant assumption in the mainstream of the antiwar movement was that politicians were in error, needing correction, and that this could be accomplished through the education and activation of a concerned citizenry. Yet a more radical minority was already beginning to see that it might take more than this, and they began to find that they had more traction than they realized. A Declaration of Conscience Against the War in Vietnam was circulated and collected four thousand signatures before it was delivered to the White House in August 1965.

> The use of the military resources of the United States in Vietnam and elsewhere suppresses the aspirations of the people for political independence and economic freedom . . . inhuman torture and senseless killing are being carried out by forces armed, uniformed, trained and financed by the United States . . . we believe that all peoples of the earth, including both Americans and non-Americans, have an inalienable right to life, liberty and the peaceful pursuit of happiness in their own way. . . . We hereby declare our conscientious refusal to cooperate with the United States government in the prosecution of the war in Vietnam.

The declaration pledged to encourage "non-violent acts, including acts which involve civil disobedience, in order to stop the flow of American soldiers and munitions to Vietnam."[60] Others made an early commitment to defy the draft. On April 25, 1964, the *National Guardian* published a statement by the May 2nd Movement. By time it was published in the *New York Herald Tribune* on May 28, it had 149 signatures.

We, the undersigned, are young Americans of draft age. We understand our obligations to defend our country and to serve in the armed forces but we object to being asked to support the war in South Vietnam. Believing the United States' participation in the war is for the suppression of the Vietnamese struggle for national independence, we see no justification in our involvement. We agree with Senator Wayne Morse, who said on the floor of the Senate on March 4, 1964, regarding South Vietnam, that "We should never have gone in. We should never have stayed in. We should get out." BELIEVING THAT WE SHOULD NOT BE ASKED TO FIGHT AGAINST THE PEOPLE OF VIETNAM, WE HEREWITH STATE OUR REFUSAL TO DO SO.[61]

It was the sudden manifestation of antiwar feeling in the streets that alerted activists to a new mood. In December 1964, SDS called for a march on Washington, scheduled for April 17, 1965. The event, expected to draw a few thousand, drew twenty-five thousand and was at that time the biggest antiwar demonstration in Washington's history. Through the remainder of the year, marches of a similar scale took place across the country, with fifteen thousand marching in Berkeley and twenty thousand in Manhattan on the same day in October. By 1967, they would be dwarfed by marches of three to five hundred thousand in New York. On October 15, 1969, a million marched against the war.[62]

It is sometimes assumed because of the prominence of younger radicals and students in the movement that antiwar activism was an elite affair, regarded skeptically by hardworking blue-collar patriots. In truth, US students had long since ceased to be the children of privilege, and a large number of even Ivy League students were recipients of financial aid. Moreover, opposition to the war was not concentrated among affluent college students. Every scientific study has shown that opposition to the war was inversely proportional to wealth and education. Blue-collar workers were doves, favoring withdrawal, while the hawks were concentrated among the college-educated high-income strata. What can also be said is that most Americans were unwilling to fight the war, pay the necessary taxes to support it, or vote for candidates who, like Barry Goldwater, pledged a fight to victory. From 1964 through to the end of the war, every candidate except Goldwater professed to be a "peace" candidate.[63]

Although the divisions between "hard hats" and students have been caricatured, they weren't fabricated. There were real grounds for antagonism between the AFL-CIO bureaucracy and the activists of the New Left. First of all, many unions had been slow to desegregate. When the AFL-CIO merger took place, pressure for immediate desegregation had been contained by anticommunist leaders like Walter Reuther and George Meany. For activists from the civil rights movement, as for African American workers, the self-satisfied complacency of the labor bureaucracy was infuriating and compelled them to seek other means of organizing.

Secondly, the AFL-CIO's history of complicity with imperialism, the extent of which was revealed in 1966 by Victor Reuther and Sidney Lens, continued with Vietnam. While SDS was castigating Johnson for bombing Vietnam—a betrayal of his promise to be the "peace" candidate in the 1964 election—the AFL-CIO hailed his "energetic retaliatory measures to halt the communist acts of provocation and aggression." In 1967, Thomas Gleason, president of the International Longshoremen's Association, went so far as to lead a pro-war parade down Fifth Avenue. When Martin Luther King Jr. spoke out against the war, the ILGWU (International Ladies' Garment Workers' Union) condemned him for "subordinating civil rights to international affairs." These differences resulted in regular run-ins, as when protesters at the AFL-CIO convention in 1965 heckled "labor fakers" and demanded an end to support for the war—George Meany responded by instructing security to "clear these kookies out of the gallery."[64]

Thirdly, the ultraleftism of some of the protesters alienated labor. Rather than being focused on building mass action, they all too often sought the most seemingly militant form of protest and in doing so repelled potential allies. Labor leaders took the opportunity to red-bait the antiwar movement, as when AFL-CIO vice president Joseph Curran claimed that they were being funded from Moscow and Beijing. So, the tensions were real. Nonetheless, there were always those in both camps who sought to keep open channels, and the spread of antiwar sentiment among workers was encouraging enough to New Left activists to raise the possibility of acting together. In response, the SDS Labor Committee produced a leaflet acknowledging that "almost everyone in the anti-war movement recognizes that students alone do not have the power to end the war."

In 1967, an alliance of trade unionists and New Leftists established the Cleveland Area Peace Action Coalition (CAPAC). The "Old Left" activists Sidney Peck, Sidney Lens, and Fred Halstead worked in the coalition to steer the more radical wing of the antiwar movement in a more conciliatory direction. In contrast to the militant but narrow forms of protest that characterized the radical wing of the student movement, they argued for peaceful mass demonstrations as the most effective way to bring new layers of the public into activism. CAPAC sponsored a series of national antiwar conferences which, bringing together dissenting unionists and New Leftists, showed the possibility of coordinating such action. This led to calls for a mass demonstration on October 15, 1969. The idea was to have a mass protest and general strike combined—though, to avoid alienating middle-class citizens, the term *strike* was replaced with *moratorium*. The national moratorium was supported by unions across the country, with forty unions backing the protest in New York City alone, and a total of one million people turned out. It was at that point the largest demonstration in US history.[65]

The critical role of the SWP in building many of the mass demonstrations should be acknowledged here. One of the key participants in CAPAC, Fred Halstead, was a leading figure in the SWP, and his book *Out Now!* is a compelling memoir of activism. Their main work was carried out in the National Mobilizing Committee to End the War (known as the "Mobe") and the New Mobilizing Committee to End the War ("New Mobe"). Despite comprising a small minority of the activists in both organizations, SWP activists did the bulk of the organizing work. Activist Brad Lyttle recalled that "they were obviously the most effective organizers. They delivered. They delivered on leaflets, they delivered on fund-raising, they delivered on banners, they delivered on sound equipment, they delivered on permits. They knew how to do it."[66]

The SWP's activism was dedicated and vital, though not unproblematic—activists accused their cadres of manipulating meetings and of cleaving to a rigid line that brooked no compromise. The major criticism they faced was that their attachment to peaceful mass demonstrations and narrow single-issue approach to the war were inhibiting the development of the movement. Their valid rejection of ultraleftism tended to shade into bolstering the moderating influence of liberals, to the detriment of the movement. As Joe Allen puts it in his history of the war,

> Fred Halstead, a Mobe leader and member of the Socialist Workers Party, blocked with the moderates because, in his words, "We supported increasing the influence of the moderates in the general publicity and tone of the event because we agreed with them that this was the best approach to turn out the largest numbers." Of course, the claims about shutting down the Pentagon and disrupting the war machine were pure hype; but the advocates of purely legal mass protest were equally wrong in their insistence that mass, legal protests (not to mention lobbying) were sufficient to stop the war.[67]

Yet, having suffered terribly from the hammer blows of McCarthyism, the SWP emerged in the 1960s engaged with the civil rights movement, placed antiracism at the center of their activity, and threw themselves into antiwar activism from early on at a time when the small "peace movement" was actually anxious to avoid discussing Vietnam. And, whether it is acknowledged or not, and whether for good or ill, their tactical and strategic guidance exerted considerable influence on the antiwar mobilizing committees.[68]

Another site of radicalization was the armed forces. The usual moral blackmail enjoined protesters to "support our troops." The implication was that protesters were morally frivolous compared to those who, in the familiar alliteration, "laid their lives on the line." Yet this was less persuasive when troops joined the insurgency. A public letter from twenty-five soldiers in Vietnam stated: "We do not want that kind of support. It is the kind of support that brought us here, keeps us here and which will bring our younger brothers or sons here or elsewhere." GIs began to form a central plank of resistance to the war. By late 1969, most of the military prisons were filled with men who had gone AWOL, and the majority of these were Black.[69]

Antiwar feeling spread among the troops. In November 1969, a unit stationed at Pleiku fasted to protest the war, boycotting Thanksgiving Day. Of 141 soldiers below the rank of Specialist 5, only eight showed up for the traditional meal. When Bob Hope introduced General Creighton Adams to thirty thousand troops assembled for the Christmas show in Long Binh on December 23, 1968, the entire throng leapt to their feet to give the peace sign. The general, mistaking it for the victory sign, returned it, and was greeted by a tremendous roar. While the antiwar movement in the United States had difficulty moving beyond symbolic actions to impeding the war, troops deserted or shot officers who ordered search-and-destroy missions, and eventually engaged in mutinies and large-scale resistance. Confirmed "fragging" incidents numbered in the hundreds, but they were part of a wider de facto policy of noncooperation and refusal, as well as episodic random violence by brutalized, bitter, angry soldiers. Enlistment consistently fell well below targets, and the retention rate for vital servicemen collapsed. The machinery of war was breaking down, and by June 1971, the *Armed Forces Journal* was reporting on "the collapse of the armed forces." The army's decision to roll back "Jane Crow" and recruit large numbers of women was largely a response to this crisis.[70]

Far from antiwar activism being an elite movement, the elites were the last to get it—particularly the liberals. In fact, the initial enthusiasm of the "vital center" liberals for intervention in Vietnam made perfect sense given their peculiar weltanschauung. It is their subsequent, judicious distancing from the policy makers whose ideas they had done so much to shape that calls for explanation. Of course, the dissent of the Cold War liberals was pragmatic rather than principled, yet even their moderate criticisms bore testimony to the breakdown of Cold War assumptions. As orthodox a Cold War liberal as Arthur Schlesinger Jr. rubbished the "domino theory," rejected the boring anticommunist line that blamed the People's Republic of China for aggression in the war, and argued for an end to the bombing. He trusted that statesmen meant well, and he shared their goals. Further, he opposed anything that looked like withdrawal, as it would send the wrong signal. It was just a better approximation of means to ends that he asked for. The anarchist intellectual Noam Chomsky pointed out that Schlesinger's argument was, in addition to being less radical than that of the Pentagon, callously indifferent to the suffering of the Vietnamese. They were—shall we say—"out of mind."

Liberal journals supportive of the Vietnam War had included *Foreign Affairs* and *Encounter*, one a mouthpiece of establishment liberalism, the other a mouthpiece of the CIA. *Dissent's* correspondent Joseph Buttinger was a defender of Diem, while Norman Podhoretz's *Commentary* magazine supported the standard anticommunist argument for the war even as the bombing of North Vietnam began. Podhoretz would later join the neoconservative reactionaries in attempting to rescue the Vietnam War from its opponents. Other liberal magazines, such as the *New Republic* and the *Nation*, were slightly more critical, though the latter was the only major publication to (eventually) support withdrawal.[71]

The effect of the anti–Vietnam War movement on American society is difficult to quantify. It derived from and fed into so many complementary liberation movements, labor struggles, and peace campaigns that it would be difficult to say how much each component of sixties radicalism contributed. What is clear is that the antiwar movement was one of the popular movements that terrorized the American ruling class. Nixon was notoriously anxious to show that "under no circumstances" would he be moved by protesters. On the day of the moratorium in October 1969, demonstrators encircled the White House. Nixon let it be known to all that he would be inside watching a football game. In fact, White House records show that Nixon, and the whole administration, was deeply afraid of the event.[72] Business reacted harshly against democracy, which had enabled a delegitimization of authority and threatened their right to rule. This theme was constantly repeated at business conferences, and vexed the authors of the Trilateral Commission's 1975 report *The Crisis of Democracy*. Corporate elites and politicians urgently sought the means to put the toothpaste back into the tube—to stop women, people of color, workers, and students from forging a viable political bloc that could threaten their interests. They considered that democracy was mainly useful as a means of creating legitimate, stable order, and would only work if the population could be restored to apathy.[73]

Politically active business coalitions would win many victories in the ensuing decades, but it was not in their power to stop the periodic awakening of radical, anti-imperialist activism from harming their interests. Reagan would try to restore the old basis for Cold War politics, but with only limited success. Today's movements still operate in terrain cleared by the pioneers of the sixties. The Vietnam campaigners worked in conditions that few protesters today would relish, and were often murdered for their trouble.

There has been repression in later antiwar movements, but luckily no equivalent to Kent State. More relevantly, the post-sixties movements were in many ways more radical than their forebears. The anti-apartheid movement, the Central American solidarity campaigns, and the opposition to war in the Middle East all deployed tactics and ideas that were well in advance of those well-meaning and optimistic souls who joined antiwar protests in 1964, believing that it was all the result of a ghastly mistake. The story of the next chapter is in many ways a story of progress, even amid a generalized turn to the right.

Chapter Five

After Vietnam

Cold War II represented a comprehensive attempt to erode the consequences of the Second World War. These consequences had been: a substantial shift of resources towards the working and other disadvantaged classes in the developed capitalist countries, through wage and welfare polices; an acceptance of the USSR as one of the two major powers in the world as a result of its prime role in the defeat of Nazism; and the replacement of colonial rule by independence in the Third World. The actions of the Reagan administration and its allies in Europe sought to reverse these consequences using the recession, anticommunism, and historical amnesia to impose a new set of values and policies on the world.

—Fred Halliday

The standard of living of the average American has to decline.
—Paul Volcker

The individual would misconceive the nuclear peril if he tried to understand it primarily in terms of personal danger, or even in terms of danger to the people immediately known to him, for the nuclear peril threatens life, above all, not at the level of individuals, who already live under the sway of

> *death, but at the level of everything that individuals hold*
> *in common. Death cuts off life; extinction cuts off birth . . .*
> *the meaning of extinction is therefore to be sought first not*
> *in what each person's own life means to him but in what the*
> *world and the people in it mean to him.*
>
> —Jonathan Schell

After Vietnam, there was to be no restoration. In the brief Carter interregnum, the executive would phrase its foreign policies in the terms of human rights and peace rather than commie-hunting. Reaganite recidivists tried, but largely failed, to reconstruct the old imperialist constituency. They could ally with apartheid South Africa, coddle the Marcos dictatorship, and run death squads in Central America, but they could not do so without experiencing vocal and often obstructive popular opposition, some of which forced its way into the press and legislature. This alarming tendency for turbulent, surging democracy to overflow the strict boundaries established for its expression and impede the doings of power was sometimes characterized as "Vietnam Syndrome," and elites spared no effort in attempting to overcome the malady.

However, something *did* change with the advent of the Reaganauts. First of all, imperial strategy shifted from the détente of the Nixon-Ford-Carter years to an aggressive reassertion of US interests. This was given ideological impetus by the Soviet invasion of Afghanistan and the Iranian hostage crisis, and authorized the "military Keynesianism" of armaments buildups centered on investment in nuclear weapons and the domination of outer space. Reagan's Strategic Defense Initiative, or "Star Wars," as it was branded, was in theory supposed to protect the United States from nuclear attack by using ground-to-space systems to create a "shield." In reality, such a shield was never viable, and its main effect was to undermine peace negotiations and trigger a global arms race.

Secondly, this aggression was implemented through various surrogates, not the US Armed Forces. Rather than attack its foes directly, the United States used networks of death squads, client armies, and guerrillas in Afghanistan, southern Africa, and Central America. Reagan did send US troops into Grenada and Lebanon. But the former was a very brief engagement, while in the latter case the troops were withdrawn under fire from Hezbollah. The major engagements involved the use of proxies. This strategy shift had its origins both in the US defeat in Vietnam, which illustrated the declining efficacy of overwhelming military force, and in the successful US-supported coup in Chile, which established the world's first neoliberal state and provided a laboratory for a new mode of US dominance. This strategy was actually first envisaged by Nixon, whose doctrine of "Vietnamization"—transferring the burden of military conflict to local elites dependent on US support—was part of a broader strategic perspective involving the use of rising regional powers to protect American interests abroad. The use of the shah's Iran as a regional bulwark in the Middle East, followed by the "tilt" toward Saddam Hussein's Iraq after the Islamic Revolution of 1979, is a classic example of this strategy.[1]

Thirdly, central to the story of changing US dominance is the neoliberal turn. This was comprised of a set of policies designed to overcome a number of problems, most centrally a slump in profitability in the kinds of Fordist industries that had dominated since World War II. The answer was to be found through a concerted attack on the organized working class, by busting unions and driving down living standards, and the financialization and the deregulation of markets, twinned with international dollar supremacy. This was tied with imperialism from the beginning, as the US-supported overthrow of the leftist Salvador Allende government in 1973 offered the first means to test the principles of the neoliberal doctrines authored by Friedrich Hayek and Milton Friedman. By violently crushing the left and dismantling popular organization, the coup d'etat enabled a team of economists trained in a Cold War program to counteract leftism in Latin America to embark on a radical restructuring of class relations. As David Harvey describes it:

> Working alongside the IMF, they restructured the economy according to their theories. They reversed the nationalizations and privatized public assets, opened up natural resources (fisheries, timber, etc.) to private and unregulated exploitation (in many cases riding roughshod over the claims of indigenous inhabitants), privatized social security, and facilitated foreign direct investment and freer trade. The right of foreign companies to repatriate profits from their Chilean operations was guaranteed. Export-led growth was favored over import substitution. The only sector reserved for the state was the key resource of copper (rather like oil in Iraq). This proved crucial to the budgetary viability of the state since copper revenues flowed exclusively into its coffers. The immediate revival of the Chilean economy in terms of growth rates, capital accumulation, and high rates of return on foreign investments was short-lived. It all went sour in the Latin American debt crisis of 1982. The result was a much more pragmatic and less ideologically driven application of neoliberal policies in the years that followed. All of this, including the pragmatism, provided helpful evidence to support the subsequent turn to neoliberalism in both Britain (under Thatcher) and the US (under Reagan) in the 1980s.[2]

In the United States, the shift toward neoliberalism was presaged by a fiscal crisis in New York City where deindustrialization produced a decline in city revenues. The withdrawal of federal funding under Nixon forced the city to borrow money from investors. In 1975, the investment banks used their leverage to force a wave of "austerity" on the city by refusing to roll over the debt. This entailed a restructuring of the city's finances, a curbing of unions, cutbacks in spending and public sector employment, and the introduction of fees for the use of public services. In this way, class relations were restructured to the advantage of Wall Street.[3] The next shift was signposted by the "Volcker shock" of 1979—in which Paul Volcker, the chairman of the Federal Reserve, drove up interest rates to combat inflation regardless of the impact on employment and growth. This was the catalyst for a deep recession lasting for two years in which a great deal of unprofitable capital was destroyed, and was followed up by the rolling out nationwide of the kinds of austerity policies that had been implemented in Chile and New York—union-busting, budget cuts, deregulation, and reduced taxes on profits and higher incomes. In addition, US capital was increasingly looking overseas for its profits—overseas trade for US companies had risen from 10 percent of output in 1965 to 31 percent in 1979[4]—which had profound ramifications for US imperialism. Again, David Harvey explains:

> The options within the US, given the depressed economic conditions and low rates of return in the mid-1970s, were not good. More profitable opportunities had to be sought out abroad. Governments seemed the safest bet because, as Walter Wriston, head of Citibank, famously put it, governments can't move or disappear. And many governments in the developing world, hitherto starved of funds, were anxious enough to borrow. For this to occur required, however, open entry and reasonably secure conditions for lending. The New York investment banks looked to the US imperial tradition both to prise open new investment opportunities and to protect their foreign operations. . . . Before 1973, most US foreign investment was of the direct sort, mainly concerned with the exploitation of raw material resources (oil, minerals, raw materials, agricultural products) or the cultivation of specific markets (telecommunications, automobiles, etc.) in Europe and Latin America. The New York investment banks had always been active internationally, but after 1973 they became even more so, though now far more focused on lending capital to foreign governments. This required the liberalization of international credit and financial markets, and the US government began actively to promote and support this strategy globally during the 1970s. Hungry for credit, developing countries were encouraged to borrow heavily, though at rates that were advantageous to the New York bankers.[5]

The use of US power to open up overseas markets for US capital was not new. In the early Cold War period, however, the United States had sought to promote a stable and noncommunist model of development that could sometimes accommodate welfare states and state direction of the economy. In the neoliberal period, the United States used its lending power to liberalize and deregulate markets, breaking the social forces—such as unions and leftist movements— capable of resisting these trends. Concurrently, the discourse of empire began to shift. A segment of neoconservatives integrated into the Reagan administration—characterized by Martin Amis at the time as "the megadeath intellectuals"—began to disseminate a new technocratic language of "democracy promotion" tied with overseas networks of patronage. Institutions such as the National Endowment for Democracy provided an ideological counterpoint to leftism, claiming to support human rights and democratic development— so long as the latter was understood to be built on a foundation of free markets and property rights. This would contribute greatly to the emergence of "humanitarian intervention" in the 1990s.[6]

These changes profoundly affected the nature of anti-imperialist movements. In the 1980s, they were mobilized less against the deployment of US Armed Forces than the use of the CIA, the IMF (International Monetary Fund), military aid, and international institutes to sustain pro-US governments and movements. This required a broader understanding of empire than that focused on the use of military force. The major domestic challenges to US power in the 1980s reflected this.

Reagan and the American Left; or, the Death Star and the Rebel Alliance

The return to Cold War hostilities in the 1980s saw a brief upsurge in protest against the thermonuclear state. The Reagan administration's nuclear policies were predicated initially on the most alarmist assumptions about Soviet military "preparedness." There were several reasons for this. One was the ideological predilections of the administration. Reagan himself had, since the end of World

War II, espoused an evangelical form of anticommunism, and he interpreted biblical prophesy to mean that there would be nuclear conflict with the Soviet Union. His advisors and colleagues, mainly belligerent Cold Warriors, shared with him this Manichaean approach. Partly for this reason, the incoming defense secretary Caspar Weinberger and his assistant secretary Richard Perle were staunch opponents of nuclear weapons controls, while Secretary of State Alexander Haig was reportedly anxious to bomb Cuba and "turn that fucking island into a parking lot."[7]

But far more important was the determination to overcome the legacy of defeat in Vietnam, which meant dropping détente and engaging in a military buildup. The nuclear escalation was the centerpiece of this military upgrade, with administration officials alarmingly blasé about the possible consequences. Lawrence Wittner describes how:

> Once in office, the Reaganites began implementing their priorities. The Pentagon's new military program called for simultaneous across-the-board modernization of all US strategic forces, including cruise missiles, the MX missile, and the Trident submarine.... In May 1982, when the administration's first Defense Guidance was leaked to the press, it revealed that the US military had been readied for a "protracted" nuclear war with the Soviet Union, in which US nuclear forces "must prevail and be able to force the Soviet Union to seek the earliest termination of hostilities on terms favorable to the United States."[8]

The "Nuclear Freeze" campaign that took off in response is considered a highly effective example of peace work. In Noam Chomsky's judgment, it was "probably the most successful campaign ever carried out in the US peace movement" in terms of achieving its stated objective. However, this was laced with the darkly ironic observation that, while it succeeded in winning the support of the general public for a "freeze" on nuclear weapons, it "had essentially zero impact on American politics."[9] In this view, then, the peace movement won the argument and lost the war. In fact, the argument was won fairly early on, as by 1981 overwhelming majorities of public opinion favored a nuclear freeze, in contrast to Reagan's early bellicose posture. Yet, by 1987, the United States and the Soviet Union had agreed upon arms control. Moreover, some would argue, this was at least partially the result of popular pressure leading to a reduction in Reagan's military expenditures and a softening of his position that allowed the Soviet Union to make its own concessions. In short, the 1987 Treaty on Intermediate-Range Nuclear Forces was, in the words of the founder of the Nuclear Freeze Campaign, "a victory for the peace movement."[10]

To establish the real impact and lessons of the 1980s peace movement, it is necessary to understand its origins, goals, tactics, and lastly, relationship to policy makers. A few points stand out here. First of all, the US anti-nuclear movement arose as part of an international response to nuclear buildup. In the United Kingdom, unprecedented numbers of people flocked to the Campaign for Nuclear Disarmament (CND), and one of its major protests in 1983 drew four hundred thousand people. Similarly, in West Germany a broad coalition of pacifists, feminists, and Greens drew three million people into activity in a week of agitation against missile deployment. Secondly, it formed one aspect of a matrix of interlocking issues, reflected in the forms of organization that arose, and in the fact that activists from the antinuclear campaign very quickly found themselves gravitating to other movements once its zenith had passed. Thirdly, it combined traditional pacifist campaigning with more limited, single-issue campaigning, and achieved extraordinarily broad political support in so doing.

So, in addition to two long-standing peace campaigns, the Committee for a Sane Nuclear Policy and Physicians for Social Responsibility (a reincarnation of the sixties formation opposing nuclear testing), the Nuclear Freeze Campaign emerged in 1980 as the major expression of the antinuclear movement in the United States. Antinuclear campaigns had been operating for decades, but usually independently of one another. Their convergence in a single campaign added to the critical mass leading to the movement's successes. The campaign for a freeze gained overwhelming public endorsement, the support of labor unions, professional associations, churches, "275 city governments, twelve state legislatures, and the voters of nine out of ten states where it was placed on the ballot in the fall of 1982." In the end, its demands were incorporated into the Democratic Party presidential platform—an issue to which we'll return presently.[11]

The issues raised by the antinuclear campaign included the ever-present risk of major nuclear accidents; the proliferation of diverse kinds of nuclear weapons, making their use more likely; that such proliferation was made possible by the spread of nuclear technology, often under the cover of developing nuclear energy; and that there were abundant renewable energy sources that were far preferable to nuclear power. Thus, the campaign intersected an array of concerns, from inter-imperialist conflict to the environment, and at the heart of it was the claim that the democratization of military policy was a necessity in order to restrain its tendencies toward escalation.[12]

The instigator behind the freeze campaign was the disarmament researcher Randall Forsberg, who began drafting a "Call to Halt the Nuclear Arms Race" in 1979. Her proposal was that all future research, development, and deployment of nuclear weapons should be halted, retaining "the existing parity between the United States and the Soviet Union" and opening the possibility of bilateral reductions in the future. Through her Institute for Defense and Disarmament Studies, Forsberg disseminated her call to a raft of peace groups, and a new Nuclear Freeze Steering Committee was convoked to implement a strategic plan for the coming years. The agenda was to begin by consolidating support among peace groups, building on that unity to reach out to "interest groups," win support in "Middle America," and then force the issue into mainstream politics.[13]

This approach lent itself to mass protests and educational activities, and both drew masses of participants. A Ground Zero Week in April 1982 involved one million people across 650 towns and cities. A demonstration in New York in June the same year attracted close to a million protesters. In addition, it succeeded in galvanizing support across a variety of influential civil society organizations. The National Council of Churches and the Conference of Catholic Bishops endorsed the freeze campaign, while professional bodies like the American Psychiatric Association added their support. In October 1983, the AFL-CIO executive unanimously endorsed the freeze campaign and called for "radical reductions" in America's nuclear arsenal—a position that it is difficult to imagine the AFL-CIO of George Meany taking. By 1982, Democratic Congressmen such as Ted Kennedy were supporting the campaign in both houses, and the House of Representatives, with a Democratic majority, overwhelmingly passed a resolution endorsing the freeze.[14]

Not all of the movement was oriented toward legislative politics. One notable tributary to the antinuclear peace campaigns that retained a degree of political independence from Congressional campaigns was women's struggles. Not only did women such as Randall Forsberg and Helen Caldicott lead the major campaigns, but a diverse array of feminist organizations participated directly. The US branch of the Women's International League for Peace and Freedom (WILPF) and the National Organization for Women (NOW) made campaigning over nuclear weapons a priority in this period. WILPF was among the most established and successful of the groups, growing to some fifteen thousand members by 1983.[15]

Women's Strike for Peace engaged in important publicity work, organizing a full-page advertisement in the *New York Times* calling for an end to the "continuing build-up of arsenals which threaten the world with nuclear extinction by plan or accident." These groups lent their support to Women's Pentagon Action, which was both a protest event in itself and an organization. At the core of Women's Pentagon Action was an ecofeminist alliance that emerged from a conference in 1980, which brought together women, antinuclear activists, and environmental movements, and included a strand of spiritualism as well as anarchism. Largely white, they made efforts to incorporate women of color into their events, though with little success. In the tradition of feminist peace campaigning, Women's Pentagon Action linked militarism to patriarchy and other forms of institutionalized violence. It was not a large group, attracting crowds in the hundreds or thousands.[16]

Their techniques relied to a considerable extent on theater and spectacle, using similar ideas to those used by Quaker groups in the 1960s, which did succeed in attracting attention. But they also included nonviolent forms of civil disobedience in their repertoire. For example, an iconic outing in mid-November 1980 involved surrounding the Pentagon and blocking the entrances in solidarity with the women's protests at the positioning of US nuclear weapons at RAF Greenham Common, England. They also set up a camp outside the Seneca Army Depot in Seneca Falls, New York. The depot was being used to send cruise missiles to the base in Greenham Common, and the women engaged in trespassing and symbolic vandalism. Realistically, none of this ever threatened to disrupt the transfer of the weapons, and the group's major success remained the solidarity that activists established with other peace campaigners and the publicity they generated.[17]

If the effectiveness of such deeds may be doubted, the emphasis on maintaining respectability and succeeding in mainstream politics also had fatal drawbacks. From the start, antinuclear campaigns devoted considerable resources to lobbying in Washington. The result of depending on the Democratic Party to implement antinuclear policies was a severe demoralization. This is entirely predictable from the history of the Democrats and the mass movements that relate to them. If social movements rely on the election of Democrats for the attainment of their goals, either the Democrats gain office and renege on their promises (Wilson and Johnson stand out here) or they are defeated and the movement is set back. In practice what happened was that Democratic congressional candidates committed themselves to very loose language about the freeze, unless they were already on the party's left wing or stood no chance of winning.

The Democratic presidential candidate Walter Mondale, for his part—and to the disappointment of Forsberg and her allies who were actively supporting Mondale's presidential bid—demonstrated only marginal policy differences with Reagan. He paid lip service to the freeze campaign while supporting the development of Trident II submarines and Midgetman missiles, and deploying Euromissiles. The activists who turned up to work for his campaign found that they couldn't abide his policies. Forsberg, to her credit, grasped what was going on. She knew that Mondale, by taking this minimal-difference approach—as he did with a whole range of peace-related and other issues—would not enthuse grassroots voters enough to win. "To tip the balance against Reagan," she said, it would not be enough for Mondale to "give lip service to the freeze while supporting traditional arms control. This is what Jimmy Carter did in 1980. Merely 'supporting arms control' does not inspire enthusiasm among the public." In the ensuing election, Reagan won 59 percent of the vote, a seven million vote lead. The turnout, however, was just 53 percent. Mondale had manifestly failed to mobilize the Democratic base, never mind "inspire enthusiasm." After 1984, the nuclear freeze campaign experienced a protracted decline.[18]

It should not be assumed that the movement is predominantly characterized by its failures and eventual decline. It is known, for example, that the Reagan White House was deeply worried by the scale and international strength of the nuclear freeze campaign. White House communications director David Gergen has described how administration officials saw the movement as "a dagger pointed at the heart of the administration's defense program." The administration responded by embarking on an unsuccessful attempt to depict the campaigners as dupes of "foreign agents" who had "instigated" the freeze policy, initially at the behest of Leonid Brezhnev. (In fact, the Soviet leadership cracked down hard on the antinuclear European Nuclear Disarmament (END) campaign for its criticisms of Russian policy). The president called the pope to see if he could reverse the position of Catholic bishops, while lobbying Republican allies in the Senate to ensure that the Democrats' freeze resolution was defeated. In the end, they were compelled to adopt the language of the freeze campaign, suggesting that the United States and NATO were the real antinuclear campaign.

And just as a number of NATO allies were compelled to retreat from stationing cruise and Pershing II missiles under the weight of popular protest, so the Reaganites began to retreat. Reagan reportedly told Secretary of State George Schultz in 1983, "If things get hotter and hotter and arms control remains an issue, maybe I should go see [Soviet leader Yuri] Andropov and propose eliminating all nuclear weapons." By 1985, having railed against nuclear controls and maintained that the Soviet Union was an "Evil Empire" that could not be reasoned with, he was in negotiations with Mikhail Gorbachev. The result was the 1987 INF Treaty.[19]

And if the antinuclear movement declined, this did not signal an end to Reagan's troubles. The activists who had been hounding the administration over nuclear weapons turned to other campaigns. Among the leading organizers for the movement were figures who would appear in similar leading positions in future antiwar struggles, such as Leslie Cagan, a Communist Party member[20] who helped organize the mass protest in New York City and who would go on to play a key role in opposition to the first Gulf War before becoming the national coordinator of United for Peace and Justice in opposition to Bush's wars. More generally, activists turned to immediately resonant causes. For example, surveys of the Central American solidarity movement found that the antinuclear coalition played a vital role in supplying its core personnel. As the freeze campaign broke down, activists migrated to the solidarity campaigns. In two groups, Sanctuary and Witness for Peace, 66 percent and 78 percent of activists, respectively, had previously been involved in agitation against nuclear weapons.[21] The antinuclear campaign was, in addition to everything else, an important base from which many other social movements of the eighties were launched.

Washington and Pretoria: For White Supremacy, Against Communism

Following the pattern established in the 1960s, the crescendo of anticolonial struggles in the 1970s converged with militancy in Europe when in 1974 the "Estada Novo" dictatorship in Portugal was overthrown by the combined battalions of revolution from the metropole and periphery. This gave Mozambique and Angola the means to their freedom, which was duly asserted the following year. The terrain of struggle in southern Africa was instantly transformed, with two new people's republics set up in the former colonies. The apartheid state itself was under renewed pressure from an independent trade union bloc and a "Black Consciousness Movement."

The United States had long defined its approach to apartheid along two vertices—Jim Crow and its perception overseas, and communism. The Eisenhower administration had worried that South African Blacks had an infantile and unrealistic appreciation of America's own racial system, and were thus susceptible to the seductions of communism. The administration went so far as to characterize the ANC (African National Congress) as a communist front, though even the white supremacist state of South Africa could not sustain this pretense. The perception of South African

Blacks as childlike and easy meat for communism was merely a localized expression of the way Washington tended to see the world that it sought to dominate. Cold War administrations feared that most of the peoples of Africa were unready for self-government and dreaded "premature independence" on the grounds that they would be prey for communist overmastery.

The Nixon administration embarked on a strategy of improving relations with the white minority governments in Mozambique, Angola, and South Africa on the pretext that the white regimes were there to stay and that cordiality with them would moderate their policies. There was also the Cold War rationale, which held that support for such regimes was essential to retard the spread of communism on the continent. Internal documents disclose that the regime was particularly vexed by the possibility that "U.S. interests will be increasingly threatened" by "violence," particularly the one-billion-dollar direct investment that "yields a highly profitable return." In response to the 1974–75 revolutions, the administration had ploughed resources into two anticommunist Angolan groups, National Union for the Total Independence of Angola (UNITA) and the National Front for the Liberation of Angola (FNLA). The Popular Movement for the Liberation of Angola (MPLA) was by far the largest political grouping in the country. The South African Army also began to intervene, starting with backup for Portuguese and Rhodesian forces before escalating into outright regional aggression. As Angola descended into civil war, the United States intensified covert aid to the rightist factions—a highly contentious policy, as Congress was worried that this intervention, justified by the same logic that had led to defeat in Vietnam, would escalate into an outright US war, with America drawn into an open alliance with the apartheid regime.[22]

Carter's "signals" on southern Africa contrasted with Nixon's more than his policies did. For example, Andrew Young, an African American with a background in the southern freedom movement and an avowed sympathy for liberation struggles in southern Africa, was sent to the United Nations as the US ambassador. This was an intelligent diplomatic move, as it helped kindle some warmth toward the United States in African states. But Young was also an advocate of US business interests on the continent, maintaining that US corporations would have a liberalizing effect in undermining segregation. In this, Carter agreed with him. And the Department of Defense and CIA continued to assist South African forces in the region under his presidency, the better to counter the MPLA. This is not to say that the "human rights" rhetoric was merely vapid. The administration's criticisms of the apartheid regime, and particularly of the brutal suppression of the Soweto uprising, as well as open support for the end of white minority rule, were not inconsequential. However, these timorous gestures tended to be overwhelmed in practice by Cold War logic and US business interests, and the overall direction of policy tended toward a rearticulation of Nixon's "constructive engagement" strategy.[23]

Reagan's approach, setting aside his predecessor's herbivorous cavils about human rights, was to amplify existing trends. The two powers would cooperate on "security" agreements and do business together, and in the resulting stable and prosperous environment it was conveniently assumed that the white supremacists in Pretoria would eventually get around to reforming their privileges out of existence.[24]

The US anti-apartheid movement can trace its origins to the Sharpeville Massacre of 1960, after which the tactics of the civil rights movement—sit-ins, protests, road blockades, and petitioning—were applied in the US. The movement pursued a campaign of targeted boycott and divestments, coinciding with the bloc boycott of white South Africa by an Asian and African alliance in the United Nations. In the afterglow of Jim Crow's overthrow, this movement grew. In 1969, as Nixon was inaugurated, growing Black electoral participation meant that there was a sizeable minority of

Black Congressmen and women who could challenge the policy of "constructive engagement." The Congressional Black Caucus was formed, and some of its members entered into an alliance with community-based Black activists, known as the National African Liberation Support Committee (ALSC). In addition, civil rights, labor, and peace groups all provided bases from which apartheid could be challenged by grassroots constituencies. The anti-apartheid American Committee on Africa (ACOA), initially formed in 1953, opened an office in Washington, DC, in 1969 to translate popular pressure into an effective lobby on the government. By 1972, the ACOA had allied with nationwide church groups to found the Washington Office on Africa (WOA) as a permanent pressure group. Strategically situated Black workers also undertook a variety of actions. For example, employees of Polaroid in Cambridge, Massachusetts, founded the Polaroid Revolutionary Workers' Movement to challenge the company's involvement in the production of film for the apartheid regime's passbook system.[25]

After the Soweto uprising, which was only one of a series of intense, spontaneous rebellions across townships in Natal, Transvaal, and the Cape Province, a group called Catalyst began to circulate speakers on university campuses favoring divestment campaigns. Part of the rationale for divestment was that the impact of capital flight following the Sharpeville Massacre showed the regime's dependence on international capital investment. Divestment could hit the junta where it hurt, forcing the issue of reform in a way that "constructive engagement" did not. However, as neither the United States nor the British government was willing to support international sanctions or otherwise imperil its preferential access to the Rand's glittering mineral resources, this campaign took a "privatized" form—targeting overseas capitalists and financial institutions to deprive the white dictatorship of loans and investment. Boycotts also imitated a strategy being deployed by black South Africans in their struggles.

Corporations responded to such campaigns by justifying their investments as both developmental aids and, in the long run, benefactors to world democracy. Thus, Chase Manhattan Bank argued that "it would endanger the free world if every large American bank deprived developing countries of the opportunity for economic growth." Corporations argued the case for "constructive engagement" by claiming that such growth would eventually erode apartheid faster than isolating the system would. As South African capitalism grew, it was maintained, the system would require more skilled black laborers, who would have more prestige, more authority, and better pay. "Frankly, we are proud of what we are doing," a Citibank official said. Opponents pointed out, using extensive case studies, that even with the integration of a small, skilled black minority, the "color bar" could still operate with the reclassification of jobs to protect the status and wage gap. By the early 1980s, divestment was a major issue on college campuses across the United States.[26]

But the movement extended well beyond campuses. Some campaigns were explicitly founded on the principles of transnational solidarity. In 1978, the Southern African Support Project (SASP) was created by a number of African American activists with the specific aim of linking US antiracist activism with anti-apartheid struggles. This organization was one of the bases for the Free South Africa Movement founded in 1984–85, which involved many civil rights veterans in large-scale, militant protests. FSAM had three goals: to fight for the release of black political prisoners, lobby for a power-sharing agreement between the South African state and liberation movements, and capsize the administration's "constructive engagement" policy. Along with other groups like TransAfrica, it sought to combine lobbying of sympathetic politicians, like Ted Kennedy and members of the Congressional Black Caucus, with disruptive tactics of the kind deployed in the sixties to compel Congress to apply sanctions. In addition to peaceful protests outside the South African embassy, they occupied consulates. During a week of protests coinciding with Desmond Tutu's visit to the United States in December 1984, police arrested labor leaders and politicians such as Representative Charles Rangel. The US press compared the militancy of this period to the civil rights movement.[27]

As the global campaign grew, a brutal tribute to its efficacy was offered by the South African government, which threatened to fine or jail any individual expressing support for sanctions. The anti-apartheid movement yielded palpable results. Local and state governments as well as universities were persuaded to participate in a boycott and divestment campaign. Congress, under popular pressure amid an increased tempo of struggle in South African townships, finally applied some limited sanctions on the regime in 1986, with the Comprehensive Anti-Apartheid Act overcoming the veto of a seemingly popular president. The movement targeted corporations, effectively and tirelessly rebutting their efforts to muddy the waters in defense of their involvement in apartheid. Hundreds of millions of dollars were rapidly withdrawn from the South African economy, and the apartheid regime was effectively delegitimized, even as intransigent policy makers continued to defend it publicly. *Delegitimization* is a key word here. Theorists of international relations operating from a "constructivist" paradigm argue that policy options for states in the international sphere are limited by socially constructed norms. The norm of racial equality, the result of anticolonial, civil rights, and anti-apartheid struggles, may still be routinely violated by imperialism, but it constrains state policies, and—as we will discuss later—can be used to make life difficult for states that violate the norm.[28]

These accomplishments were significant but hard won, and tactical difficulties provoked wide-ranging debate. In retrospect, some of the tactics assumed to be effective at the time were unproductive. Sarah Soule argues, for example, that the tactic of "shantytown" protests, wherein students built ramshackle living quarters on the grounds of target colleges and lived in them, was far less efficacious than was widely assumed at the time. Media reports connected divestment with the shantytown campaign, and the tactic fit in with existing student repertoires—yet colleges targeted with this tactic divested more slowly than others did. This is not to assert that the shantytown tactic was responsible for colleges divesting more slowly. Nor is it to minimize the uses to which the shantytowns could be put as centers for organizing divestment campaigns. However, it is a warning to resist the belief that because certain protest strategies resonate in the media as spectacle, this necessarily makes them effective.[29]

The movement was also divided along race and class lines. Put simply (too simply), white middle-class activists engaged in nationally oriented lobbying, directing their energies at Washington-based politicians, while working-class black activists ran local divestment campaigns. White liberals, it may be argued, were inhibited by their unwillingness to relate the fight against apartheid to the struggle against racism in the United States, thus proving themselves unable to attract African Americans in numbers to the national organizations they ran. Some anti-apartheid activists argued that a popular front was necessary, combining the different levels of activism as complementary rather than competing aspects of the struggle. Kevin Danaher was one of those to offer a clear strategic and political basis for such an articulation. He maintained that the core of moral outrage against apartheid should be leavened with an appeal to self-interest. Most Americans, he said, would benefit from the overthrow of apartheid. Its successful pursuit would involve fundamentally democratizing foreign policy, opening policy making to wider layers of people. "We will never reach broad masses of people with our message," Danaher wrote, if "we ignore issues of practical self-interest to average Americans."[30] Further, the campaign should seek to persuade corporations that their interests would be best pursued in a peaceful, prosperous post-apartheid South African system. Companies should be enticed with the prospect that a "post-apartheid

South Africa would need large infusions of capital to develop sectors of the population currently deprived of education, health facilities, housing, agricultural inputs, and much more. This would provide many opportunities for US investors." This proposal resembled, in some ways, the Popular Front strategy of the old CPUSA-dominated left, involving a multiclass coalition in an attempt to occupy some of the traditional language and territory of the right.

However, there were other bases on which a new unity could be forged. The accent could be placed on the rational self-interest of African Americans and other oppressed minorities in opposing racism and US imperialism, rather than the self-interest of capitalists. Workers could be involved in the struggle in a way that stressed their commonality with South African labor, rather than in a way that implied a competition between them—such was the approach of SASP, for example. There was a contradiction here, moreover, as Danaher also maintained that the divestment campaign challenged a central component of capitalism, namely that "investment decisions are best handled (undemocratically) by the wealthy minority that owns most of the capital." One can see why capital would respond to the offer of profits in a post-apartheid South Africa, but not why they would consent to the erosion of their power.[31]

Nevertheless, the problem this argument addressed was real, and continues to recur in social and political movements in the United States: how to achieve unity, and on what basis? The next movement we will consider brings up other problems: chiefly, how to sustain militant movements in the face of state repression, and to what extent anti-imperialist alliances in the United States depend on, and respond to, the initiative of their would-be beneficiaries.

The Central American Solidarity Movement

The Reagan gang had come to power, armed with a critique of the Carter administration's "human rights" policy—which they claimed weakened America's defense of its interests abroad and allowed the Soviets to begin penetrating Central America, as well as "losing" Iran. They reversed this forthwith, primarily by defending the authoritarian regimes of Central America. Such authoritarianism was, at any rate, always preferable to its "totalitarian" alternative, communism. In El Salvador, for example, a military junta sending death squads after nuns, peasants, and human rights activists was the beneficiary of Reaganite largesse. The Salvadoran ruling class, it was known to the Reagan regime, was disposed toward a genocidal solution of its conflict with leftist peasants and workers, favoring the "cleansing" of up to half a million people.[32]

In Nicaragua, a civilian, left-wing government run by a coalition known as the Sandinistas was to be attacked by proxy. This took place through CIA-trained and -armed "Contra" ("Contra" was an abbreviation of *contrarrevolución*, meaning "counterrevolution") death squads, who directed their terror toward "soft targets"—these being the populations who supported the Sandinistas, whose whereabouts were disclosed by CIA intelligence. The Contra riffraff were exceptionally good at rape and creative with mutilations, and managed to kill in the region of fifty thousand people through their calculated outrages. Yet they were often too random in their violence for the United States. As a result, CIA contractors frequently had to be parachuted in to carry out more targeted attacks.[33]

This fresh wave of counterrevolutionary violence, blessed by the Reaganauts, called into being a new generation of activists who learned the methods and ideas of international solidarity. In addition to the old peace networks, such as the Fellowship of Reconciliation (FOR) and the American Friends Service Committee (AFSC), arose a series of movements with a decidedly militant approach. The origin and nature of these movements was at the time partially obscured by propaganda disseminated through the state and the media—an issue to which we will return. Unfortunately, the effect of this has been to polarize discussion between those who stress the "foreign" (allegedly "terrorist" linked) roots of the movement in order to criminalize it and those who focus on its genuinely domestic roots, and in particular the involvement of white, middle-class Americans in such radical action. In fact, the Central America solidarity movement stands in the tradition of internationalism, in which the agency of Central American activists themselves has been of considerable importance in stimulating solidarity campaigns.

The social scientist Héctor Perla Jr. has warned against the danger of discounting the agency of the oppressed, arguing that these mobilizations were decisively seeded by the Central American diaspora in the 1970s, before Reagan's war began. For example, US-based Salvadoran activists retained close contacts with repressed popular movements in El Salvador, and were thus a conduit through which revolutionaries could communicate information to where it could have a strategically significant effect. Using a "signal flare" strategy, they brought testimonials and information first to immigrant communities themselves, then to wider American audiences in order to galvanize solidarity actions and subvert the Reagan administration's policy in ways that those facing death squads could not.[34]

Whereas many previous peace movements had been based most significantly on the Eastern Seaboard, these alliances sprang up first on the West Coast of the United States. The Committee in Solidarity with the People of El Salvador (CISPES), the National Network in Solidarity with the Nicaraguan People (NNSNP), and the Network in Solidarity with the People of Guatemala (NISGUA) were all national organizations that had roots in the West Coast. But the campaign was truly national as it grew, developing fifteen hundred solidarity groups in fifty states, often based in churches. Witness for Peace was a vital national movement that brought four thousand American activists to the war zones of Nicaragua to gain a firsthand understanding of the struggle. In addition to the above organizations were the Pledge of Resistance, Sanctuary, the SHARE Foundation, Christians for Peace in El Salvador (CRISPAZ), the National Agenda for Peace in El Salvador, Voices on the Border, and the Center for Global Education.[35] Some examples should illustrate how these groups drew on traditions of radicalism and religious nonconformism in US history, as well as how they were prompted by the struggling men and women they encountered to take the actions they did.

Sanctuary, an important organization set up to defend Central American refugees from the Reaganites' onslaught, was founded by the Quaker activists Jim Corbett and Jim Dudley. Initially motivated by an enraging experience attempting to protect a Salvadoran asylum seeker who was illegally deported by the US government, they began to think about ways they could intervene to help the victims of the death squads. They decided, in Corbett's words, that "if Central Americans' rights to political asylum are decisively rejected by the US government, or if the US legal system insists on ransom that exceeds our ability to pay, *active resistance* will be the only alternative to abandoning the refugees to their fate." They began to develop a network of supporters and fundraisers on both sides of the US-Mexico border, which eventually involved seventy thousand Americans in helping Central American refugees cross the border in defiance of immigration laws.[36]

Witness for Peace began as the initiative of Gail Phares, a former nun who had long experience with antipoverty work in Central America. Urged on by her Central American colleagues, she moved back to the United States to fight US policy from, as it were, the belly of the whale. From North Carolina, she created the Carolina Interfaith Taskforce on Central America, and took a number of her religious acquaintances to Nicaragua when the Contra war began so that they could survey the situation. They learned that the Contras would not attack the group of Nicaraguans they were with because "you are here with us," and that the residents of the village they visited did not want them to leave. In one house they were taken to, they found a shocked, weeping mother sitting in a room covered with the blood of her children and her own mother, who had been injured in a recent Contra assault. Their feelings of guilt and shame over having to leave were second only to the nausea of knowing that their tax dollars were subsidizing this slaughter. They decided that they should appeal for a group of volunteers, some fifteen hundred people to travel to parts of Nicaragua where people were endangered. This would serve the twin purposes of retarding the assaults and collecting information that could be used to raise awareness in the United States. Beginning with dozens rather than thousands of volunteers, they accessed friendly religious networks such as the American Friends Service Committee and began to send delegations. Having seen that the Nicaragua of real life was quite unlike the "totalitarian" nightmare depicted by the US media, they embarked on an awareness campaign called "Project Witness." It was highly effective, inasmuch as it garnered national and local press coverage and resulted in a *New York Times* essay countering the myths about Nicaragua. The networks of religious support expanded such that churches across the United States, whether Catholic, Presbyterian, or Methodist, were providing material and financial support. They were consistently able to mobilize thousands of people within the United States, in addition to the four thousand Americans they took to visit Nicaragua directly. Their actions included a call-in to Congress in advance of a vote on Contra aid, which generated eleven thousand phone calls to members of congress.[37]

In addition to direct solidarity work, there was an immense variety of propaganda, awareness-raising initiatives, and agitation for direct action. The Pledge of Resistance, for example—again, emerging from the religious left—garnered eighty thousand signatures on a pledge of civil disobedience. The whole movement over the course of the 1980s involved hundreds of thousands of

Americans. Solidarity actions included propaganda-by-deed such as throwing blood over government buildings, tax resistance, aid shipments, newspaper editorials, buying Nicaraguan-grown coffee, hunger strikes, candlelit vigils, and protests.[38] The total effect of this movement is difficult to gauge. The United States was eventually able to negotiate a series of political settlements favorable to its interests in all of the countries under attack. But it was certainly restrained in the extent of its violence and in its ability to maintain popular support for its imperialist policies.

The US government, of course, did not take this challenge lightly. The FBI, recapitulating its traditional role of repressing the left, launched a major campaign against CISPES when it was founded in 1980. The ostensible aim was to detect links between CISPES and a Salvadoran guerrilla group, the Farabundo Martí National Liberation Front (FMLN). If it could establish links, then the FBI could charge that CISPES was merely a front organization and thus in violation of the Foreign Agents Registration Act of 1938. This campaign was made easier by an executive order signed by Reagan, which resulted in a new set of guidelines relaxing restrictions imposed on the FBI's domestic surveillance following the revelations about COINTELPRO. (The FBI's counterintelligence program, a program of subversion aimed at leftist and civil rights groups, ran from 1956 until it was finally exposed in 1971.)

The basis of the initial suspicion, astonishingly, was a rumor published in the John Birch Society publication *Review of the News*, which was passed on to the FBI by a Republican staffer at the House of Representatives. The rumor had it that Shafik Handal, a Palestinian-Salvadoran negotiator for the FMLN, had been in contact via his brother Farid with Sandy Pollack of the Soviet-infiltrated World Peace Council and the CPUSA for the purposes of creating a solidarity movement with the Central American rebels. This was classic fifties-style right-wing paranoia, the technique of designating domestic dissenters as "front groups" for foreign meddlers drawn directly from the Cold War. On that basis, the FBI began to penetrate and gather information on the group.

Frank Varelli, son of the former chief of El Salvador's national police, infiltrated the group under the guise of a refugee whose family had been murdered by state militias, and began passing names, addresses, and license plate numbers to the FBI. Despite a two-year investigation producing no evidence and compelling the FBI to shut its operation down, yet another investigation began just over a year later, lasting another two years. Released documents showed that though the FBI was acting under antiterrorism legislation, its motives were political—it was the legitimate fundraising and campaigning activities of CISPES that galvanized its actions. And the investigation did not stop with surveillance. Information later disclosed showed that the FBI was actively involved in disruption and attempts to discredit CISPES. The FBI thought it essential to develop and implement "some plan of attack against CISPES," and that it did. In a sinister twist, Varelli later disclosed that he had been passing the names and arrival dates of deported Salvadoran refugees and American activists traveling to the country to the El Salvadoran national police.[39]

While the FBI's own investigation of the affair naturally exonerated the bureau of any wrongdoing, the Senate's investigation also accepted the FBI's version of events. It did emerge, however, that the CISPES investigation was just one of half a dozen similar investigations being pursued by the FBI, and that the broad remit of these investigations ensured that thousands of groups and individuals would come under the scope of the FBI's surveillance. Left uninvestigated are a series of death threats and break-ins experienced by activists, as well as the cost to refugees deported back to El Salvador by the administration. Among the corpses left lying in ravines and unmarked graves were many of those returning refugees, and it seems more than plausible that Varelli's information led to some of those deaths. Meanwhile, the lack of evidence against CISPES did not prevent a series of propagandistic books and articles being produced alleging that the organization had "terrorist" connections.[40]

Given the ruthlessness with which the solidarity movements were targeted, it is worth noting that after the wars in Central America, the solidarity networks did not collapse. Rather, the axis of their intervention shifted to building movements to oppose the kinds of policies that the conservative Salvadoran party ARENA, President Violeta Chamorro, and their US backers favored imposing. CISPES is still active today, and the kinds of struggles it supports have fed into the global anticapitalist movements that asserted themselves at the tail end of the twentieth century.[41]

Desert Storm and the "End of History" Interregnum

They thought it was all over. The slow-motion collapse of the Soviet Union, hastened by its losses in Afghanistan and portended by perestroika, told a gloomy Francis Fukuyama and an elated US media that history had arrived at its terminus, and it wasn't the Finland Station. Just because history was deemed to be at an end, however, didn't mean that there couldn't still be fun with war and the great games of geopolitics. The Panamanian dictator Manuel Noriega had recently gotten on the wrong side of his client and, in mid-1990, it was the turn of Saddam Hussein to find himself jilted by a realpolitik "tilt." Hussein, a chicken thief from Tikrit, leader of the Arab Socialist Ba'ath Party, esteemed dictator of Iraq, and butcher of the Kurds, offended Washington's sense of propriety only when he sent an army under the command of Ali Hassan al-Majid to invade Kuwait over a dispute concerning the possession of oil fields on the border. He did so for a number of reasons. His regime was decaying from within, debts incurred during the Washington-backed invasion of Iran hanging around its neck.

Criticisms from the United States and the dissolution of the Warsaw Pact left the dictatorship increasingly isolated internationally.

In this situation, Hussein bet on one of the remaining planks of his legitimacy, his claim to represent the aspirations of Arab nationalism against imperialism and Zionism. An exemplary exertion of regional strength would solve many of his problems at a stroke—or rather, it would if he was correct in understanding that the United States would be unlikely to punish his venture. He was not correct. Whether or not they understood Hussein's intentions, the United States had sent signals through its ambassador April Glaspie that strongly implied a lenient attitude on the part of the American behemoth. But George Bush the elder very quickly moved to a war footing once the invasion was under way, sending troops to "protect" the meek and retiring Saudi Arabia in Operation Defensive Shield. He explained that he was at this point doing nothing but defending an ally, and was ready to exhaust all peaceful remedies to the conflict. In fact, he decided early on in favor of war, evaded all possible diplomatic solutions, and embarked on an extensive propaganda campaign to excite American passions against the former ally.[42]

The antiwar movement began in a reasonably strong position where public opinion was concerned, inasmuch as people were deeply skeptical about what was perceived as Bush père's rush to war. A brief summary of some the polls confirms this. In October 1990, 69 percent of Americans wanted the UN sanctions campaign to be given time to work, and only 46 percent favored war if the sanctions failed, with 48 percent against. By November, 70 percent still opposed war. In the same month, 47 percent of Americans said that Bush had been too eager to send in troops, while only 38 percent believed he had taken sufficient diplomatic steps to avoid war. This followed Bush's decision, as the Democrats took control of Congress, to increase coalition troop levels in the Gulf to four hundred thousand—an invasion force, for sure, and hardly likely to be returned home if the president could avoid it. All surveys of the data confirm much the same trend in the buildup to war—growing skepticism and a desire to get out of the Gulf.[43]

There should then have been no difficulty in assembling an antiwar majority once the invasion began, or at least in winning the support of a significant minority of Americans. But as ever, opinion polls offer only a shallow register of deeply held attitudes. When the war began, the same polls detected *overwhelming* public support for the war and the president, who climaxed in the polls at 89 percent with a bullet. This would not be the last time American antiwar activists would face such an apparent brick wall of inexplicable, yet undeniable, jingoism. Not that this support was distributed evenly among all sectors of the population. As usual, African Americans were the least gung ho, with 48 percent supporting the war, compared to 84 percent of whites who supported it.[44] However, given the very rapid buildup of support for war, it is necessary to briefly address the issue of how the Bush administration successfully operated on public sentiments to manufacture consent for the venture, and thus how the antiwar movements sought to project alternative frames, disseminating oppositional knowledge and communicating a collective identity that could undermine media derision.

Where the Bush case was strongest was in the argument that Saddam Hussein represented a danger because of "weapons of mass destruction" and because of reported atrocities in Kuwait, which were salaciously hammed up and falsified by the public relations firm Hill & Knowlton. Otherwise the public was uninterested in fighting a war for oil or for the defense of the Kuwaiti royal family. For this reason, antiwar campaigners were justified in investing a great deal in the slogan "No Blood for Oil" and in the execration of the Al-Sabah dynasty.

The "yellow ribbon" campaign was another soft-sell hegemonic operation, intended to bind a skeptical public to those waging the war, to appeal to their latent nationalism, and override their objections to war through sentimental nudzhing. In this vein, the US mass media engaged in an illuminating instance of revisionism. In the run-up to war, it sought to depict the anti–Vietnam war movement as an anti-troop movement that had treated ordinary grunts disgracefully. This was plainly meant to force antiwar activists onto the defensive about their attitude to the troops. The success of the propaganda could be measured in the fact that many anti–Gulf War protesters accepted this "memory" as fact and sought to legitimize their actions by distancing themselves from their forebears.[45]

Such media framing was part of a wider attempt to construe the protesters as an "enemy within." Such depictions of the sixties antiwar movements had depended on spotlighting the real or imagined communist and "Viet Cong" sympathies of some protesters. In winter and spring 1991, protest was depicted as a public order issue, with anticipated violence and "anarchy" foregrounded. Protesters were also considered "treasonous," inasmuch as their actions were construed as an unsavory slur on troops who were bravely fighting for the extension of the very democracy of which activists availed themselves. If all else failed, peaceniks could be reviled as an irresponsible and intolerant minority unable to work within the existing representative institutions of democracy.

Projecting their own identity meant that protest groups such as the Rainbow Coalition, AFSC, FOR, Pax Christi, the Southern Christian Leadership Conference, and WILPF had to work largely outside the dominant media institutions. However, they sent "official statements" and press releases to the papers in the optimistic anticipation that some outlets would pick up on them and report them faithfully. In doing so, they offered insights into their legitimization strategies. Long-standing pacifist organizations highlighted their longevity and humanitarian work. Far from being the semi-criminal ingrates depicted in the media spectacle, they were responsible, civic-minded people. Religious organizations espoused a ministry of peace and the sacredness of every human life. Larger organizations emphasized their representative clout, stressing their strong grass roots. I need hardly note that the media did not oblige with these framing strategies.[46]

Despite their difficulties with the media and the polls, antiwar campaigns managed some impressive mobilizations and maintained a critical space against compelling pressures that sought to effectively close down debate. Protests were relatively large. In the month of January 1991, when the war began, it is estimated that a total of half a million people engaged in antiwar activism. Importantly, many of the same alliances that were struck up over Desert Storm would be revisited over Operation Iraqi Freedom.[47] The dark side of this was the disabling divisions between the liberal and radical wings of the antiwar movement which emerged first in the context of Desert Storm and continued to have an impact ten years later. As the *International Socialist Review* argued:

> Then, two national antiwar coalitions emerged, one controlled by the International Action Center (IAC)—the precursor to ANSWER; the other, the liberal-controlled National Campaign for Peace in the Middle East. The two rival groups called competing national demonstrations just one week apart in January 1991, with the start of the war only weeks away. The Workers World–led protest called for U.S. troops out of the Gulf. The Campaign also supported withdrawal of U.S. troops from the Gulf. But in the name of building the "broadest" movement, the Campaign insisted on demanding an Iraqi pullout from Kuwait, and pandered to organizations such as Sane-Freeze (the predecessor of today's Peace Action) that supported UN sanctions against Iraq as an "alternative" to war.[48]

Even so, the antiwar movement could claim to be a mass movement. The war fever that had sent Bush to the top of the polls was short-lived, his little Caesar moment enervated within months of the war's end, and he lost the 1992 election to an oleaginous southern Democrat. The major source of Bush's decline, and Clinton's rise, was the recession that shook the US economy in the first years of the 1990s. It was the first major crisis within the neoliberal settlement, a warning of tremors to come, and Clinton's subsequent popularity depended to a considerable extent on his undertaking policies to restore Wall Street's dynamism and create a finance-led boom. War fever didn't have to last long—it never does, and its effects are necessarily superficial. It relies on a certain forgetting, an "innocence" (as we sometimes call willful ignorance) about America's role, against which the best antidote is the condensed knowledge and traditions of internationalist political movements.

Chapter Six

From the End of History to the "War on Terror"

The huge anti-war demonstrations around the world this weekend are reminders that there may still be two superpowers on the planet: the United States and world public opinion.
—*New York Times*

We, the participants in the Cairo meetings, launch the International Campaign against U.S. Aggression on Iraq. . . . U.S. global strategy, designed to ensure enduring economic and military ascendancy, is now fully operationalized in a post-9/11 era. . . . We declare our total opposition to war on Iraq. . . . We affirm the rights of the Iraqi and Palestinian people to resist external occupation.
—*"The Cairo Declaration"*

The vast majority of people living in the US have nothing to gain from this occupation. In fact, not only do we have nothing to gain, but we suffer more because of it. We lose limbs, endure trauma, and give our lives. Our families have to watch flag-draped coffins lowered into the earth. Millions in this country without healthcare, jobs, or access to education must watch this government squander over $450 million a day on this occupation. Poor and working people in this country are sent to kill poor and working people in another

country to make the rich richer, and without racism soldiers
would realize that they have more in common with the Iraqi
people than they do with the billionaires who send us to war.
                                                    —Corporal Mike Prysner

To the troops, I want to say that there is a way out. We
signed a contract, and we swore to protect the constitution
and to fight for freedom and democracy, but that's not what
we're doing in Iraq. And if it means jail, or if it means dis-
grace or shame, then that's what it's going to take. . . . There
is no higher freedom that can be achieved than the freedom
we achieve when we follow our conscience, and that's some-
thing that we can live by and never regret.
                                                    —Staff Sergeant Camilo Mejía

In the spirit of the post-historical age, the Clinton era was a time
of laughter and forgetting for many. Wall Street graduated from
obscenely rich to unbearably so, the "Goldilocks economy" grew
at a reasonable pace, and Clintonite triangulation pleased "everyone." There were, to be sure, those for whom this conviviality rang
hollow, and not just those about whom *Time* magazine invented
the "whine of '99: everyone's getting rich but me!" However, there
was little in the way of an organized leftist opposition, and certainly
little antiwar activism.

Part of the reason for this was the ascendancy of "humanitarian
intervention," a doctrine that, under a Democratic executive, gained
considerable traction among liberal activists. The framing of US
interventions in Yugoslavia as operations to protect human rights
generated assent from those who would be best placed to mobilize
opposition. Clintonite foreign policy tended to be criticized more
for what it did not do than what it did; "too little, too late" was the
tenor of much criticism when Clinton finally did get around to a
major air war in Kosovo. Right-wing libertarians were disproportionately evident in the antiwar movements that did arise, and

rightist Republicans were among the most vocal critics of Clinton's Yugoslavia policies, largely due to the vacation of the left.

However, the ideology of "humanitarian intervention" would have gained little traction were it not for the global transformations consequent to the dismantling of Russia's European empire and subsequently of the Stalinist system itself. In the post–Cold War world system, the United States swiftly sought to adapt its imperial strategies toward ensuring its dominance in the absence of a major rival, ensuring that allies who had thus far remained loyal due to collective security did not abandon the United States or form hostile alliances. The Pentagon's Defense Planning Guidance in 1992, drafted under the guidance of Paul Wolfowitz and Dick Cheney, with the involvement of Zalmay Khalilzad, laid out the problem as follows:

> Our first objective is to prevent the re-emergence of a new rival, either on the territory of the former Soviet Union or elsewhere, that poses a threat on the order of that posed formerly by the Soviet Union. This is a dominant consideration underlying the new regional defense strategy and requires that we endeavor to prevent any hostile power from dominating a region whose resources would, under consolidated control, be sufficient to generate global power. These regions include Western Europe, East Asia, the territory of the former Soviet Union, and Southwest Asia.
>
> There are three additional aspects to this objective: First, the U.S. must show the leadership necessary to establish and protect a new order that holds the promise of convincing potential competitors that they need not aspire to a greater role or pursue a more aggressive posture to protect their legitimate interests. Second, in the non-defense areas, we must account sufficiently for the interests of the advanced industrial nations to discourage them from challenging our leadership or seeking to overturn the established political and economic order. Finally, we must maintain the mechanisms for deterring potential competitors from even aspiring to a larger regional or global role. An effective reconstitution capability is important here, since it implies that a potential rival could not hope to quickly or easily gain a predominant military position in the world.[1]

The strategy laid out here, though coming from the Republican intelligentsia, was not very dissimilar in its cold elaboration of realpolitik calculations to that commended by Democratic strategist Zbigniew Brzezinski, a key figure in the Carter administration and an adviser to the Obama campaign. Brzezinski saw the key objective as being one of warding off any rivals for control of "Eurasia." As he put it:

> How America "manages" Eurasia is critical. A power that dominates Eurasia would control two of the world's three most advanced and economically productive regions. A mere glance at the map also suggests that control over Eurasia would almost automatically entail Africa's subordination, rendering the Western Hemisphere and Oceania geopolitically peripheral to the world's central continent. About 75 percent of the world's people live in Eurasia, and most of the world's physical wealth is there as well, both in its enterprises and underneath its soil. Eurasia accounts for about three-fourths of the world's known energy resources.
>
> . . .Two basic steps are thus required: first, to identify the geostrategically dynamic Eurasian states that have the power to cause a potentially important shift in the international distribution of power and to decipher the central external goals of their respective political elites and the likely consequences of their seeking to attain them; . . . second, to formulate specific U.S. policies to offset, co-opt, and/or control the above. . . . To put it in a terminology that harkens back to the more brutal age of ancient empires, the three grand imperatives of imperial geostrategy are to prevent collusion and maintain security dependence among the vassals, to keep tributaries pliant and protected, and to keep the barbarians from coming together.[2]

These strategies for global domination were not merely aggressive, though coercion through military dominance in a number of grand areas was clearly intended. They were statements of *hegemonic* intent. In Gramscian terms, a social class achieves hegemony when it leads an alliance of other classes by incorporating their interests and providing moral and intellectual direction. As Giovanni Arrighi explained, in international terms, this involves the hegemonic power in an effort to expand not only its own power but also, simultaneously, that of allied states.[3]

The establishment and protection of a new order accommodating the interests of major potential competitors would center first and foremost on the former Soviet Union and Warsaw Pact states. There, under the leadership of Jeffrey Sachs, IMF economists worked to implement "shock therapy"—a drastic feat of social engineering in both its measures and consequences. This transition was quite consciously conducted in such a way as to exclude popular forces, such as the syndicalists and advocates of workers' self-management in Solidarność. Rather than an open-ended journey to a new, free society, the architects of neoliberalism insisted that there was but one route: the creation of a private capitalist class (often comprising much of the old *nomenklatura*), the concurrent development of a normal labor market with mass unemployment, foreign direct investment and export-led growth, institutional stabilization, and eventually—perhaps in the *longue durée* of capitalist development—a thriving civil society as well.[4]

The transition in the former Yugoslavia brought with it certain challenges, for Yugoslavia was a multinational state with considerable disparities of wealth and power among its constituents. The neoliberal restructuring of Yugoslavia created competition between the elites over the future distribution of property and political power, as well as social crises (soaring unemployment, for example), which they sought to manage to their advantage. An obnoxious political corollary was the revival of nationalist ideologies with a reactionary pedigree. In Croatia, for example, the political leadership of Franjo Tudjman, which began pressing for secession in the late 1980s, was organized on an ultranationalist basis, with a virulently anti-Serb politics and a sideline in Nazi chic and Holocaust revisionism. In each constituent bloc, in fact, the nationalist forces were riddled with ethnic chauvinism, and it was those forces that came to predominate as Yugoslavia disintegrated and headed toward civil war.[5]

The United States approached Yugoslavia on the basis of its determination to manage and suppress emerging rivalries with the European powers and retard any Russian reassertion in Eastern Europe. This meant finding a new role for NATO and expanding it eastward rather than winding it down as a Cold War relic. It would involve the Euro-American alliance in military projection well beyond its traditional area of operation—as Senator Richard Lugar put it, NATO must go "out of area, or out of business." The ongoing operation in Afghanistan is an example of just such an attempt to move beyond the European North Atlantic theater. But the first area of consolidation was to be in Yugoslavia. First of all, the United States made a client of the Bosnian leadership, supporting its push for secession, arming it through an alliance with Iran as well as a network of jihadists left over from the conflict with Russia in Afghanistan, and encouraging it to turn down negotiated settlements that it deemed unsatisfactory. It also permitted Croatia to settle accounts with the Serbs in Krajina through a bout of ethnic cleansing known as Operation Storm. Finally, having negotiated the boundaries of the new Bosnian entity in the Dayton Accords, which would thereafter be governed by a UN-appointed high representative in the manner of the Raj, the United States began to shift its sights to Kosovo, where a separatist guerrilla movement known as the Kosovo Liberation Army was launching an insurgency against the Serbian state that governed the province. While the CIA armed and trained the guerrillas, the United States prepared an aerial assault on the former Yugoslavia under the rubric of NATO to ensure Kosovo's separation under UN tutelage. The result of all this was that in place of the former Yugoslavia was a patchwork of pro-"Western" free-market states, with NATO troops and US advisors sited in the southeast of Europe.[6] David Benjamin, a member of the US National Security Council under Clinton, explained the rationale in response to George W. Bush's criticisms of the war: "Mr. Bush showed a misunderstanding of a major strategic achievement of the

Clinton administration. . . . In particular [he] missed the intrinsic connections between enlargement and the conflict in the Balkans. . . . NATO enlargement advanced US interests in dealing with one of the country's foremost strategic challenges: coping with a post-communist Russia whose trajectory remains in question."[7]

The transformation of the global situation created a crisis for antiwar activists. The "framing" that they had used to interpret the world system had been shaped by the bipolar arrangement of powers in the Cold War. Even if the majority did not view the Soviet Union as a progressive alternative to US imperialism, the existence of a nominally postcapitalist bloc seemed to uphold the historic possibility of transcending capitalist social relations and imperialism. In its absence, and with the defeat of a swathe of leftist forces in the Global South, a spurious "end of history" triumphalism was regnant in the dominant ideological institutions. With ideas of progress cast into doubt, and with liberal capitalism now presented as the terminus to which all historical movements tended, the United States depicted itself as the major force of progress in world affairs. In that sense, global problems tended to present themselves as pathologies of the transition to liberal capitalist modernity, which could and should be managed by a benign hegemon. Beginning in Somalia with Operation Restore Hope, this perspective was expressed as "humanitarian intervention." From now on wars were less about material interests than about developing liberal institutions that could contain ethnic and national conflict while promoting prosperity. This ideology had considerable influence on segments of the left, and not only the liberal left, resulting in minimal opposition to US intervention in Yugoslavia when it came.

In addition, without two competing superpowers pointing nuclear weapons at one another, the dangers of global conflict seemed to decline. As a result, mobilizations against militarism fell dramatically. One study concludes that between 1988 and 1992, 35 percent of existing peace movement organizations ceased to operate.[8] Nor was it just the lack of apparent danger that impeded the peace movement. The 1990s were, briefly, a belle epoque for US capitalism. Driven by speculative bubbles on Wall Street and unprecedented private and corporate debt, the United States experienced a period of growth, with profit rates for a time higher than they had been since the mid-1970s. And within the world system, America's unchallenged dominion meant that there were few serious divisions apparent among the dominant states. The process of developing and spreading neoliberal institutions, led by the United States and culminating in the emergence of the World Trade Organization in 1995, was broadly supported by the core capitalist states. US hegemony had been conserved and expanded. In such circumstances of both domestic and international strength, oppositional movements had little on which to operate.

Opposing the War before the War

From the great movements beginning in the sixties and cresting in the eighties, there continued to flow tributaries that would be important in future struggles. The campaign against sanctions in Iraq, involving groups such as Voices in the Wilderness, was one such. Voices in the Wilderness was founded by a number of peace activists from the Gulf Peace Team, a delegation that camped on the Iraq-Saudi border to protest the buildup to the first Gulf War. Leading among them was Kathy Kelly, a long-standing antiwar activist with experience in the antinuclear campaign as well as solidarity work in Haiti.[9] Kelly chaired the organization throughout its existence from 1996 to 2003.

The chief raison d'être of Voices was to break the sanctions regime that was imposed on Iraq after Desert Storm, ostensibly as a coercive measure to ensure that Iraq cooperated with the UN-supervised destruction of its "weapons of mass destruction." The regime was understood to be causing widespread malnutrition by maintaining a comprehensive blockade, withholding vital food and medicine supplies from Iraq, and keeping its oil revenues in an escrow account. The nation's annual GDP fell by between 50 and 75 percent, while between 1990 and 1995 some $265.3 billion in growth was lost. The impact of this was predictable. Iraq was uniquely vulnerable to the kinds of sanctions being imposed, as it was overwhelmingly dependent on importing food and other basic goods, which it did not produce, through revenues from oil, which it did produce. The country's vital infrastructure, including sewage, electricity, and clean water, was never permitted to recover to its pre-war robustness. By 1997, a million children under five were malnourished, and by 1998 some 70 percent of Iraqi women were anemic. In all, at least half a million children died as a result of sanctions between 1990 and 2003.[10]

The strategy of Voices was to accumulate medicines and food supplies to take to Iraq, breaking the sanctions, and then publicize that they had broken the law merely by bringing much-needed humanitarian supplies to the people of Iraq. Their publicity particularly directed attention to those Iraqis who, uncontroversially, bore no responsibility for anything the Hussein regime had done yet suffered most from sanctions: the children of Iraq. As Voices put it, responding to Madeleine Albright's callous claim regarding infant mortality in Iraq that "the price is worth it": "Iraqi children are totally innocent of oil power politics. All those who prevent lifting the sanctions, including Madeleine Albright, are not. . . . According to the UN itself [Iraqi children] died as a direct result of the embargo on commerce with Iraq. Many United Nations members favored significantly easing these sanctions. The US government and Madeleine Albright as its spokesperson prevented that from happening."[11]

The activists were potentially subject to severe punishment. Kathy Kelly received a warning letter from the US Treasury Department warning that any breach of the sanctions could be risking twelve-year prison terms and up to $1 million fines.[12] Similar punishments were available to the UK government. In practice, such threats were rarely followed up, no doubt in part because of the risks of putting such activists on very public trial, and of testing the legal circumstances of the sanctions regime in a court of law. As Voices in the Wilderness activists Kirsty Gathergood and Dave Rolstone explained:

> On April 29 we broke these sanctions by taking medical sup-plies, medical journals, and toys into Iraq without export li-cences from the British Government. . . . We deliberately and openly broke the sanctions of an act of civil disobedience against a policy to which the deaths of thousands of children every month are attributable. We risk a maximum 5-year prison sen-tence if prosecuted.
>
> In March, 1998, two delegates of Voices of the Wilderness were arrested and threatened with prosecution. HM Customs and Excise concluded that there was "sufficient evidence to sup-port criminal proceedings" and yet no prosecution was brought. Why not? We believe that any jury hearing all the evidence would have no option but to acquit us and find the British Gov-ernment guilty of crimes against humanity.[13]

In fact, the US government did eventually apply a $20,000 fine to the Voices campaign, though the organization refused to pay.[14]

In addition to sanctions, the US government routinely led bombing campaigns over the most trivial pretexts relating to Sad-dam Hussein's noncompliance with weapons inspections. The reg-ular bombing campaigns, despite being relatively brief in duration, also mobilized surprisingly wide coalitions of activists at short no-tice. For example, the aerial assault on Iraq in December 1998, known as Desert Fox, provoked demonstrations across the United States. In January 1999, a "Call to Action" against sanctions was disseminated by Robert Jensen at the University of Texas, gaining the support of a number of antiwar activists. The intention was to generate signatures for an ad in the *New York Times*, but it acquired far broader political support than anticipated, with some fifteen hundred signatures from politicians, journalists, and activists; it attracted new layers of people to antisanctions activism. The persistence of organizations committed to stopping the war on Iraq ensured that by February 2001, a new National Network to End the War Against Iraq could be launched. Its goals were to work toward ending the sanctions, stopping the "no fly zones" and the relentless bombing campaigns, and communicating information about Iraqis to Americans.[15]

These campaigns were small, and may have been perceived as insignificant at the time, but movements tend to begin in this way. The existence of a core of activists already organized on this issue meant that they were well placed to amplify dissenting voices from within the political establishment. For example, by the end of the nineties, three UN officials had resigned in protest against the sanctions. Two of them, Denis Halliday and Hans von Sponeck, had been the UN humanitarian coordinators responsible for administering "oil for food" programs, which were supposed to mitigate the effects of sanctions. On the basis of their experiences, they accused the United States and the UN Security Council of knowingly imposing policies that were tantamount to genocide. In addition, former UN Special Commission (UNSCOM, a body set up to assess Iraq's decommissioning of weapons) inspector Scott Ritter was telling anyone who would listen that the Hussein regime had been effectively disarmed, with remaining equipment unusable and not capable of being constituted into "weapons of mass destruction."[16] This did a great deal to erode the perceived moral advantage enjoyed by the United States in relation to Iraq and prepared much of the general public for the mass opposition that arose in response to preparations for invading Iraq in 2002.

The Return of Systemic Opposition

In addition to work on Iraq, there were ongoing solidarity campaigns supporting East Timor, Colombia, the Kurds, and Haiti, the struggle for which was strengthened when the Clinton administration called

off the US-supported death squads and permitted Jean-Bertrand
Aristide to take his position as the elected president (albeit under severe restrictions that effectively left him having to implement the
agenda of his opponent).[17]

But it was the return of a different kind of activism and ideology toward the end of the millennium that saw a new movement
challenging imperialism in another key. The social movements that
arrived en masse in Seattle in fall 1999 were at the tip of a wedge
aimed in part at US dominance, which had been secured increasingly through the spread of neoliberal arrangements harmful to
labor, women, peace, and the environment. There is, however, little
agreement as to the long-range origins of the movement, which
suffered a lack of definition from the beginning.

The civil society coalitions against the Multilateral Agreement
on Investment—which prefigured many of the privatizing, neoliberal measures that would be rolled out by the World Trade Organization—anticipated those that took shape in the early 2000s. The
Zapatista movement, which emerged to challenge the effects of neoliberalism in the form of the North American Free Trade Agreement (NAFTA) in the Chiapas region of Mexico, validated the
ideas of "autonomism"—a form of organization based on the idea
that the working class and the oppressed can achieve radical
changes outside of the traditional structures of parties, trade
unions, and the state—for many anticapitalist activists. The People's Summits that developed in response to the Free Trade Area
of the Americas, meanwhile, could be said to have been germinal
forms of the Social Forums that would be a characteristic of the
anticapitalist movement.[18] Certainly, long before the movement
became a global spectacle, patient work was carried out by relatively small groups of activists elaborating analyses and tactics in
response to neoliberalism.

However, the movement's debut as a world-historic campaign
was most certainly in Seattle, where one hundred thousand union-

ists, environmentalists, socialists, and peace activists converged to successfully disrupt the World Trade Organization (WTO) talks in November 1999. The following year, mass protests took place in Davos, Montreal, Nice, Prague, London, Melbourne, and—in the United States—Washington, Los Angeles, and Philadelphia. Both the Republican and Democratic Party conventions attracted demonstrations. The following year saw a similar wave of activity, peaking with three hundred thousand people protesting in Genoa at the G8 summit. Ralph Nader's radical presidential candidacy in 2000 partially reflected the impact of these movements. Nader, by no means an anticapitalist, had nonetheless participated through his Public Citizen group in the buildup to the Seattle demonstrations, and saw the movements congregated there as representing a "fork in the road."[19] His campaign, championing the labor and environmental concerns of those movements, garnered close to three million votes.

What was distinctive about this movement was its "interconnection of different issues through the systemic logic of capitalism . . . by contrast with earlier campaigns that concerned themselves with more specific (though hugely important) issues such as nuclear weapons, apartheid, and even the environment."[20] The object of their critique was not merely a particular policy, nor even a set of exploitative relations between the West and the Rest, but rather the existence of "a global capitalist class benefiting at the expense of a global working class."[21] The existence of such an antisystemic movement was in one sense an amazing fact, and produced a euphoric mood around the first protests in recognition of how the celebrated "end of history" had been made history. There was, moreover, a sense of limitless possibility in the diversity and creativity of these movements.

This brought with it certain weaknesses, however. The movement's breadth meant that a baseline for any sort of programmatic unity was difficult to achieve. Moreover, there were those, informed by distrust of the traditional left, who felt it was important to *avoid* arriving at a shared political agenda. There was a spirit of DIY anarchism in the protest movements, tending to favor a diversity of agendas, tactics, and styles.[22] This has its strengths, but its inadequacy in taking on well-organized opponents with considerable cohesion and the advantages of state power should be obvious. A related difficulty faced by the anticapitalist movement, particularly when New York was defiled on September 11, 2001, was that it lacked a body of theory on imperialism that was capable of explaining the sorts of policies that the United States would undertake in the coming years. Indeed, one of the core anticapitalist texts, *Empire* by Michael Hardt and Tony Negri, maintained that the system no longer had a center from which imperialism could be organized.[23] Even so, the anticapitalist movements would play a key role in developing the mass antiwar demonstrations that began to erupt in 2002, particularly in the three European states most closely allied to the Bush administration—Italy, Spain, and the United Kingdom.[24] From some of these roots would grow the largest antiwar movement in the history of the world.

American Insurgents and the "War on Terror"

A gift from the skies, the very public demolition of the World Trade Center, gave President George W. Bush a degree of definition that he had hitherto lacked. From the stolen election to the Enron scandal, the Bush presidency seemed to combine weakness, illegitimacy, and corruption—until his very own Pearl Harbor licensed the high-octane aggression of the "war on terror." This multilayered set of domestic and international policies included crackdowns on civil liberties in the United States (based on legislation prepared well in advance of the 9/11 attacks), extralegal detentions within US borders, the development of an international system of "extraordinary renditions" and secret prisons used to torture "suspects," and two major-theater wars in Iraq and Afghanistan. The leftward drift of US public opinion was halted, a small but significant revival of union organization was put into reverse, and the global anticapitalist movements were temporarily derailed.

The Bush administration held al-Qaeda responsible for the attacks. Moreover, it charged the Taliban regime with enabling those attacks by hosting the al-Qaeda network in Afghanistan. It was preparing a casus belli focused on national security, yet it also drew upon "humanitarian interventionism" in framing the ideological arguments for war. The Taliban ran an oppressive, barbaric state, and its overthrow by military force would, claimed the war's supporters, be a deliverance for the people of Afghanistan, particularly the women suffering under the restrictive form of patriarchy that the Talibs ordained. Yet, at the same time, it is now apparent, the Bush administration sought early on to connect the attacks with Saddam Hussein in order to justify an adventurist strike into the Middle East, taking out a senescent and weakened holdout of Arab nationalism, and build a pro-American, free-market state on its ruins.

It should be said that this, far from breaking with the precedents established by Clinton, took the logic of Democratic policy to a new extreme. Although the strongest pressure for an invasion of Iraq had always come from the right, it was a Clintonite policy to seek Saddam's overthrow even if by nonmilitary means.[25] In general, Bush's policies were more aggressive versions of those that Clinton had already institutionalized. As Gopal Balakrishnan put it:

> The key development was the proclamation of the legitimacy of military intervention—regardless of national sovereignty or absence of aggression—to defend human rights, to stamp out terrorism, or to block nuclear proliferation. In the name of the first, Clinton launched a full-scale war in Yugoslavia; of the second, bombed Sudan, Iraq and Afghanistan; and of the third, came within an ace of unleashing a preemptive attack on North Korea in 1994 (holding off only for the reasons that have so far restrained Bush—the consequences for Seoul). The Republican administration, for all its glaring contrasts of style, has essentially operated within the same framework.[26]

To this one might add that if Bush did not obtain UN backing before invading Iraq, neither did Clinton obtain UN backing before bombing Yugoslavia. This posed potential problems for antiwar organizing. The liberals who had endorsed the Clintonite framework, or criticized him largely for not intervening, were now deprived of any basis from which to assail Bush's foreign policy. As Stephen Holmes put it, "Having supported unilateralist intervention outside the UN framework during the 1990s, liberals and progressives are simply unable to make a credible case against Bush today."[27] And indeed, there were those liberals—such as Paul Berman and Christopher Hitchens—who, having supported Clintonite humanitarian intervention, defended Bush's "war on terror."[28]

On top of this, the militant anticapitalist movements that provided a focus for such rowdy opposition in the early months of Bush fils's reign collapsed in the United States under the weight of the Twin Towers. The nationalist surge and the escalation of police brutality in dealing with protests after 9/11 meant that it was dubious, initially, whether there would even be an organizational basis for a mass antiwar movement in the United States.[29]

The Meek and the Militant

Despite the difficulties activists faced, even before the bombs began to fall, a peace movement was in the advanced stages of early development. In the absence of the mass global justice movements, the vacuum was filled by left-wing activists in the Workers World Party (WWP) and the International Action Center (IAC), who helped form the Act Now to Stop War and End Racism (ANSWER) coalition. They organized one of the first national antiwar demonstrations, attracting thousands to Washington, DC, on September 29, 2011. Among its key organizers were those such as Brian Becker, who had led a faction of the antiwar movement during Operation Desert Storm in 1991. Among the activists it attracted were many who had recently been participants in the anticapitalist movements of the turn of the millennium. Yet overall public support for the war remained high, as long as the war was restricted to Afghanistan. When it became clear that the Bush administration intended to wage war on Iraq, activists decided to form United for Peace and Justice (UFPJ). Launched in October 2002, it was a self-consciously broad coalition from its inception, whose organizational spine was made up of veterans from anti–Vietnam War, antinuclear, anti-apartheid, and anti–Gulf War campaigns. Here, the leading figure was Leslie Cagan, who had also led a faction in the struggle against the Gulf War. Both campaigns were large grassroots initiatives capable of attracting more support than any other antiwar groups. Their approaches, and their differences, therefore decisively shaped the tone of the antiwar activism to come.[30]

The antiwar movement in the United States over the last decade has drawn strength from a number of sources. First of all, it was related to and codependent on other mass movements linking together a network of interests and struggles, thus adding to its social depth and weight. As T. V. Reed writes: "to speak of a contemporary US peace movement is to speak of two interrelated phenomena: an anti-war movement focused on US intervention in Iraq, and a peace movement that is part of a worldwide set of forces arrayed against 'neo-liberal globalization' policies and practices."[31] This isn't entirely novel. Opposition to US imperialism from the Mexican War to the Vietnam War has involved activists attempting to explain the injustice of war by reference to the objectionable features of American society.

But the antiwar movement over Iraq was the largest such movement in the history of the world, reflecting a deep global revolt against US domination that had already been at the very least latent and usually explicit in the anticapitalist movements, the WTO protests, the Zapatista revolt, the Bolivian "water wars," the protests by Indian farmers against "patenting seeds," and so on. Indeed, antiwar activists educated in the New Left tradition specifically argued for preparedness to address the multiple issues intersecting with war. As Michael Albert writes:

> It is easier to defeat a specific war with a movement that is actively expanding its focus than with a movement that is narrowly prioritizing only war, much less only that specific war. . . . The former type of broad and diversifying movement that makes links and connections, that is radicalizing people about a range of concerns and priorities, is far more threatening to elites, because it challenges their basic positions and power . . . we need to be multi-issue because if we aren't, we are unlikely to be good on matters of race, gender, class, sexuality, etc., and if the antiwar movement isn't good on these issues, it will be hampered in reaching out to, communicating with, and involving diverse constituencies.[32]

Secondly, the Iraq antiwar movement was a self-consciously international one, transnational rather than nationally centered. Barbara Epstein argues that this was a positive strength:

> Opposition to the war in Vietnam took place in many countries, but it was centered in the United States; the antiwar movement in the United States tended to overshadow antiwar movements elsewhere. This time not only was the opposition to the war outside the United States of extraordinary proportions, but the movement as a whole understood itself as an international movement, to the extent that protests came to be internationally coordinated. The international character of the antiwar movement helps to account for one of the differences between the movement against the war in Iraq and the movement against the first Gulf War, in 1991. At that time there was strong protest until the war began; when public opinion in the United States turned decisively in favor of the war, the antiwar movement collapsed. This time protest was sustained well into the war. The strength of international protest was no doubt an important factor in sustaining protest inside the United States, even as the media and public opinion were shifting toward unquestioning support of the war.[33]

The basis of opposition to the war has been radical. If activists focused on the Bush administration as the *diabolus ex machina* causing the war, they were also less likely to think of the war as an error than to consider it an act of outright aggression, fought for power and resources, and a danger to peace and democracy. This opened a space for more explicitly anti-imperialist analyses.[34] The scale of the movements in the United States, though smaller than in some other countries, certainly rivaled those during the Vietnam War. A series of national networks reflecting different political approaches worked against the war. UFPJ and ANSWER were the largest,[35] but initiatives such as Not in Our Name gained celebrity support, while Win Without War coalesced relatively moderate but influential antiwar opinion, including Democrats, pacifists, Greens, and Christian and Jewish peace groups. On February 15, 2003, in New York alone, four hundred thousand activists marched against war. On the same day, at least a hundred and fifty thousand marched in San Francisco, and tens of thousands marched in Hollywood, Colorado Springs, and Seattle.[36] Ten million people protested worldwide.[37]

In addition to the big battalions of antiwar activism were class- or gender-based responses. US Labor Against the War did important work in building solidarity with Iraqi trade unionists. The feminist peace organization CODE PINK engaged in highly visible, theatrical activities partly intended to satirize the masculinist, chauvinist culture of imperialism and thus undercut the "imperial feminism" that was being used to justify war. More than that, CODE PINK and its well-known spokesperson Medea Benjamin have formed a vital link among various antiwar groups, punching well above its numerical weight in the movement and brokering between the big two at key moments.[38] The Campus Antiwar Network, founded just prior to the invasion of Iraq, brought together students from seventy colleges and universities when it was first founded. It spearheaded the student presence on demonstrations, organized teach-ins, and engaged in "counter-recruitment" on campuses. The latter involved a number of successful campaigns to get military recruiters kicked out of colleges while also presenting alternatives to young people who might be tempted by military service to pay for college. In addition there were the usual local networks and initiatives, such as the People's Non-Violent Response Network based in the San Francisco Bay Area.[39]

Throughout this narrative, a prized place has been reserved for troops who refuse to fight, "frag" officers, or defect. This is not only because of the difficulties, pressure, and punishment that resistant soldiers can face, but because their resistance is strategically well placed. When soldiers resist, the consequences are direct and palpable. Today's army is not a conscript army. Unlike those who resisted the Vietnam War, the only coercion that causes Americans to join today's army is economic. For that reason, it has actually been more difficult for antiwar soldiers to speak plainly in opposition to US policies or risk undertaking disruptive action.[40]

Even so, a significant aspect of the antiwar movement has consistently been the presence of refuseniks, such as GI Mike Prysner, former specialist Victor Agosto, and Staff Sergeant Camilo Mejía, a founder of Iraq Veterans Against the War (IVAW). Geoffrey Millard, Adam Kokesh, Sergio Kochergin, Kristopher Goldsmith, Luis Montalvan, Jason Lemieux, Scott Ewing, Ash Woolson, Jeff Key, Ehren Watada, and innumerable others still have either refused to fight or protested against the war and worked toward its end once they returned to the United States. Perhaps most striking is the clarity of their vision when they speak, as they have done at IVAW events, "Winter Soldier" testimonials, and other forums.

Importantly, for the first time in a major way, the US antiwar movements began to place emphasis on Palestine. Left-wing support for Palestine can be traced back to some minority elements of the New Left and their response to the 1967 war, though most white leftists had relatively little to say about Palestine at the time. Americans had been organized in support of the Palestinians since the First Intifada began in 1988, and the campaign against the Gulf War in 1991 galvanized many left-wing Americans, notably Jewish Americans, in support of the Palestinians. But organization in support of Palestine by antiwar groups after 2000, when the Second Intifada began, attracted larger numbers of activists than had hitherto been the case. However, the two main antiwar groups diverged sharply over this issue. While UFPJ generally attempted to keep the issue of Palestine separate from antiwar activism, to the dismay of some, ANSWER proactively embraced the cause and connected it to the Iraq War.[41] People of color, principally Arab American and Asian American communities, supplied many of the activists in local pro-Palestine activism.

A remarkable initiative known as the International Solidarity Movement (ISM) has sprung up in the last decade. Led by Palestinians, the ISM involves international activists in nonviolent intervention in the occupation, though it also advocates the right of Palestinians to resist occupation through "legitimate armed struggle." It represents the culmination of several initiatives set up to fulfill a Palestinian Authority request in September 2000, following the Israeli killing of dozens of unarmed people, for foreign monitors to be placed on the ground so that Israeli violence could be documented (and thus, perhaps, deterred). The ISM is genuinely international in scope, but recruits chiefly from the United States and United Kingdom—one half of the recruits are American, a quarter of those Jewish American. By being situated among Palestinian populations whom Israel had done its utmost to isolate, ISM activists both bear witness and provide protection, and over time have insinuated the fate of Palestine intimately into the social and cultural lives of their countries of origin.[42]

But in addition to the ISM, a flotilla of organizations has emerged to challenge the US-Israel axis at a number of points. Students for Justice in Palestine (SJP) was launched in Berkeley, California, in 2001. Initially campaigning to force the University of California to divest from its holdings in Israel, it subsequently engaged in educational and publicity actions, and most of its activists joined the Berkeley Stop the War Coalition to protest against the bombing of Afghanistan. The movement spread and by the following year there were twenty-five chapters of the SJP in the United States. Its recent successes include the divestment decision by Hampshire College—the first college to divest from South Africa. It attempts to pursue Palestinian justice in a way that doesn't risk dividing over the fraught question of one-state or two-state solutions, while also rejecting "attempts to equate principled criticism of Zionism, or of the character or policies of Israel, with anti-Semitism."[43]

Other initiatives include the aid campaign US Boat to Gaza and a number of divestment campaigns such as that initiated by Jewish Voice for Peace, with the support of the US Campaign to End the Israeli Occupation. In 2009, the US Campaign for the Academic and Cultural Boycott of Israel was launched as part of a series of initiatives respecting the Palestinian campaign for such boycotts.[44] Importantly, like the anti-apartheid boycott and divestment campaigns that flourished throughout American churches, campuses, labor unions, and solidarity groups in the 1980s, this is being driven by Palestinians themselves rather than being something that is imposed from without.

Long Division

The weaknesses besetting the American antiwar movement, however, became more obvious as the war went on. To begin with, the active cadres in the movement were disproportionately white, despite the fact that African Americans were far more opposed to the war than their white counterparts. The white-run progressive movements that dominated the scene had work to do to align with organizations run by people of color. Many activists regrettably saw racism as secondary and unrelated to antiwar activism. Second, the movement had been susceptible to the animating illusion that, as the socialist activist and writer Paul D'Amato put it, "somehow mass protest would be enough" to stop the war this time, and thus were disillusioned when it was not enough. Third, sections of the movement muted or suppressed their criticisms of the Democratic Party during the run-up to the 2004 presidential election, subordinating antiwar activism to the needs of Democratic electoralism, and little was heard from the antiwar movement during the Kerry campaign. This was particularly true of UFPJ.

This was a catastrophic missed opportunity. Kerry was an unappealing candidate on most days, and he had long since dropped his former reputation as an anti–Vietnam War "dove" like so much baggage; before a soporific nation, he "reported for duty" as a patriotic militarist. He felt, at most, that the war had been waged badly, and needed to be fought better. No note of antiwar opinion was allowed to sour the Democratic campaign, particularly after the media's demolition job on the stolidly centrist and skeptical Howard Dean, whose theatrical yawp before an audience one evening was interpreted as a sign of potential instability. As a consequence, those who channeled their antiwar activism into support for the Kerry presidential bid not only backed a hopeless candidate but also set themselves up to be disappointed losers no matter who won.[45]

Worse still, at a crucial tipping point in 2005, two of the largest antiwar groups, UFPJ and ANSWER, split over political and strategic differences. Weeks after a successful joint demonstration, and at the moment of Bush's lowest poll ratings to date, UFPJ announced that it would not coordinate with ANSWER in the future. There was a terrible irony in this because one of the movement's features that activists of the sixties vintage agreed was a great improvement on past enterprises was its openness to coalition-building. The basis for the split was UFPJ's charge that ANSWER operated in an unaccountable and disruptive way in the coordination of protests. UFPJ also indicated that its aim was to stage focused demonstrations based around issues directly relating to US "empire building," whereas they did not believe ANSWER shared this approach. (In this respect, UFPJ bears some resemblance to the coalition behind the New Mobilization Committee to End the War in Vietnam, whose narrow single-issue focus placed it at odds with the radical wing of the antiwar movement). ANSWER's response was that UFPJ's problem was chiefly political. They aimed, ANSWER charged, to split the progressive antiwar coalition in favor of a "left-center" alliance involving conservative Democrats like John Murtha and right-wing libertarians such as Ron Paul. Many of their leaders supported the Democratic Party and worked hard to get Kerry elected. It might be added that they have largely supported President Obama, maintaining that he is "largely keeping to his campaign promises, and that is a good thing."[46]

At any rate, this is a classic case of what "social movement" theorists call a "framing dispute." In such a scenario, participants in a coalition apply a contrasting and competing ideological "frame" to the situation they are working in, and thus define that situation in ways that lead to incompatible approaches. The "frame" will mainly affect the kind of demographic that each party wishes to mobilize. One study of the UFPJ-ANSWER split maintains that the chief difference in principle between the organizations was that UFPJ tended to try to "segregate the Iraq war from other foreign policy issues," since its aim was to build the broadest possible coalition. ANSWER, by contrast, maintains that Iraq must be addressed in the wider context of US imperialism, including in Haiti and elsewhere. Demographically, the former attracts a more "moderate" caliber of activist, while the latter attracts radicals. Organizationally, UFPJ is closer to the Democratic Party than is ANSWER. These differences were sufficient to alarm many rank-and-file UFPJ supporters, for whom the coalition between the two groups was always controversial, especially in light of the constant media attacks on ANSWER. And, perhaps most interestingly, UFPJ's larger core network of activists meant that unity was more advantageous to ANSWER than to its partner. Perhaps this explains why the differences between the organizations impelled UFPJ to initiate the schism.

This split in the antiwar movement continued while the administration and its war became ever more unpopular.[47]

However, it would be mistaken to attribute the long-term decline of the US antiwar movement to these divisions. Rather, the divergence between ANSWER and UFPJ condenses deeper problems inhibiting the antiwar movement. Alexander Cockburn listed among them the fact that the United States no longer had the draft, thus limiting the effect of the war on working-class communities and containing the spread of insurgency among the troops.

Cockburn also pointed out that unlike the Central American solidarity campaigns, the Iraqi resistance was given no "human face" in American society. Any expressions of solidarity in that direction risked being howled down with censorious patriotism, if not stamped on under the powers of the PATRIOT Act. There are other reasons for this. While many of the twentieth-century movements that gained support from US antiwar activists, from the Viet Minh to the Sandinistas, saw themselves as part of a global left, the Iraqi resistance was a disarticulated movement coordinated by easily reviled Islamist leaderships. Nevertheless, the internationalism of any antiwar movement that has nothing to say about those directly combating imperialist aggression has certainly been compromised. It has been a mainstay of this book that successful antiwar movements are those that have been able to make direct links with those in the flight path of US aggression and bring their struggles and concerns directly into the US political arena. Indeed, direct comprehension of their urgent struggles has often been a radicalizing factor in antiwar campaigns.[48]

Cockburn was also sharply critical of the cozy, celebrity-laden, nonthreatening atmosphere of protests organized by UFPJ and the latter's links with the Democrats, meaning that "the mainstream anti-war movement, as represented by UFPJ, is captive to the Democratic Party." That captivity ensured that antiwar sentiment was bound to the sinking ships of Howard Dean and Dennis Kucinich in the Democratic primaries, and later John Kerry in the presidential race. The influx of Democrats into Congress in the 2006 midterm elections did nothing to alter this trend.[49]

A study conducted by Michael T. Heaney and Fabio Rojas confirmed some of this picture. Combining the results of "5,398 surveys of demonstrators at antiwar protests, interviews with movement leaders, and ethnographic observation," the study established that the main factor contributing to demobilization of the antiwar movement between 2007 and 2009 was the withdrawal of Democratic activists. The election of Barack Obama undermined the broad coalitions that survived for much of the Bush era and "thwarted the ability of the movement to achieve critical mass." This is because Democratic activists placed their faith in the Democratic Party to adopt antiwar measures. In fact, as the authors write:

> Democrats leveraged antiwar sentiment in the 2006 midterm congressional elections, allowing them to regain majorities in both houses of Congress, with self-identified Democrats and independents taking a much more critical view of the war than taken by self-identified Republicans. . . . While most Democrats took advantage of a general public sentiment against the war, some, such as 2006 US Senate candidate Jim Webb (D-VA), reaped direct rewards from the work of antiwar activists on their campaigns. . . .
>
> Once in control of Congress, Democrats voted in favor of antiwar resolutions, but were unable to attain the supermajorities necessary to override Republican objections. . . . Democratic leaders never resorted to Congress's "power of the purse" as a blunt instrument to defund the war immediately. When Obama became President-Elect, he quickly ruffled feathers in the antiwar movement by retaining Bush appointees in his government, such as Defense Secretary Robert Gates. . . . As president, Obama maintained the occupation of Iraq and escalated the war in Afghanistan. The antiwar movement should have been furious at Obama's "betrayal" and reinvigorated its protest activity. Instead, attendance at antiwar rallies declined precipitously and financial resources available to the movement dissipated.[50]

This was not unexpected. A recurring theme of this book has been the tendency of peace movements to lose momentum through being co-opted into the electoral strategies of one of the dominant parties, usually the Democratic Party. Still, exogenous factors also played their part. By 2007, for example, the occupation of Iraq was beginning to stabilize. The Bush administration claimed that its "surge," a sudden increase in military forces in Iraq, was responsible for this. In reality, this owed itself to a characteristic US geopolitical "tilt," this time toward the Iraqi Sunni leadership. Former insurgents were recruited en masse and paid to battle the resistance. Meanwhile, after a series of difficult battles with the Shi'ite Mahdi Army, a truce was reached in 2008. The rate of insurgent attacks on US troops fell sharply.[51] Finally, the credit crunch arising from certain long-term pathologies in the US economy and leading to a worldwide recession directed political attention from the international to the domestic plane.

Notwithstanding these difficulties, the US antiwar movement has played an honorable role as part of a transnational anti-imperialist movement, delivering some of the aspirations of the Global South for freedom and autonomy in the political contest in the United States. In so doing, it helped intensify the political crisis for the US ruling class, which has still not been resolved, and created openings for other oppositional forces.

Conclusion

The United States that Obama leads is a much weaker imperialist power than that which Bush inherited. The confluence of the crisis of US hegemony resulting from the invasion of Iraq, and the crisis of global capitalism catalyzed by a financial meltdown, has undermined the major bases for US dominance in the world system. In addition, the limits of US power were disclosed in the Georgia crisis of 2008, during which the latter invaded South Ossetia, attacking

Russian peacekeepers and thus provoking a devastating Russian counterattack. Georgia, which was supported by Washington and being groomed to join NATO, may or may not have acted with permission from the White House. But the inability of the United States to do anything to protect its regional ally was a stark reminder of the limits of American capabilities. There is little sign of these problems disappearing. The global system continues to have a massive surplus of capital that cannot find profitable investment. While the United States initially took the lead in global bailouts, divisions have opened up with erstwhile allies over the timing of rollback and "austerity," meaning that Clinton-era hegemony may still be out of America's grasp, even with a comparatively popular president.

Obama is also unfortunate enough to have come to power just as US imperialism was about to face a major crisis in the Middle East. The global antiwar movement has played a small role in assisting genuine movements for democracy in the Middle East, forming a small but significant tributary of the democratic revolutions that stampeded the entrenched dictatorships of Ben Ali and Mubarak in 2011. These ecstatic but grimly serious undertakings showed Arab masses organizing themselves to take on not only the police, internal security, and armed forces of their ruling despots, but also their imperialist backers. Tahrir Square in Cairo was turned into a metropolis within a metropolis, the city in the city, a commune that recalled 1871 with the degree of spontaneous self-organization, vigilance, and grassroots democracy involved. This was the moment that Iraq was denied in the name of democracy and freedom, Bush-style.

And yet, of course, Obama did not come to power to wind down the empire. Ever opportunistic, the United States is once more positioning itself as the parent and protector of democratic revolution through its intervention in Libya—even as it sustains bloody repression in Yemen. But US anti-imperialists have seen this routine before, just as they've heard the old refrain "but this time, it's different." The question is whether, with so many having placed their faith in the Democrats, they will regain sufficient independence of political initiative to challenge this president in the same way that they challenged Bush.

Revolution in the Middle East

Anti-Imperialism in the Course of American History

I have argued that anti-imperialism has been shaped by the specificities of America's development as a capitalist state and by the phases of its imperial expansion. The early anti-imperialists were often radical liberals who took the ideals of the American Revolution to their logical conclusion. In particular, they took seriously the ideal of "free labor," which led them to oppose slavery. As egalitarians, they rejected racial supremacy and sometimes women's oppression. As libertarians, they opposed the concentrations of political power that wars of expansion entailed. Partly, this was a sectional contest, as struggles by predominantly northern activists dovetailed with the strategic battles of northern capital against a largely southern, rural Democratic power bloc based on slaveholders and farmers. Exploiting strategic divisions within the ruling class continues to be an important element of anti-imperialist practice. On that basis, they opposed the expansion of the southern slaveocracy, the colonization of "Indian country," and the annexation of Mexico. Often, they formed links with those in the path of US colonial aggression, chiefly Native Americans whose struggles for freedom complemented their own battles for justice within the United States.

With the closing of the frontier and the settlement of the Civil War in favor of the North, the dynamics of imperialism altered. Northern capital was now the dominant expansionist bloc, while some elements in the South could oppose further imperial expansion on sectional and racist grounds. The latter joined forces with liberals, businessmen, and labor in the Anti-Imperialist League in opposing the colonial turn in 1898. The dominant note in the league's propaganda was liberal, again developing ideas from the revolutionary legacy, operating on the antagonism between democracy and imperialism. The league did not hesitate to make connections with resistant Filipinos as they fought with US troops. But the league's Achilles' heel was its attachment to parliamentarist politics, resulting in its endorsement of the Democratic candidacy of William Jennings Bryan, whose failure left the league greatly depleted. Even with its manifest limits, and despite its dominance by a minority of wealthy white men, the league represents a high-water mark of anti-imperialism in the United States.

The emergence of a labor movement led to a new phase of anti-imperialism, as transnational labor solidarity, such as that between workers in the United States and Mexico, became a basis for resistance to empire. Socialists argued that global working classes had more in common than divisions, and attempted to develop trends toward solidarity and radicalization. In the face of a European continental conflagration that would come to be known as World War I (because there was a sequel), they attempted to rally workers to the idea of a general strike to stop the war. US socialists divided once "their" nation entered the war, just as their European counterparts had. And following the Russian Revolution, many of those socialists who remained opposed to imperialism joined or supported the CPUSA, which played a leading role in anti-imperialist activity throughout the 1920s and 1930s as part of its wider activism in the labor movement.

The degeneration of the Russian Revolution into dictatorship, the emergence of fascism as a world power, and the defeat of antifascist forces in Europe constituted a series of world-historic defeats for the left. The ensuing world war left the United States at the apex of the imperialist chain. This was not an accidental outcome but the result of a deliberate shift in policy. The United States already had tremendous advantages over competitive rivals—a vast internal market, access to abundant raw materials, and productive superiority, exemplified by its booming car industry. Following Hitler's invasion of France, FDR decided that the United States would turn this productive advantage into the basis for global military supremacy.[1] This was an announcement of intended succession—the European colonial empires were doomed in the long term, and the United States emerged as a global power claiming to be on the side of anticolonialism, a revolutionary power supporting freedom struggles (as long as they were not communist). Moreover, it strengthened the repressive capacity of the American state, as FDR tended from early on to treat critics of his rearmament program and subsequent US entry into the war as treasonous.[2]

After the war, then, a greatly strengthened American ruling class waged war on its domestic left and advanced its global reach, both under the impress of anticommunism. Anti-imperialist forces in the United States were shattered. The CPUSA, which had been at the heart of the "Popular Front" left, was witch-hunted. The party's uncritical support for Moscow helped undermine its position. Socialists, just like liberals before them, operated on ambiguities in America's founding liberal revolutionary ideals, drawing out their more radical side. But this was less plausible if they were seen as "alien" elements, agents of a "foreign" power, especially when their anti-imperialist agenda could be represented as an attempt to weaken the homeland for the alien interlopers. Paranoia about infiltration and espionage has rarely needed much sustenance in the United States, and the CPUSA's support for Stalinism was devastating for it. In addition, the labor movement was co-opted by the CIA for much of the Cold War, such that the union bureaucracy was usually on the side of imperialism, if not actively complicit with imperialism, up to the Vietnam War.

As a result, a New Left had to be birthed into existence, initially by a combination of radical students and civil rights activists, before anti-imperialism could take shape as a major force in US politics again. This New Left, emerging from the struggles against Jim Crow, became the leading force in the movement against the Vietnam War. One of the major reasons why this movement was comparatively successful is that US power was encountering serious limitations. Though high military expenditure had a certain stabilizing effect on the US economy, as the war dragged on it also began to drain revenues from productive investment. Moreover, the disciplined resistance of the Viet Minh demonstrated the limits of sheer military superiority. As the war went on, sections of business as well as sections of the dominant political parties began to call for its end. The antiwar movement was again in the position of exploiting strategic divisions within the ruling class while also leveraging exposed weaknesses in US imperialist power. The New Left suffered from certain limitations. Its relations to organized labor were strained as a result of the latter's support for the war and the involvement of some of the unions in supporting segregation. This took some time to remedy and weakened its response to LBJ's escalation. The New Left remained constantly divided between its liberal and radical wings, with the former eventually corralled into the Democratic fold while the latter occasionally resorted to hype-driven adventurism. Yet the scale of its mobilizations was unprecedented in US history, and its campaigns educated a generation of people in the techniques of organizing and solidarity. Many of the same activists went on to lead campaigns against Reaganite aggression in the 1980s.

However, one of the weaknesses mentioned above came to be important here. A large section of the anti-Reagan coalition tended to rely on the Democrats in Congress, to its ultimate disadvantage. Later, while they would oppose wars prosecuted by both Reagan and Bush, the mainstream of the antiwar left simply vacated the streets when a Democrat took the Oval Office. Part of the problem was the drastic narrowing of political options in light of the collapse of the Soviet Union. This was a decisive symbolic terminus to a string of painful defeats endured by the left and labor movements in the United States since the mid-1970s. It heralded the ascendancy of neoliberalism, whose greatest champions were now in the leadership of the Democratic Party. In global terms, this meant the continued defeat of the left, usually retailed as a move "beyond left and right." As a result, with a weak domestic left, absent major Third World leftist currents, and with the end of the Soviet Union as an orienting pole in world politics, many activists could come to see the United States not as an imperialist power but as the last best hope for suffering populations. Third World populations were no longer seen as potential agents of their own liberation but as suffering innocents at best and atavistic killers at worst.

Even the mass revival of antiwar movements in the 2000s did not entirely escape this logic. The movement never found a way to relate to the anti-US insurgency in Iraq, despite the ludicrous injustice of the US occupation. They could not see past the greatly exaggerated claims of brutality on the part of insurgents.[3] Many also took the view that the United States could potentially be a benign hegemon if led by good, wise people. The existence of strategic cleavages in the US ruling class over the invasion of Iraq allowed the Democrats to capitalize on antiwar sentiment, particularly as the occupation degenerated into chaos after 2005. Much of the antiwar movement was thus channeled into electing Democrats. This culminated in Barack Obama's historic victory, which, far from encouraging antiwar activists and giving confidence to their campaigns, actually demobilized and fatally weakened the antiwar coalition.

The United States never wholly overcame the Vietnam Syndrome, and there is now the Iraq Syndrome to compound it. Further, Obama has taken the executive at a most inopportune moment for any imperialist revival to take place. A series of revolutions has shaken America's most stable allies in the Middle East, that most strategically significant zone. Moreover, the natural sympathy of most Americans with the overthrow of such dictators proved highly inconvenient for those in the administration trying to protect them. We will now conclude this history by turning to Obama's Middle East crisis, the war in Libya, and the left's response.

Revolution: Obama Administration in Crisis

"You can get much farther with a kind word and a gun," Al Capone reportedly said, "than you can with a kind word alone." This is a sentiment the US government understands. In 2009 Senator George Mitchell was sent to Tunisia to convey Obama's warm regard for dictator Zine El Abidine Ben Ali. Obama made good his word by seeking Congressional authorization for the sale of military equipment to Ben Ali the same year. In November 2010 Secretary of State Hillary Clinton expressed her warm regard for the dictator Hosni Mubarak, whose relationship with the United States was a "cornerstone of stability and security."[5] Months later, when protests against the regime erupted, US vice president Joseph Biden insisted that Mubarak was an "ally" of America and by no means "a dictator." Tony Blair, the Middle East envoy for the Quartet (the United Nations, the European Union, the United States, and Russia), described the dictator as "immensely courageous and a force for good."[6]

The Egyptian state had been the glad recipient of aid, arms, and torture equipment from the United States since signing the Camp David Accords in 1978, which confirmed Egypt's alliance with Israel and thus with the region's pro-US forces. Through this donated ordnance and material, Mubarak had maintained control over the country since 1981. Thirty years later, his decrepit rule, along with that of Ben Ali in Tunisia, was dispatched to the furnace of history. Given that Egypt was second only to Israel in the regional strategic importance it held for American planners, the overthrow of Mubarak and the destruction of his party and security apparatus were a serious threat. Unsurprisingly, US officials backed the regime until its tenure became untenable. They presently rely on the Egyptian military, which retains close links with the US armed forces, to contain the ongoing revolutionary process.

The question of how to control the Middle East has troubled American policy makers since the British Empire went into receivership. World War II left British capitalism in a precarious state, its colonial authorities struggling to contain a series of anticolonial rebellions. In some cases the United States was happy to exploit this. In Egypt, for example, Washington acquiesced in the Free Officers' rebellion led by Nasser against the pro-British monarch King Farouk in 1952. By contrast, Washington supported another pro-British ruler, King Idris of Libya, until the Free Officers of the Royal Libyan Army overthrew him in 1969. The difference between 1952 and 1969 was that, in the interim, independent Middle East states showed an alarming propensity toward the nationalization of resources, particularly oil.

Matters became more difficult for the United States when, at the gruesome height of the Vietnam War, the British Empire relinquished its "East of Suez" responsibilities. This meant the withdrawal of the British Navy from the Gulf, which had been used to support a network of sterling-based regional clients. The US Navy's "Middle East Force" took over these imperial duties, and in place of sterling patronage came dollar diplomacy. In the post–Cold War world the US right sought to exploit the absence of a major rival to reshape the region in US interests, uniting around an agenda of overthrowing Saddam and building a pro-US, "free-market" state on its ashes. The culmination of this venture was the first serious dent in Washington's regional hegemony, the first major fractures in the Euro-American alliance, and the first signs of Russian re-assertion. Obama's mission was to repair the damage.

So, it was particularly unfortunate for the Obama administration that revolutions broke out in a number of allied Middle East states—Tunisia, Egypt, Yemen, and Bahrain among them. Tunisia and Egypt fell remarkably quickly despite US support. Yemen's regime clung on with US weapons, and Bahrain was saved by Saudi intervention and US military equipment. Obama adapted to the new situation, issuing a series of sermons on liberty that it would be too generous to call half-baked even as he continued to support repression. But this was subterfuge—Washington was clearly losing its prized hegemony in the Middle East.

Libya: Antiwar Movement in Abeyance

The first sign of an attempt to cohere a response to the revolutions that fitted with US interests emerged with the calls for intervention in Libya, where an initially successful rebellion was facing defeat at the hands of Gaddafi. January 2011 saw Libyan protesters organize over corruption and the shortage of housing, mainly in eastern coastal towns and cities like Benghazi and Darnah. But some political activists, viewing the spectacular revolutions in neighboring coun-tries, began to press for more. By early February, middle-class human rights activists such as the journalist Jamal al-Hajji and lawyer Fathi Terbil began to organize protests in favor of greater political liberty. On the evening of February15, the night the revolt began, police vi-ciously beat and injured protesters in Benghazi.

In normal circumstances the combination of threats and re-pression would have been sufficient to isolate anyone foolhardy enough to protest. But in the afterglow of the Egyptian revolution, the protests spread to normally loyal towns such as al-Baydah. Tribes such as the Barassa, which had hitherto filled up the security apparatus, defected. Importantly, sections of local security and po-lice broke with the regime. Exiles in the National Conference for the Libyan Opposition coordinated with dissidents to plan a "Day of Rage" for February 17. On that day the government set snipers loose on the protesters, and turned a political struggle into an armed struggle. By February 25, it looked as if Libya was mostly in opposition hands, barring the capital, Tripoli, and Gaddafi's home town, Sirte. A transitional council was formed, largely comprised of elites and regime defectors—military officials, politicians, businessmen, academics, and other professionals—to try to organize the social forces involved in the uprising into a single body.

Gaddafi had suppressed all signs of organized opposition to his regime, so the civil society that was now in revolt had no trade unions or political parties to lead the opposition. People's committees arose across the country, but these were fragmented forms of popular power. In these circumstances it was natural that well-organized elites should try to fill the vacuum. However, their aspiration to get delegations from across the country was not fulfilled; they did not stamp their authority on the revolt, and remained narrowly based in the urban centers of the eastern coast.

Moreover, the personnel making up the council continued to be drawn from the elites, and they were given to fractiousness over strategy as well as individual power struggles—between Mahmoud Jibril, who coordinated Gaddafi's privatization programs, former justice minister Mustafa Abdul Jalil, and former interior minister General Abdul Fattah Younis. Later the arrival of Khalifa Hefta from the United States raised further divisions as he assumed leadership of the rebel army. Hefta was once an ally of Gaddafi's, but broke with the regime in 1987 and is reported to have longstanding ties to the CIA.

Notwithstanding the early military successes, moreover, it was not long before Gaddafi appeared to have the upper hand again, and the weaknesses of the revolt were brutally exposed. Significant tribes like the Warfalla, which had appeared to back the rebels, were won back to the government's side. This gave the United States and some of its European allies the opportunity to cohere around a strategy that had so far eluded them. They could take control of this process and shape it in a manner that suited their interests.

The United States had long attempted to destabilize the Libyan state through sanctions and bombings, but by the 2000s had every reason to expect that Gaddafi would go on ruling indefinitely. Since the revolution Gaddafi's regime had adeptly used patronage to gain the support of conservative rural elites, entrepreneurs in the oil, banking, and imports sector, and technocratic state managers. Three major tribes—the Gadhadhfa, Warfalla, and Margharha—formed the backbone of the regime and populated the security forces. A US diplomatic cable from 2009, disclosed by Wikileaks, paid tribute to Gaddafi's "mastery of tactical maneuvering," as he shifted patronage between different social layers as well as between his competing sons.

So, when Gaddafi decided that sanctions were costing his regime too much—an estimated thirty billion dollars through the 1990s—and sought to realign his regime with Washington, the United States had no reason to believe that this new relationship would blow up in its face. Bush and Blair began the nuptials with Gaddafi in 2004, and Libyan elites began to circulate among their Euro-American counterparts—for example, Gaddafi's son and London School of Economics graduate al-Islam became a close friend of Prince Andrew and Peter Mandelson.

Even so, the United States was not so vested in the Libyan regime that it could not abandon the alliance. The former regime elements who occupied the spearhead of the revolt had been participants in the alliance with the United States and European Union, and were known to be "pro-Western." Some elements among the transitional council favored an alliance with the United States to topple Gaddafi early on. For example, General Abdul Fattah Younis stated on March 1 that he would welcome targeted air strikes against Gaddafi's forces, but not a ground invasion.

But the social forces on which the revolt was based were not immediately disposed to accept this. As US politicians and security experts began to talk of intervention, signs appeared in rebel-controlled areas saying clearly "No Foreign Intervention." Hafiz Ghoga of the transitional council put it just as bluntly: "We are completely against foreign intervention. The rest of Libya will be liberated by the people and Gaddafi's security forces will be eliminated by the people of Libya." When Special Air Service (SAS, a special forces unit attached to the British Army) forces arrived in Benghazi to offer help on March 6, they were arrested, for fear that Gaddafi would gain support if he could depict the rebellion as an imperialist plot.

Only when the rebellion began to experience serious military reversals in major cities such as Zawiya did the argument for imperialist intervention begin to prevail. Once the rebels had been forced to give up on the idea of spreading the revolt to Tripoli and Sirte and decisively fracturing the regime, imperialist support seemed to be a way to make up for the weakness of the rebel alliance and for the lack of authority of the transitional council itself.

This circumstance complicated matters for the antiwar left. The majority was supportive of the rebellion when it emerged, and relished the embarrassment of those who had recently become allies of Gaddafi. But when the rebel leadership turned to the United States, citing the prospect of coming massacres if they were defeated, antiwar opinion fractured. Opinion polls have shown a majority of Americans opposed to war on Libya.[7] But this sentiment, far from stimulating a tumult of activism, has largely remained passive.[8] As previously noted, the energies of a great section of the movement had already been canalized into the electoral strategies of the Democratic Party. As a result, the antiwar left had lost funding, members, and prominence. But the confusion and division on the left has also been important.

The division between UFPJ and ANSWER developed along predictable ideological lines. One could oppose the war on the basis of defending Gaddafi's regime as a relatively "progressive" one. AN-SWER has effectively taken that stance, to widespread dismay. This reflects the politics of some of its organizers—the Workers' World Party, for example, to which steering committee member Brian Becker belongs, has a record of praising Gaddafi's regime. While ANSWER's position allowed it to be uncompromising in its opposition to war and thus provided a basis for it to engage in meetings and protests, it also alienated potential allies and narrowed the political base for mobilization.[9] An alternative was to oppose intervention by arguing that it would not serve the real interests of the rebels. A version of this stance was taken by UFPJ, who argued that the United States' motives were "questionable" and that negotiations would better meet the demands of the rebels.[10] Yet UFPJ has largely been absent from antiwar organizing.

More disorienting still, many hitherto vocal antiwar intellectuals spoke out in favor of intervention in Libya. Juan Cole, for example, declared that he was "unabashedly cheering the liberation movement on, and glad that the UNSC [Security Council] authorized intervention has saved them from being crushed." The "gold standard" for intervention that he felt had been reached was the support of the United Nations.[11] The appeal to international law has a particular place in the history of US antiwar movements, related to pacifist attempts to constrain the warmongers. But in effect what it means is that the morality of war is settled by the geopolitical determinations of the great powers that dominate UN decision making. By Cole's rationale, it would have been difficult to object to the Korean War or Operation Desert Storm, for example, despite their bloody consequences. By the same token, the horrific results of the 2004 occupation of Haiti would have been validated by a UN mandate.[12]

Another rationale was offered by Gilbert Achcar, generally an opponent of imperialism, who took the view that opposition to the intervention should be temporarily withheld on pragmatic humanitarian grounds, with a view to preventing the demolition of the

Libyan uprising. "Western governments," he said, "like everybody else for that matter, became convinced that with Gaddafi set on a counter-revolutionary offensive and reaching the outskirts of Libya's second largest city of Benghazi (over 600,000 inhabitants), a mass-scale slaughter was imminent." This would have forced the United States "to impose sanctions and an oil embargo on his regime," which would have been untenable in a global market conditioned by historically high energy prices. Thus, it became in the interests of US imperialism to overthrow Gaddafi. Moreover, had they allowed Gaddafi to continue his repression and perpetrate a massacre, they would have undermined the plausibility of humanitarian pretexts for intervention in future. In this case, the interests of imperialism coincided with those of a legitimate rebellion. For that reason, to oppose the intervention was to oppose the legitimate aspirations of the Libyan people. So much the worse if such a step is made in the name of mechanically applied principles.[13]

In light of such arguments, it is worth stressing again that antiimperialists in the United States have encountered American power in its missionary, humanitarian mien many times before. In fact, while the humanitarian arguments for conquest can be traced back to the nineteenth century, the United States has a particular history of framing its global subventions as emancipatory exercises. From the "Saxons" delivering "freedom" in Mexico, Cuba Libre, and Wilsonian internationalism to the Cold War for democracy, the "Alliance for Progress," and "humanitarian intervention," US imperialism is rarely without a moral pretext.

But what of the pretext for intervention in Libya? The argument that "a mass-scale slaughter" would be afoot if the rebel-controlled city of Benghazi was captured—with the number already dead perhaps as high as ten thousand—is no longer as compelling as it may initially have seemed. Firstly, if, as Obama maintained, the issue motivating intervention was the avoidance of bloodshed, then the obvious question is why a war was launched *before* a negotiated settlement was discussed. The exhaustion of nonmilitary solutions may also be considered a "gold standard" in the justification of war. In the case of Libya, there wasn't even a hollow performance of diplomacy, a remarkable fact that largely passed unremarked upon.

Secondly, Amnesty International, having investigated the situation, has discovered no evidence of mass killings on the scale being warned about. Gaddafi certainly engaged in brutal repression, much of it killing civilians. But the scale is indicated by this Amnesty International report on the targeting of the rebel-held city, Misratah, over a five-week period: "Misratah . . . suffered weeks of relentless and indiscriminate shelling by al-Gaddafi forces in April and early May. Scores of Misratah residents and several African migrants were killed and many other people were injured in the attacks." Similarly, Alan J. Kuperman cited Human Rights Watch figures to suggest that Gaddafi was unlikely to perpetrate a massacre on a genocidal scale in Benghazi because "he did not perpetrate it in the other cities he had recaptured either fully or partially—including Zawiya, Misurata, and Ajdabiya, which together have a population greater than Benghazi."[14]

What remains is the argument that, in the absence of intervention, Gaddafi would have been able to finish off a genuine uprising and despoil the hopes for democratic revolution across the Middle East. However, the deal between a rebel leadership comprised of former regime elements and the imperialist powers signaled that the initiative had *already* fallen out of the hands of the population. A revolution is by definition a process that is driven by the self-activity of the masses. The alliance between NATO, as well as US, British, and French intelligence, and a revamped rebel leadership simply cut the majority of Libyans out of the process. And as the war dragged on, the idea that a quick rescue (from a hypothetical massacre) might restore the revolution's lost initiative looked increasingly forlorn.

By the end of July, Gaddafi controlled more of Libya than he had when the NATO-led bombing campaign began.[15] The revolt failed to spread to the capital, Tripoli—a necessary condition for Gaddafi's overthrow. Increasingly, the rebel leadership had come to behave in a mercenary, fratricidal fashion, with the assassination of former rebel army leader General Abdul Fattah Younis believed to be the work of elements in the transitional council. The resulting fiasco saw the chair of the council, Mustafa Abdul Jalil, a former Libyan government minister, sack the entire "cabinet." Such maneuvering reflects internecine power rivalries rather than any matter of principle.[16]

Moreover, as the emancipatory content was sucked out of the rebellion, it turned increasingly to racism and repression. A painted slogan of rebels in Misrata read: "the brigade for purging slaves, black skin." Rumors that Gaddafi was using "African" (that is, black) mercenaries, spread by the rebels, have never been supported—much like the rumors of Viagra-fuelled Gaddafi loyalists raping throughout Libya. Yet they have been used to justify the rounding up, brutalization, and sometimes lynching of "African" migrant workers that has characterized rebel conduct in some key cities.[17] Nor did this racist violence abate after Tripoli fell to the opposition. If anything, it seems to have intensified, with group killings and even ethnic cleansing taking place.[18] Of course, this does not exhaust the conduct of the rebels, nor does it attenuate the despotic nature of the Gaddafi regime. It does, however, suggest that a serious degeneration in the original emancipatory impulse has taken place.

It is likely that the vast majority of Libyans welcomed the downfall of the Gaddafi regime in late August. Yet, to a considerable extent, the victory they sought belongs to NATO. NATO powers determined the military pace and strategy of rebel offensives. They decided whether the transitional council could sell oil or buy weapons. They decided how, when, and under what circumstances the rebels could gain international recognition as the authentic government of Libya. This meant that they effectively dictated the politics of the opposition by late March. With the masses thus excluded, it was no longer realistic to call the overthrow of Gaddafi a revolution. The new regime preserves intact the apparatus of the old regime with different personnel, and a promise of political liberalization. It also promises to protect US and European interests and will form a "pro-Western" pole of influence in a region in revolt against US dominance. This constitutes not a victory for the original rebellion but its effective annexation.

The situation of anti-imperialists in the United States in this context has not been easy, and is not about to become easier. Largely unable to influence events due to the mass evacuation of antiwar activists under a Democratic executive, they have been faced with the task of developing a political analysis that is capable of accommodating the legitimate aspirations of insurgent populations while also maintaining an uncompromising opposition to US imperialism. The fact that opinion has fractured in what is a qualitatively novel situation is to be expected. But the battle of ideology and analysis matters, as the appraisals developed today will shape how people respond to future wars. It will also determine how effectively anti-imperialists can relate to the Arab mass movements that have already weakened US dominance.

The revolutionary process in the Middle East has sufficiently complex dynamics as to allow further US subventions, ostensibly on the side of democracy. While, for example, the United States is decidedly hostile to the pro-democracy movement in Yemen, there have been ongoing negotiations with sections of the Syrian opposition.[19] In the latter case, those calling for external intervention are allied with the Syrian Muslim Brotherhood and exile groups. This is not to say that a bombing campaign is necessarily afoot in Syria. Unlike the Libyan uprising, Syria's movement has a left wing. The left-nationalist National Committee for Democratic Change has opposed talk of intervention, as have the Local Coordination Committees representing the grass roots of the revolt.[20] Nonetheless, the formation of a pro-imperialist faction in the Syrian opposition was made possible by the success of the intervention in Libya—an *outstanding* success from the US perspective, costing little in Pentagon terms, involving minimal military commitment, resulting in no loss of lives on the NATO side, and establishing a friendly regime within a few months. The overthrow of Gaddafi has opened up regional opportunities for the United States and its allies to insinuate themselves into future struggles.

The question is whether anti-imperialists will respond by simply defending the targeted regimes, or by defending imperialism— or whether they can develop a superior approach rooted in the traditions of international solidarity that have characterized US anti-imperialism at its finest moments.

Notes

Preface

Mark Twain, "To the Person Sitting in the Darkness," *North American Review*, February 1901, available at people.virginia.edu/~sfr/enam482e/totheperson.html.

1. See Bill Kaufman, *Ain't My America: The Long, Noble History of Anti-war Conservatism and Middle American Anti-Imperialism* (New York: Metropolitan Books, 2008); Justin Raimondo, *Reclaiming the American Right: The Lost Legacy of the Conservative Movement* (Wilmington, DE: ISI Books, 2008); Bill Kaufman, (2010), *Bye Bye, Miss American Empire: Neighborhood Patriots, Backcountry Rebels, and Their Underdog Crusades to Redraw America's Political Map* (White River Junction, VT: Chelsea Green Publishing, 2010); for a defense of "progressive" imperialism against its Marxist oblocutors, see Lewis S. Feuer, *Imperialism and the Anti-Imperialist Mind* (Piscataway, NJ: Transaction Publishers, 1989).

2. Michael Ignatieff, *Empire Lite: Nation-Building in Bosnia, Kosovo and Afghanistan* (New York: Vintage, 2003).

3. See Niall Ferguson, *Empire: How Britain Made the Modern World* (London: Penguin, 2004); Niall Ferguson, *Colossus: The Rise and Fall of the American Empire* (London: Penguin, 2004).

4. Max Boot, "American Imperialism? No Need to Run Away from Label," *USA Today*, May 6, 2003.

5. James Atlas, "The World: Among the Lost; Illusions of Immortality," *New York Times*, October 7, 2001.

6. For a stringent critique of Realist precepts, see Justin Rosenberg, *The Empire of Civil Society: A Critique of the Realist Theory of International Relations* (New York and London: Verso, 1994).

7. For a judicious summary of the Lenin/Bukharin thesis and its flaws and strengths, see Alex Callinicos, *Imperialism and Global Political Economy* (Cambridge: Polity Press, 2009), 25–66; Anthony Brewer, *Marxist Theories of Imperialism: A Critical Survey* (London: Routledge and Kegan Paul, 1990), 111–16.

8. See Ellen Meiksins Wood, *Empire of Capital* (New York and London: Verso, 2002) for a concise discussion of the peculiar dynamics of capitalist imperialism; on the geographical shifts of the twentieth century, see Neil Smith, *American Empire: Roosevelt's Geographer and the Prelude to Globalization* (Berkeley and Los Angeles: University of California Press, 2004).

9. See Sankar Muthu, *Enlightenment Against Empire* (Princeton, NJ: Princeton University Press, 2003).

10. Laura L. Toussaint, *The Contemporary US Peace Movement* (Philadelphia: Taylor & Francis, 2008), 39, 48, 100.

11. Moynihan quoted in *The Neoconservative Vision: From the Cold War to the Culture Wars*, ed. Mark Gerson, (Lanham, MD & London: Madison Books, 1996), 109; on working-class and African American antipathy to the Vietnam War, see Marvin Gettleman et al., eds., *Vietnam and America: The Most Comprehensive Documented History of the Vietnam War* (New York: Grove Press, 1995), 297–99.

12. Ron Paul, *A Foreign Policy of Freedom: Peace, Commerce, and Honest Friendship* (Auburn, AL: Ludwig von Mises Institute, 2007), 33–34, 45, 48, 247; on Pat Buchanan's involvement in mobilizing support for the Contra aggression in Nicaragua, see Bruce Cameron's insider memoir. Bruce P. Cameron, *My Life in the Time of the Contras* (Albuquerque: University of New Mexico Press, 2007), 147, 217; see also Peter B. Levy, *Encyclopedia of the Reagan-Bush Years* (Westport, CT: Greenwood Press, 1996), 54–55.

Chapter One

1. This is not to reduce the complex revolutionary ferment to its liberal capitalist components. The radicalization leading up to the revolution had roots in the working class as well as the bourgeoisie. Samuel Adams, who represented the left wing of the revolution, reached back to more radically egalitarian ideologies to frame the social struggles brewing in the mid-eighteenth century, to the Diggers and Levellers of the English Revolution. Nonetheless, the leadership of the revolution was mostly comprised of liberal capitalists who largely dictated the terms on which the new polity would be formed. On the influence of

British political philosophy, particularly concerning ideas of liberty and equality, see Gordon S. Wood, *The American Revolution: A History* (London: Phoenix Paperbacks, 2002), 56–61, 96–103. Wood's "Neo-Whiggian" account has tended to stress the influence of the "pre-capitalist" Republican ideology of England, in contrast to older historians such as Louis Hartz who placed the accent on Lockean influence. But here Wood acknowledges the crucial role of Enlightenment thought in providing a grounding for the combination of patrician elitism and egalitarianism that characterized the American revolutionary leadership. On the more radical ideas of the revolution, see Marcus Rediker and Peter Linebaugh, *The Many-Headed Hydra: Sailors, Slaves, Commoners and the Hidden History of the Revolutionary Enlightenment* (Boston: Beacon Press, 2000), 211–47; and Ray Raphael, *The American Revolution: A People's History* (London: Profile Books, 2001).

2. Wood, *American Revolution*, 1; Herbert Aptheker, *The American Revolution, 1763–1783* (New York: International Publishers, 1960), 25.

3. Robin Blackburn, *The American Crucible: Slavery, Emancipation and Human Rights* (New York and London: Verso, 2011), 131.

4. Wilson quoted in Bernard Baylin, *The Ideological Origins of the American Revolution* (Cambridge, MA: Harvard University Press, 1992), 154–55; Washington quoted in Sidney Lens, *The Forging of the American Empire: From the Revolution to Vietnam; A History of US Imperialism* (Chicago: Pluto Press and Haymarket Books, 2003), 2, and Richard H. Immerman, *Empire for Liberty: A History of American Imperialism from Benjamin Franklin to Paul Wolfowitz* (Princeton, NJ: Princeton University Press, 2010), 1.

5. Baldwin quoted in Hermann Wellenreuther, Maria Gehrke, and Marion Stange, *Revolution of the People: Thoughts and Documents on the Revolutionary Process in North America, 1774–1776* (Göttingen: Universitätsverlag Göttingen, 2006), 115.

6. Gordon S. Wood, *Empire of Liberty: A History of the Early Republic, 1789–1815* (Oxford: Oxford University Press, 2009).

7. For a detailed exposition of this analysis, see Charles Post, "The American Road to Capitalism," *New Left Review* I, no. 133 (May–June 1982); and Charles Post, *The American Road to Capitalism: Studies in Class Structure, Economic Development and Political Conflict, 1620–1877* (Leiden, Netherlands: Brill Academic Publishers, 2011).

8. A relatively recent example of this tendency is the Libertarian writer Justin Raimondo's essay on the revolutionary roots of "non-interventionism," though it would be mistaken to classify this as anti-imperialist. Justin Raimondo, "Defenders of the Republic: The Anti-Interventionist

Tradition in American Politics," in *The Costs of War: America's Pyrrhic Victories*, ed. John V. Denson (Piscataway, NJ: Transaction Books, 1999).

9. Alfred W. Blumrosen and Ruth G. Blumrosen, *Slave Nation: How Slavery United the Colonies and Sparked the American Revolution* (Naperville, IL: Sourcebooks, 2007); Duncan J. Macleod, *Slavery, Race and the American Revolution* (Cambridge: Cambridge University Press, 1975); see also David R. Roediger, *How Race Survived US History: From Settlement and Slavery to the Obama Phenomenon* (New York and London: Verso, 2009), 73–74.

10. Quoted in R. Van Alstyne, *The American Empire: Its Historical Pattern and Evolution* (London: The Historical Association/Routledge and Kegan Paul, 1960); Raphael, *The American Revolution*; Andrew K. Frank, "'The Times Have Turned Everything Upside Down': Native Americans and the American Revolution," in *American Revolution: People and Perspectives*, ed. Andrew K. Frank and Peter C. Mancall, (Santa Barbara, CA: ABC-CLIO, 2008).

11. On this aspect of liberalism, see Domenico Losurdo, *Liberalism: A Counter-History* (New York and London: Verso, 2011). Losurdo points out that the liberal revolutions in England, France, and the United States were coterminous with the rise of racial tyranny and argues that at the heart of liberalism is the logic of *exclusion*—all of its seemingly universal principles meet limits to their realization within the capitalist political economy that liberalism validates.

12. Lens, *Forging of the American Empire*, 62–86; Murray Polner and Thomas E. Woods Jr., *We Who Dared to Say No to War: American Antiwar Writing from 1812 to Now* (New York: Basic Books, 2008), 1–2.

13. Polner and Woods, *We Who Dared*, 1–20; David Mayers, *Dissenting Voices in America's Rise to Power* (Cambridge: Cambridge University Press, 2007), 43–55; on Southern, Republican support for the war, see Roger H. Brown, *The Republic in Peril: 1812* (New York: Norton, 1971).

14. C. Edward Skeen, *Citizen Soldiers in the War of 1812* (Lexington: University Press of Kentucky, 1999), 148–49; Lens, *Forging of the American Empire*, 66.

15. Donald R. Hickey, *The War of 1812: A Forgotten Conflict* (Champaign: University of Illinois Press, 1995), 27, 32–3; Adam Rothman, *Slave Country: American Expansion and the Origins of the Deep South* (Cambridge, MA: Harvard University Press, 2005), 38.

16. Reginald Horsman, "British Indian Policy in the Northwest, 1807–1812," *Mississippi Valley Historical Review* 45, no. 1 (June 1958).

17. Quoted in Alan R. Velie, *American Indian Literature: An Anthology* (Norman: University of Oklahoma Press, 1991), 150–51.

18. Quoted in Howard Zinn, *A People's History of the United States: From 1492 to the Present* (New York: Pearson Longman, 1996), 126.

19. Peter Lamphere, "The Life of Tecumseh: A Native War of Independence," *International Socialist Review* 39, January–February 2005.

20. Hickey, *War of 1812*, 25–26.

21. Eugene M. Wait, *America and the War of 1812* (Hauppage, NY: Nova Biomedical, 1999), 263; Carl Benn, *The Iroquois in the War of 1812* (Toronto: University of Toronto Press, 1998), 29–67, 263; Hickey, *War of 1812*, 139; Robert S. Allen, *His Majesty's Indian Allies: British Indian Policy in the Defence of Canada* (Toronto: Dundurn Press, 1993), 88–122.

22. David Brion Davis, *Inhuman Bondage: The Rise and Fall of Slavery in the New World* (Oxford: Oxford University Press, 2006), 269–70.

23. Frank A. Cassell, "Slaves of the Chesapeake Bay Area and the War of 1812," *Journal of Negro History* 57, no. 2 (April 1972).

24. Lens, *Forging of the American Empire*, 83; Hickey, *War of 1812*, 303; Rothman, *Slave Country*, 42.

25. See Arthur M. Schlesinger, *The Age of Jackson* (New York: Back Bay Books, 1988); Arthur M. Schlesinger, "The Ages of Jackson," *New York Review of Books*, December 7, 1989. For examples of sycophantic popular and schoolchildren's histories, see Carol H. Behrman, *Andrew Jackson* (Minneapolis, MN: Lerner, 2005); Barbara Somervill, *Andrew Jackson* (Minneapolis, MN: Compass Point Books, 2003); Carol Marsh, *Andrew Jackson: The People's President* (Peachtree City, GA: Gallopade International, 2003); John Meacham, *American Lion: Andrew Jackson in the White House* (New York: Random House, 2008); also consult the pro-Jackson histories of the Clintonite historian Sean Wilentz, written in response to leftist challenges and largely in defense of Schlesinger's themes, for example, Sean Wilentz, "On Class and Politics in Jacksonian America," in "The Promise of American History: Progress and Prospects," special issue, *Reviews in American History* 10, no. 4 (December 1982); on historiographical controversies about Jackson and the Jacksonians, particularly the leftist challenge of the sixties to Schlesingerian apologia, see Edward Pessen, *Jacksonian America: Society, Personality, and Politics* (Champaign: University of Illinois Press, 1985).

26. See Mayers, *Dissenting Voices*, 80–105.

27. For a detailed account of Jackson's war against the Seminoles and Creeks, see Sean Michael O'Brien, *In Bitterness and in Tears: Andrew Jackson's Destruction of the Creeks and Seminoles* (Westport, CT: Greenwood Press, 2003); for a typical example of apologetic revisionism, see F. P. Prucha, "Andrew Jackson's Indian Policy: A Reassessment," *Journal of American History* 56, no. 3 (December 1969), 527–39.

28. Mary Hershberger, "Mobilizing Women, Anticipating Abolition: The Struggle Against Indian Removal in the 1830s," *Journal of American History* 86, no. 1 (June 1999).

29. John Ashworth, *Slavery, Capitalism, and Politics in the Antebellum Republic*, vol. 1 (Cambridge: Cambridge University Press, 1996), 371.

30. Ashworth, *Slavery, Capitalism, and Politics*, vol. 1, 289–347.

31. Alfred A. Cave, "Abuse of Power: Andrew Jackson and the Indian Removal Act of 1830," *Historian* 65, no. 3 (December 2003); Amy H. Sturgis, *The Trail of Tears and Indian Removal* (Westport, CT: Greenwood Press, 2006), 86; Mayers, *Dissenting Voices*, 86–90.

32. Quoted in Michael L. Krenn, *The Color of Empire: Race and American Foreign Relations* (Dulles, VA: Potomac Books, 2005), 23–24, 114–16.

33. Quoted in Mayers, *Dissenting Voices*, 86.

34. On Locke's arguments for empire, property rights, and slavery, see Barbara Arneil, "Trade, Plantations, and Property: John Locke and the Economic Defense of Colonialism," *Journal of the History of Ideas* 55, no. 4 (October 1994), 591–609; see also Ellen Meiksins Wood, *The Origin of Capitalism: A Longer View* (New York and London: Verso, 2002), 96–100; Robin Blackburn, *The Making of New World Slavery: From the Baroque to the Modern, 1492–1800* (New York and London: Verso, 1997), 264; R. Bernasconi and A. Maaza Mann, "The Contradictions of Racism: Locke, Slavery and the Two Treatises," in *Race and Racism in Modern Philosophy*, ed. Andrew Valls (Ithaca, NY: Cornell University Press, 2005), 91.

35. Stephen J. Rockwell, *Indian Affairs and the Administrative State in the Nineteenth Century* (Cambridge: Cambridge University Press, 2010), 174–77.

36. Hershberger, "Mobilizing Women, Anticipating Abolition"; Catherine E. Beecher, *An Essay on Slavery and Abolitionism, with Reference to the Duty of American Females* (Virginia, 1837), available from the Electronic Text Center at etext.virginia.edu; Angelina Emily Grimké, *Letters to Catherine E. Beecher* (Massachusetts: 1838), available through Google Books at books.google.com.

37. Christine Bolt, *American Indian Policy* (London: Routledge, 1989), 58–59; on the relation between abolitionism and early feminism, see Blackburn, *American Crucible*, 376–80.

38. Quoted in Natalie Irene Joy, "Hydra's Head: Fighting Slavery and Indian Removal in Antebellum America," (unpublished PhD dissertation, University of California, 2008); and Patrick Neale Minges, *Slavery in the Cherokee Nation: The Keetoowah Society and the Defining of a People, 1855–1867* (London: Routledge, 2003), 48–49.

39. Sturgis, *Trail of Tears*, 94–95.

40. Alisse Portnoy, *Their Right to Speak: Women's Activism in the Indian and*

Slave Debates (Cambridge, MA: Harvard University Press, 2005), 166; see extracts from Frelinghuysen's speech in *The American Spirit: United States History as Seen by Contemporaries*, vol. I, ed. David M. Kennedy and Thomas A. Bailey (Florence, KY: Wadsworth, 2010), 302–304.

41. Hershberger, "Mobilizing Women, Anticipating Abolition"; Joy, "Hydra's Head."

42. Mayers, *Dissenting Voices*, 86.

43. Michael D. Green, *The Politics of Indian Removal: Creek Government and Society in Crisis* (Lincoln: University of Nebraska Press, 1982), 48.

44. Tim Allan Garrison, *The Legal Ideology of Removal: The Southern Judiciary and the Sovereignty of Native American Nations* (Athens: University of Georgia Press, 2009), 108–112; Victoria Sherrow, *Cherokee Nation v. Georgia: Native American Rights* (Berkeley Heights, NJ: Enslow Publishers, 1997).

45. Mayers, *Dissenting Voices*, 90–103; V. G. Kiernan, *America: The New Imperialism; From White Settlement to World Hegemony* (New York and London: Verso, 2005), 39.

46. David E. Stannard, *American Holocaust: The Conquest of the New World* (Oxford: Oxford University Press, 1992), 122–23.

47. Mayers, *Dissenting Voices*, 90–103; Kiernan, *America: The New Imperialism*, 39; Joe Knetch, *Florida's Seminole Wars, 1817–1858* (Charleston, SC: Arcadia Publishing, 2003), 104.

48. Quoted in Howard Zinn and Anthony Arnove, *Voices of a People's History of the United States* (New York: Seven Stories Press, 2004), 140–41.

49. Quoted in Helen Addison Howard, *Saga of Chief Joseph* (Lincoln: University of Nebraska Press, 1965), 330.

50. Historian Tim J. Todish, quoted in Hector Saldaña, "'The Alamo' Turns 50," *MySanAntonio.com*, October 23, 2010.

51. For a typical apologetic account of Austin and his views on slavery, see Eugene C. Barker, *The Life of Stephen F. Austin, Founder of Texas, 1793–1836: A Chapter in the Westward Movement of the Anglo-American People* (Austin: University of Texas Press, 1969). For an alternative perspective, see Randolph B. Campbell, *An Empire for Slavery: The Peculiar Institution in Texas, 1821–1865* (Baton Rouge: Louisiana State University Press, 1991), 10–34; Stephen L. Danver, ed., *Revolts, Protests, Demonstrations, and Rebellions in American History: An Encyclopedia* (Santa Barbara, CA: ABC-CLIO, 2010), 305–306.

52. Quoted in Campbell, *Empire for Slavery*, 10–49.

53. Reginald Horsman, *Race and Manifest Destiny: The Origins of American Racial Anglo-Saxonism* (Cambridge, MA: Harvard University Press, 1986), 210.

54. Lens, *Forging of the American Empire*, 117–26.
55. Gregory S. Hospador, "The Home Front in the Mexican-American War," in *Daily Lives of Civilians in Wartime Early America: From the Colonial Era to the Civil War*, ed. David S. Heidler and Jean T. Heidler (Westport, CT: Greenwood Press, 2007), 116–17
56. Horsman, *Race and Manifest Destiny*, 233; Zinn, *People's History*, 5.
57. Polner and Woods, *We Who Dared*, 30–33
58. Toombs quoted in L. Pierce Clark, *Lincoln: A Psycho-Biography* (New York: C. Scribner & Sons, 1933), 96.
59. Joshua Reed Giddings, *Speeches in Congress 1841–1852* (1853; repr. Scholarly Publishing Office, University of Michigan Library, 2005), 197.
60. Zinn, *People's History*, 151–52; Lens, *Forging of the American Empire*, 129–32.
61. Quoted in *Voices of a People's History*, ed. Arnove and Zinn, 160.
62. David W. Blight, *Frederick Douglass' Civil War: Keeping Faith in Jubilee* (Baton Rouge, LA: Louisiana State University Press, 1989), 28.
63. Robert S. Levine, *Martin Delany, Frederick Douglass, and the Politics of Representative Identity* (Chapel Hill: University of North Carolina Press, 1997), 34.
64. Zinn, *People's History*, 153
65. Polner and Woods, *We Who Dared*, 33–45.
66. Henry David Thoreau, *Civil Disobedience* (1849). Available through The Thoreau Reader at thoreau.eserver.org/civil.html.
67. Zinn, *People's History*, 155; Frederick Douglass, "Address to the New England Convention," May 31, 1849, in *Voices of a People's History*, ed. Arnove and Zinn, 159.
68. See Post, "The American Road to Capitalism."

Chapter Two

Quoted in Jim Zwick, ed., *Mark Twain's Weapons of Satire: Anti-Imperialist Writings on the Philippine-American War*, (Syracuse, NY: Syracuse University Press, 1992), 5; W. E. B. Du Bois, *The Souls of Black Folk* (Oxford: Oxford University Press, 2007), 15; Address by George S. Boutwell, "Address by the President," first annual meeting of the Anti-Imperialist League, November 25, 1899. Available at www.antiimperialist.com.
1. For a succinct account of the massacre and its context, see Marty Gitlin, *Wounded Knee Massacre* (Santa Barbara, CA: ABC-CLIO Press, 2010); on the Turner thesis, see Frederick Jackson Turner, *The Frontier in American History* (Mineola, NY: Dover Press, 1996); Richard Slotkin, *The Fatal Environment: The Myth of the Frontier in the Age of Industri-*

alization, 1800–1890 (Norman: University of Oklahoma Press, 1998); Richard White, "Western History," in *The New American History*, ed. Philip S. Foner (Philadelphia: Temple University Press, 1997).

2. Quoted in Richard Slotkin, *Gunfighter Nation: The Myth of the Frontier in Twentieth-Century America* (Norman: University of Oklahoma Press, 1998), 29.

3. Marilyn Lake and Henry Reynolds, *Drawing the Global Colour Line: White Men's Countries and the International Challenge of Racial Equality* (Cambridge: Cambridge University Press, 2008), 100–101.

4. Quoted in Edward J. Renehan Jr., *The Monroe Doctrine: The Cornerstone of American Foreign Policy* (New York: Infobase, 2007), 103.

5. Neil Smith, *The Endgame of Globalization* (New York and London: Routledge, 2005), 53–81.

6. See John Bellamy Foster, *Naked Imperialism: The U.S. Pursuit of Global Dominance* (New York: Monthly Review Press, 2006), 99–103.

7. See Callinicos, *Imperialism and Global Political Economy*, 144–64.

8. On the "Yellow Peril" anti–Asian immigrant hysteria and ethnic cleansing, see Matthew Frye Jacobson, *Barbarian Virtues: The United States Encounters Foreign Peoples at Home and Abroad* (New York: Hill & Wang, 2000), 73–88; Jean Pfaelzer, *Driven Out: The Forgotten War Against Chinese Americans* (New York: Random House, 2007); Krenn, *Color of Empire*, 51–55.

9. Louis A. Perez Jr., *The War of 1898: The United States and Cuba in History and Historiography* (Chapel Hill: University of North Carolina Press, 1998); Paul A. Kramer, *The Blood of Government: Race, Empire, the United States, and the Philippines* (Chapel Hill: University of North Carolina Press, 2006), 10–11; Richard Gott, *Cuba: A New History* (New Haven, CT: Yale University Press, 2004), 97–104; Krenn, *Color of Empire*, 44–48.

10. William George Whittaker, "Samuel Gompers, Anti-Imperialist," *Pacific Historical Review* 38, no. 4 (November 1969); Zinn, *People's History*, 299–300.

11. Zwick, *Mark Twain's Weapons*, 4.

12. Gompers quoted in Whittaker, "Samuel Gompers"; R. Kent Rasmussen, *Critical Companion to Mark Twain: A Literary Reference to His Life and Work* (New York: Infobase, 1987), 140–41; James quoted in Graham Clarke, *Henry James: Critical Assessments*, vol. 2 (New York and London: Routledge, 1992), 219; Robin Kadison Berson, *Jane Addams: A Biography* (Westport, CT: Greenwood Publishing, 2004), 67; for a great deal of detail on the attitudes of contemporary business groups, chambers of commerce, financial publications, and so on, see

Julius W. Pratt, "Business and the Spanish-American War," *Hispanic American Historical Review* 14, no. 2 (May 1934).

13. Winslow Warren, *The White Man's Burden*, Anti-Imperialist League, Boston, 1899. Available at www.antiimperialist.com.

14. Quoted in Lens, *Forging of the American Empire*, 178.

15. Quoted in Bellamy Foster, *Naked Imperialism*, 69–70; see also Charles A. Conant, "Can New Openings Be Found for Capital?" *Atlantic Monthly* 84, no. 505, 1899.

16. Spencer C. Tucker, ed., *The Encyclopedia of the Spanish-American and Philippine-American Wars: A Political, Social and Military History*, vol. I (Santa Barbara, CA: ABC-CLIO, 2009), 480; Jim Zwick, "The Anti-Imperialist League and the Origins of Filipino-American Oppositional Solidarity," *Amerasia Journal* 24, no. 2, 1998.

17. John R. Eperjesi, *The Imperialist Imaginary: Visions of Asia and the Pacific in American Culture* (Lebanon, NH: Dartmouth College Press, 2004), 10–12.

18. Marilyn Fischer, Carol Nackenoff, and Wendy Chmielewski, *Jane Addams and the Practice of Democracy* (Champaign: University of Illinois Press, 2009), 172. It is not clear what Addams made of the profoundly racist aspects of Hobson's theory—predictably, his account of finance capital was anti-Semitic and, unlike Addams and her colleagues, he was not in favor of self-government for the "lower races." For a concise discussion of Hobson's theory, its origins in the critique of the Boer War, and its racist aspects, see Callinicos, *Imperialism and Global Political Economy*, 44–49.

19. George E. McNeill, "The Poor Man's Burden," *Boston Globe*, March 30, 1899 cited in *Anti-Imperialism in the United States, 1898–1935*, ed. Jim Zwick. This was published at www.boondocksnet.com. It is, alas, no longer available.

20. See Edwin Burrett Smith, *The Constitution and the Inequality of Rights* (Chicago: American Anti-Imperialist League, 1901). Available at www.antiimperialist.com.

21. E. Berkeley Tompkins, "Scylla and Charybdis: The Anti-Imperialist Dilemma in the Election of 1900," *Pacific Historical Review* 36, no. 2 (May 1967).

22. For background on Bryan's politics, see Robert W. McCherny, *A Righteous Cause: The Life of William Jennings Bryan* (Norman: University of Oklahoma Press, 1994); Tompkins, "Scylla and Charybdis: The Anti-Imperialist Dilemma"; Willard H. Smith, "William Jennings Bryan and Racism," *Journal of Negro History* 54, no. 2 (April 1969).

23. McCherny, *A Righteous Cause*, 77–78; Gary B. Nash and Carter Smith,

Atlas of American History (Dallas, TX: Media Projects Inc., 2007, 207; Mark Twain, "Municipal Corruption," address at the City Club Dinner, January 4, 1901. Available at www.antiimperialist.com.

24. For a caustic demolition of the Democrats' pacific posture, see Dennis Perrin, *Savage Mules: The Democrats and Endless War* (New York and London: Verso, 2008). For a general critique of the Democrats, see Lance Selfa, *The Democrats: A Critical History* (Chicago: Haymarket Books, 2008).

25. Kramer, *Blood of Government*, 153.

26. Twain quoted in E. San Juan Jr., "An African American Soldier in the Philippine Revolution: An Homage to David Fagen," *Cultural Logic* (2009).

27. "Fourth Annual Meeting of the New England Anti-Imperialist League," November 29, 1902, New England Anti-Imperialist League, Boston; "Report of the Seventh Annual Meeting of the Anti-Imperialist League," November 25–27, 1905, Anti-Imperialist League, Boston. Available at www.antiimperialist.com; Richard E. Welch Jr., "Atrocities in the Philippines: The Indictment and the Response," *Pacific Historical Review* 43, no. 2 (May 1974).

28. Address by George S. Boutwell, "Fourth Annual Meeting of the New England Anti-Imperialist League," November 29, 1902, New England Anti-Imperialist League, Boston. Available at www.antiimperialist.com.

29. Welch, "Atrocities in the Philippines."

30. See Christopher Lasch, "The Anti-Imperialists, the Philippines, and the Inequality of Man," *Journal of Southern History* 24, no. 3 (August 1958); Eperjesi, *Imperialist Imaginary*, 10–12.

31. Joseph A. Fry, *Dixie Looks Abroad: The South and U.S. Foreign Relations, 1789–1973* (Baton Rouge: Louisiana State University Press, 2002), 130.

32. Frank Ninkovich, "Anti-Imperialism in US Foreign Relations," in *Vietnam and the American Political Tradition: The Politics of Dissent*, ed. Randall B. Woods (Cambridge: Cambridge University Press, 2003); Nina Silber, "Emancipation without Slavery: Remembering the Union Victory," in *In the Cause of Liberty: How the Civil War Redefined American Ideals*, ed. William J. Cooper and John M. McCardell Jr. (Baton Rouge: Louisiana State University Press, 2009), 116.

33. Carl Schurz, "The Policy of Imperialism," Anti-Imperialist Conference, Chicago, October 17, 1899; Mark Twain, "China and the Philippines," address at a dinner given in the Waldorf-Astoria Hotel, New York, December 1900; Twain was also an ardent supporter of labor, and even came to evince revolutionary enthusiasms. See Helen Scott, "The Mark Twain They Didn't Teach Us About in School," *International Socialist Review* 10 (Winter 2000).

34. "Report of the Fifteenth Annual Meeting of the Anti-Imperialist League," Boston, November 29 and December 19, 1913.

35. On Gompers's racism, see Paul Buhle, *Taking Care of Business* (New York: Monthly Review Press, 1999), 40–46; Lasch, "The Anti-Imperialists, the Philippines, and the Inequality of Man."

36. Michelle Mitchell, "'The Black Man's Burden': African Americans, Imperialism and Notions of Racial Manhood, 1890–1910," in *Complicating Categories: Gender, Class, Race and Ethnicity*, ed. Eileen Boris and Angelique Janssens (Cambridge: Cambridge University Press, 2004), 77–101.

37. Charles F. Howlett, "Anti-Imperialist League," in *The American Economy: A Historical Encyclopedia*, ed. Cynthia Clark Northrup (Santa Barbara, CA: ABC-CLIO, 2003), 20–22.

38. J. Dallas Bowser, "Take Up the Black Man's Burden," *Colored American*, April 8, 1899.

39. Erin L. Murphy, "Women's Anti-Imperialism, 'The White Man's Burden,' and the Philippine-American War," *Asia-Pacific Journal* 23, no. 2 (July 6, 2009).

40. Hazel V. Carby, "On the Threshold of Woman's Era: Lynching, Empire, and Sexuality in Black Feminist Theory," in *Dangerous Liaisons: Gender, Nation, and Postcolonial Perspectives*, ed. Anne McClintock, Aamir Rashid Mufti, and Ella Shohat (Minneapolis: University of Minnesota Press, 1997).

41. Du Bois, *Souls of Black Folk*, 40.

42. Mitchell, "'The Black Man's Burden,'" 77–101; San Juan, "African American Soldier"; Gill H. Boehringer, "Black American Anti-Imperialist Fighters in the Philippine American War," *Black Agenda Report*, September 15, 2009.

43. Berson, *Jane Addams*, 67–68.

44. Murphy, "Women's Anti-Imperialism."

45. Kristin L. Hoganson, "'As Badly off as the Filipinos': U.S. Women's Suffragists and the Imperial Issue at the Turn of the Twentieth Century," *Journal of Women's History* 13, no. 2 (Summer 2001).

46. Murphy, "Women's Anti-Imperialism."

47. David Montgomery, "Workers' Movements in the United States Confront Imperialism: The Progressive Era Experience," *Journal of the Gilded Age and Progressive Era* 7, no. 1 (January 2008); Ira Kipnis, *The American Socialist Movement 1897–1912* (Chicago: Haymarket Books, 2004), 297.

48. Montgomery, "Workers' Movements."

49. Kipnis, *American Socialist Movement*, 297.

50. Montgomery, "Workers' Movements."

51. Zinn, *People's History*, 300, 310

52. Daniel Bell, *Marxian Socialism in the United States* (Ithaca, NY: Cornell University Press, 1996), 55–56.

53. For a rather tart, condescending review of the socialists in the Spanish-American War, see Howard H. Quint, "American Socialists and the Spanish-American War," *American Quarterly* 10, no. 2, part 1 (Summer 1958).

54. Quoted in Eperjesi, *Imperialist Imaginary*, 11; Krenn, *Color of Empire*, 43–44.

55. See Rubin Francis Weston, *Racism in US Imperialism: The Influence of Racial Assumptions on American Foreign Policy, 1893–1946* (Columbia: University of South Carolina, 1972), 1–15, 32–49.

56. On the literary impact of US peace movements, see Cynthia Wachtell, *War No More: The Antiwar Impulse in American Literature, 1861–1914* (Baton Rouge: Louisiana State University Press, 2010). For background on the women's peace movements, see Carrie A. Foster, *The Women and the Warriors: United States Section of the Women's International League for Peace and Freedom, 1915–46* (Syracuse, NY: Syracuse University Press, 1995); John Whiteclay Chambers, ed., *The Eagle and the Dove: The American Peace Movement and United States Foreign Policy, 1900–1922* (Syracuse, NY: Syracuse University Press, 1992), 4–10.

57. On the colonial roots of international law, see Antony Anghie, *Imperialism, Sovereignty and the Making of International Law* (Cambridge: Cambridge University Press, 2004); and Martti Koskenniemi, *The Gentle Civilizer of Nations: The Rise and Fall of International Law 1870–1960* (Cambridge: Cambridge University Press, 2001). China Miéville, whose arguments I have sampled above, is the author of by far the superior Marxist work on international law, *Between Equal Rights: A Marxist Theory of International Law* (Chicago: Haymarket, 2006).

Chapter Three

John Reed, "What About Mexico?" *Masses* (June 1914), available from History Matters at http://historymatters.gmu.edu/d/4948; Randolph Bourne, "The State" (1918), quoted in Zinn and Arnove, *Voices of a People's History*, 299.

1. A fairly typical summary of this sort of argument can be found in Lloyd E. Ambrosius, "Woodrow Wilson and World War I," in Robert Schulzinger, ed., *A Companion to American Foreign Relations* (Malden, MA: Wiley-Blackwell, 2006), 149–67. For a more detailed version of the analysis that follows, see Richard Seymour, *The Liberal Defence of Murder* (New York and London: Verso, 2008), 97–101.

2.   Zinn, *People's History*, 293.

3.   Smith, *Endgame*, 71–72.

4.   On Wilson's segregationist politics, see Kenneth O'Reilly, "The Jim Crow Policies of Woodrow Wilson," *Journal of Blacks in Higher Education* 17 (1997), 117–21; his support for the KKK was cited in D. W. Griffiths's film *Birth of a Nation*: "The white men were roused by a mere instinct of self-preservation . . . until at last there had sprung into existence a great Ku Klux Klan, a veritable empire of the South, to protect the Southern country." Having seen the film, Wilson remarked: "It is like writing history with lightning, and my only regret is that it is all so terribly true." Quoted in D. Flamming, *Bound for Freedom: Black Los Angeles in Jim Crow America* (Berkeley and Los Angeles: University of California Press, 2005), 88; quoted in Derek Heater, *National Self-Determination: Woodrow Wilson and his Legacy* (New York: St. Martin's Press, 1994), 15; Ronald J. Pestritto, ed., *Woodrow Wilson: the Essential Political Writings* (Lanham, MD: Lexington Books, 2005), 32–35.

5.   Niels Aage Thorsen, *The Political Thought of Woodrow Wilson 1875–1910* (Princeton, NJ: Princeton University Press, 1988), 164–65; Heater, *National Self-Determination*, 24–25.

6.   Thorsen, *Woodrow Wilson*, 174–75.

7.   Curry, "Woodrow Wilson and Philippine Policy," *Mississippi Valley Historical Review* 41, no. 3 (1954), 435–52; Arthur S. Link, *Woodrow Wilson and the Progressive Era, 1910–1917* (New York: Harper & Brothers, 1954), 227–28.

8.   Erez Manela, *The Wilsonian Moment: Self-Determination and the International Origins of Anticolonial Nationalism* (Oxford: Oxford University Press, 2007), 30.

9.   Ibid., 24.

10. Miéville, *Between Equal Rights*, 20–21.

11. Quoted in Thorsen, *Woodrow Wilson*, 179.

12. See Richard F. Grimmett, "Instances of Use of United States Armed Forces Abroad, 1798–2009," (RL32170; January 27, 2010), US Congressional Research Service; for a detailed account of the counterrevolutionary interventions in Latin America, see Jenny Pearce, *Under the Eagle* (Boston, MA: South End Press, 1982).

13. Quoted in Zinn and Arnove, *Voices of a People's History*, 252.

14. Michael J. Gonzales, *The Mexican Revolution, 1910–1940* (Albuquerque: University of New Mexico Press, 2002), 60–71.

15. Dan LaBotz, "U.S. Socialists and the Mexican Revolution," *Against the Current* 149 (November–December 2010).

16. Gilbert G. González, *Mexican Consuls and Labor Organizing: Imperial*

Politics in the American Southwest (Austin: University of Texas Press, 1999), 11–12.

17. Gonzales, *Mexican Revolution*, 60–71; LaBotz, "U.S. Socialists and the Mexican Revolution."

18. Gonzales, *Mexican Revolution*, 71–74.

19. Stuart Easterling, "Mexico's Revolution: A Look Back in the Centennial Year," part 1, *International Socialist Review* 74 (November–December 2010).

20. Alan Knight, "The Working Class and the Mexican Revolution, c. 1900–1920," *Journal of Latin American Studies* 16, no. 1 (May 1984).

21. Gonzales, *Mexican Revolution*, 73.

22. Stuart Easterling, "Mexico's Revolution: A Look Back in the Centennial Year," part 2, *International Socialist Review* 75 (January–February 2011).

23. Ibid.; see also Stuart Easterling, "Mexico's Revolution: A Look Back in the Centennial Year," part 3, *International Socialist Review* 76 (March–April 2011).

24. Teresa A. Meade, *A History of Modern Latin America: 1800 to the Present* (Malden, MA: Wiley-Blackwell, 2010), 163–64; John A. Britton, *Revolution and Ideology: Images of the Mexican Revolution in the United States* (Lexington: University of Kentucky Press, 2006), 5–6; on the role of the Texas Rangers, see Charles H. Harris and Louis R. Sadler, *The Texas Rangers and the Mexican Revolution: The Bloodiest Decade, 1910–1920* (Albuquerque: University of New Mexico Press, 2007); Rodolfo Rocha, *The Influence of the Mexican Revolution on the Mexico-Texas Border, 1910–1916* (PhD dissertation, Texas Tech University, 1981).

25. Montgomery, "Workers' Movements"; LaBotz, "U.S. Socialists"; Norman Caulfield, "Wobblies and Mexican Workers in Mining and Petroleum, 1905–1924," *International Review of Social History* 40 (1995); Philip S. Foner, "The IWW and the Black Worker," *Journal of Negro History* 55, no. 1 (January 1970).

26. Montgomery, "Workers' Movements"; LaBotz, "U.S. Socialists"; Shelley Streetby, "Labor, Memory, and the Boundaries of Print Culture: From Haymarket to the Mexican Revolution," *American Literary History* 19, no. 2 (Summer 2007).

27. Britton, *Revolution and Ideology*, 5, 30–32; Lens, *Forging of the American Empire*, 220–28.

28. Lens, *Forging of the American Empire*, 231–22.

29. Ibid., 232–24; Clifford W. Trow, "Woodrow Wilson and the Mexican Interventionist Movement of 1919," *Journal of American History* 58, no. 1 (June 1971).

30. LaBotz, "U.S. Socialists."

31. Montgomery, "Workers' Movements"; LaBotz, "U.S. Socialists."
32. John Reed, *Insurgent Mexico* (New York: International Publishers, 1969).
33. Reed, "What About Mexico?"
34. Quoted in Cole Brassier, *The Hovering Giant: U.S. Responses to Revolutionary Change in Latin America* (Pittsburgh: University of Pittsburgh Press, 1985), 102.
35. Mary A. Renda, *Taking Haiti: Military Occupation and the Culture of U.S. Imperialism, 1915–1940* (Chapel Hill: University of North Carolina Press, 2001), 10–13; Hans Schmidt, *The United States Occupation of Haiti, 1915–1934* (New Brunswick, NJ: Rutgers University Press, 1995), 9.
36. Krenn, *Color of Empire*, 76.
37. Quoted in David Brion Davis, "Impact of the French and Haitian Revolutions," in *The Impact of the Haitian Revolution in the Atlantic World*, ed. David Patrick Geggus (Columbia: University of South Carolina, 2001), 3.
38. Davis, "Impact," 3–4.
39. Montgomery, "Workers' Movements"; Seymour, *Liberal Defence of Murder*, 96; Brenda Gayle Plummer, "The Afro-American Response to the Occupation of Haiti, 1915–1934," *Phylon* 43, no. 2 (1982); Henry Lewis Suggs, "The Response of the African American Press to the United States Occupation of Haiti, 1915–1934," *Journal of African American History* 87 (Winter 2002).
40. Plummer, "Afro-American Response"; Suggs, "Response of the African American Press."
41. Seymour, *Liberal Defence of Murder*, 98–97; Schmidt, *United States Occupation of Haiti*, 120–22.
42. See Joyce Blackwell, *No Peace Without Freedom: Race and The Women's International League for Peace and Freedom 1915–1975* (Carbondale: Southern Illinois University Press, 2004); Foster, *Women and the Warriors*, 162; Renda, *Taking Haiti*, 268. The radical pacifist War Resisters' League (WRL) was created in the same year as a result of the pioneering efforts of the socialist activist Dr. Jessie Wallace Hughan, and would go on playing an honorable role in antiwar movements throughout the Korean and Vietnam Wars. Scott H. Bennett, *Radical Pacifism: The War Resisters League and Gandhian Nonviolence in America, 1915–1963* (Syracuse, NY: Syracuse University Press, 2003).
43. Renda, *Taking Haiti*, 268–70; Margaret Stevens, "'Hands Off Haiti!' Self-Determination, Anti-Imperialism, and the Communist Movement in the United States, 1925–1929," *Black Scholar* 37, no. 4 (2008); Laurie F. Leach, *Langston Hughes: A Biography* (Westport, CT: Greenwood Publishing, 2004), 63–65.

44. Seymour, *Liberal Defence of Murder*, 50–57; Ross F. Collins, *World War One* (Westport, CT: Greenwood Press, 2008), 9; Mayers, *Dissenting Voices*, 222.

45. Philip S. Foner, *Labor and World War I, 1914–1918* (New York: International Publishers, 1987), 4–7.

46. Foner, *Labor and World War I*, 7.

47. Ibid., 4, 40–42.

48. Lloyd E. Ambrosius, *Woodrow Wilson and the American Diplomatic Tradition: The Treaty Fight in Perspective* (Cambridge: Cambridge University Press, 1990), 25; James D. Ciment and Thaddeus Russell, eds., *The Home Front Encyclopedia: United States, Britain, and Canada in World Wars I and II* (Santa Barbara, CA: ABC-CLIO, 2006), 460.

49. Markku Ruotsila, *John Spargo and American Socialism* (Hampshire, UK: Palgrave MacMillan, 2006); Foner, *Labor and World War I*, 66–67, 99.

50. John A. Thompson, *Reformers and War: Progressive Publicists and the First World War* (Cambridge: Cambridge University Press, 1987); Mark Ellis, *Race, War, and Surveillance: African Americans and the United States Government during World War I* (Bloomington: Indiana University Press, 2001); Zinn, *People's History*, 354.

51. Eugene V. Debs, "The Canton, Ohio, Anti-War Speech," *Call*, June 16, 1918, available at the E. V. Debs Internet Archive, www.marxists.org/debs.

52. Nick Salvatore, *Eugene V. Debs: Citizen and Socialist* (Champaign: University of Illinois Press, 1987), 290.

53. Zinn, *People's History*, 355.

54. On the response of Debs and the Socialist Party to the Russian Revolution, see Dan LaBotz, "American 'Slackers' in the Mexican Revolution: International Proletarian Politics in the Midst of a National Revolution," *Americas* 62, no. 4 (April 2006); Salvatore, *Eugene V. Debs*, 286–91.

55. Jeremy Brecher, *Strike!* (Boston, MA: South End Press, 1997), 119.

56. For the best history of the strike, which traces its origins from socialist radicalism, IWW unionism, opposition to US involvement in World War I, and jubilation over the Russian Revolution, see Harvey O'Connor, *Revolution in Seattle* (New York: Monthly Review Press, 1964).

57. See Philip S. Foner, *The Bolshevik Revolution: Its Impact on American Radicals, Liberals and Labor* (New York: International Publishers, 1967).

58. Zinn, *People's History*, 381–82; Paul Dickson and Thomas B. Allen, *The Bonus Army: An American Epic* (New York: Walker and Company, 2004).

59. For an instructive account of this process of degeneration and counterrevolution, see Kevin Murphy, *Revolution and Counterrevolution: Class Struggle in a Moscow Metal Factory* (Chicago: Haymarket Books, 2007); for the classic account of Stalinist Russia as a "state capitalist"

society, see Tony Cliff, *State Capitalism in Russia* (London: Pluto Press, 1974); for an interesting study of this and competing accounts, see Marcel van der Linden, *Western Marxism and the Soviet Union: A Survey of Critical Theories and Debates Since 1917* (Leiden, Netherlands: Brill Academic Publishers, 2007).

60. For the best guide to Communism and African Americans in 1930s America, see Mark Solomon, *The Cry Was Unity: Communists and African Americans, 1917–1936* (Jackson: University Press of Mississippi, 1996).

61. Fraser M. Otanelli, *The Communist Party of the United States: From the Depression to World War II* (New Brunswick, NJ: Rutgers University Press, 1991), 55–56; David Adams, *The American Peace Movements* (2002), available at http://www.culture-of-peace.info, 8–10; Charles Chatfield, "Alternative Antiwar Strategies of the Thirties," *American Studies* 13, no. 1 (Spring 1972).

62. Andy Durgan, *The Spanish Civil War* (Hampshire, UK: Palgrave Macmillan, 2007), 7–30, 62–66.

63. Peter N. Carroll, *The Odyssey of the Abraham Lincoln Brigade: Americans in the Spanish Civil War* (Palo Alto, CA: Stanford University Press, 1994), 9–10; Durgan, *Spanish Civil War*, 62–74; Joseph Kip Kosek, *Acts of Conscience: Christian Nonviolence and Modern American Democracy* (New York: Columbia University Press, 2009), 153–54.

64. Harry Fisher, *Comrades: Tales of a Brigadista in the Spanish Civil War* (Lincoln: University of Nebraska Press), 1998, 23–24; James Yates, *Mississippi to Madrid: Memoir of a Black American in the Abraham Lincoln Brigade* (Greensboro, NC: Open Hand, 1993), 105.

65. On the buildup to World War II, see Callinicos, *Imperialism and Global Political Economy*, 156–61; and Paul N. Hehn, *A Low Dishonest Decade: The Great Powers, Eastern Europe, and the Economic Origins of World War II, 1930–1941* (London: Continuum, 2006). On the inter-imperialist rivalries involved in World War II, see Ernest Mandel, *The Meaning of the Second World War* (New York and London: Verso, 2011) for a useful if flawed historiography.

66. Marian Mollin, *Radical Pacifism in Modern America: Egalitarianism and Protest* (Philadelphia: University of Pennsylvania Press, 2006), 14–19.

67. Leon Trotsky, "Some Questions on American Problems," *Fourth International* 1, no. 5 (October 1940), available at the Marxists Internet Archive, www.marxists.org/archive/trotsky/1940/08/american.htm.

68. Alex Callinicos, *Trotskyism* (London: Polity Press, 1990).

69. Otanelli, *Communist Party*, 159–69.

70. Ibid., 163.

71. Ibid., 197–206. For a full discussion of the CPUSA's role during World War II, see Maurice Isserman, *Which Side Were You On? The American Communist Party during the Second World War* (Champaign: University of Illinois Press, 1993).

Chapter Four

Simon Hall, *Peace and Freedom: The Civil Rights and Antiwar Movements in the 1960s* (Philadelphia: University of Pennsylvania Press, 2006), 1; Gerald Horne, *Black and Red: W. E. B. Du Bois and the Afro-American Response to the Cold War, 1944–1963* (Albany: State University of New York Press, 1985), 19; Quoted in Terry H. Anderson, *The Movement and the Sixties: Protest in America from Greensboro to Wounded Knee* (Oxford: Oxford University Press, 1995), 146; Manic Street Preachers, lyrics from the song "Love of Richard Nixon," from the album *Lifeblood* (London: Sony Music UK, 2004).

1. On Cold War bipolar competition and its implications for shifting US strategies, see Callinicos, *Imperialism and Global Political Economy*, 165–87. For a detailed account of the geographical calculations behind America's postwar imperial planning, see Smith, *American Empire*; and Smith, *Endgame of Globalization*, 82–121. On the postwar boom and the impact of military spending, see Chris Harman, *Zombie Capitalism: Global Crisis and the Relevance of Marx* (Chicago: Haymarket Books, 2010).

2. Niels Bjerre-Poulsen, *Right Face: Organizing the American Conservative Movement 1945–65* (Copenhagen, Denmark: Museum Tusculanum Press, 2002), 88.

3. Robbie Lieberman, *The Strangest Dream: Communism, Anticommunism, and the U.S. Peace Movement, 1945–1963* (Charlotte, NC: Information Age, 2010), 32.

4. Alan Yarnell, *Democrats and Progressives: The 1948 Presidential Election as a Test of Postwar Liberalism* (Berkeley and Los Angeles: University of California Press, 1974), 90.

5. Ibid., 32–33. On Cold War anticommunism and its focus on espionage and sabotage, see Ellen Schrecker, *Many Are the Crimes: McCarthyism in America* (New York: Little, Brown & Co., 1998), 159–67. On Kennan's role in this, see Joel Kovel, *Red Hunting in the Promised Land: Anticommunism and the Making of America* (London: Cassell, 1997), 43–49.

6. Yarnell, *Democrats and Progressives*, 87; Lieberman, *Strangest Dream*, 52.

7. Mayers, *Dissenting Voices*, 297.

8. For an excellent discussion of Cold War hegemony and the dominance of Fordist capital, see Mark Rupert, *Producing Hegemony: The Politics*

of Mass Production and American Global Power (Cambridge: Cambridge University Press, 1995).

9. Odd Arne Westad, *The Global Cold War* (Cambridge: Cambridge University Press, 2007), 66; S. Lee, *The Korean War* (New York: Pearson Longman, 2001), 21; Charles K. Armstrong, *The North Korean Revolution, 1945–1950* (Ithaca, NY: Cornell University Press, 2003), 2, 12–14, 17, 142–45, 244; Bruce Cummings, *The Origins of the Korean War, vol. I: Liberation and the Emergence of Separate Regimes, 1945–1947* (Princeton, NJ: Princeton University Press, 1981), xx–xxi, 199, 209–13; Hugh Deane, *The Korean War, 1945–1953* (Melbourne, Australia: China Books, 1999), 12–14; J. Merrill, "Internal Warfare in Korea, 1948–1950: The Local Setting of the Korean War," in *Child of Conflict: The Korean–American Relationship: 1943–1953*, ed. Bruce Cummings (Seattle: University of Washington Press, 1983), 136.

10. Stanley Sandler, *The Korean War: No Victors, No Vanquished* (Lexington: University Press of Kentucky, 1999), 9; Mayers, *Dissenting Voices*, 298. For some background and more detail on Shachtman's idiosyncratic approach to the Korean War, see Seymour, *Liberal Defence*, 134–35.

11. Barry Sheppard, *The Party: The Socialist Workers Party, 1960–1988, volume 1; The Sixties, A Political Memoir* (Chippendale, Australia: Resistance Books, 2005), 18–19; Workers' League, *Desert Slaughter: The Imperialist War against Iraq* (Detroit, Michigan: Labor Publications, 1991), 410–13; the analysis of the postwar system by the Socialist Workers Party is contained in James P. Cannon, "The Road to Peace: According to Stalin and According to Lenin," *Militant*, 1951, available through the Marxists Internet Archive at www.marxists.org.

12. Steven Casey, *Selling the Korean War: Propaganda, Politics, and Public Opinion 1950–1953* (Oxford: Oxford University Press, 2008), 75, 139, 205–06.

13. Lieberman, *Strangest Dream*, 32–35; Maurice Isserman, *If I Had a Hammer: The Death of the Old Left and the Birth of the New Left* (Champaign: University of Illinois Press, 1995), 3–31; Michael R. Belknap, *Cold War Political Justice: The Smith Act, the Communist Party, and American Civil Liberties* (Westport, CT: Greenwood Press, 1977), 41.

14. Joseph R. Starobin, *American Communism in Crisis, 1943–1957* (Cambridge, MA: Harvard University Press, 1972), 205–11.

15. Lawrence S. Wittner, *The Struggle against the Bomb*, vol. 2 (Palo Alto, CA: Stanford University Press, 1993), 86–92; William B. Stueck, *The Korean War: An International History* (Princeton, NJ: Princeton University Press, 1997), 124.

16. Rebecca Mina Schreiber, *Cold War Exiles in Mexico: U.S. Dissidents*

and the Culture of Critical Resistance (Minneapolis: University of Minnesota Press, 2008), 12.

17. Quoted in Mary Young, *W.E.B. Du Bois: An Encyclopedia* (Santa Barbara, CA: ABC-CLIO, 2001), 215.

18. See Young, *W.E.B. Du Bois*, 215; Joyce Gleason Carew, *Blacks, Reds, and Russians: Sojourners in Search of the Soviet Promise* (New Brunswick, NJ: Rutgers University Press, 2008), 56–57; Gerald Horne, *Black and Red: W. E. B. Du Bois and the Afro-American Response to the Cold War, 1944–1963* (Albany: State University of New York Press, 1985), 128–32.

19. Bennett, *Radical Pacifism*, 192.

20. An aspect of the rising anticommunism was that even imperialist liberals like Harry Truman were criticized by the right for "losing" China. David R. McCann and Barry S. Strauss, eds., *War and Democracy: A Comparative History of the Korean War and the Peloponnesian War* (Armonk, NY: M.E. Sharpe, 2001), 206.

21. Mayers, *Dissenting Voices*, 298–311.

22. Kennedy and Morgenstern quoted in Murray N. Rothbard, *For a New Liberty: The Libertarian Manifesto* (Auburn, AL: Ludwig von Mises Institute, 2006), 343–47.

23. Garet Garrett, *The People's Pottage* (Caldwell, Idaho: The Caxton Printers, 1953), available through the Ludwig von Mises Institute at www.mises.org.

24. Casey, *Selling*, 139–41.

25. Casey, *Selling*, 75, 200–02; Peter B. Levy, *The New Left and Labor in the 1960s* (Champaign: University of Illinois Press, 1994), 50.

26. Casey, *Selling*, 292–93, 334–35.

27. Mark Ellis, *Race, War, and Surveillance: African Americans and the United States Government during World War I* (Bloomington: Indiana University Press, 2001); Gerald Horne, *Race War! White Supremacy and the Japanese Attack on the British Empire* (New York: New York University Press, 2004); Gerald Horne, "Civil Rights/Cold War," *Guild Practitioner* 48 (1991).

28. Kovel, *Red Hunting*, 18.

29. David S. Foglesong, *The American Mission and the "Evil Empire"* (Cambridge: Cambridge University Press, 2007), 58.

30. Bolshevism is, in fact, as anti-racial as it is anti-social. To the Bolshevik mind, with its furious hatred of constructive ability and its fanatical determination to enforce leveling, proletarian equality, the very existence of superior biological values is a crime. Bolshevism has vowed the proletarianization of the world, beginning with the white peoples. To this end it not only foments social rev-

olution within the white world itself, but it also seeks to enlist the colored races in its grand assault on civilization. . .

Bolshevism thus reveals itself as the arch-enemy of civilization and the race. Bolshevism is the renegade, the traitor within the gates, who would betray the citadel, degrade the very fiber of our being, and ultimately hurl a rebarbarized, racially impoverished world into the most debased and hopeless of mongrelizations.

Therefore, Bolshevism must be crushed out with iron heels, no matter what the cost. If this means more war, let it mean more war. We know only too well war's dreadful toll, particularly on racial values. But what war-losses could compare with the losses inflicted by the living death of Bolshevism? There are some things worse than war, and Bolshevism stands foremost among those dread alternatives.

Lothrop Stoddard, *The Rising Tide of Color Against White World-Supremacy* (New York: Charles Scribner's Sons, 1920), 96.

31. Jeff Woods, *Black Struggle, Red Scare: Segregation and Anti-Communism in the South, 1948–1968* (Baton Rouge: Louisiana State University Press, 2004), 19–21; Manning Marable, *Race, Reform, and Rebellion: The Second Reconstruction and Beyond in Black America, 1945–2006* (Jackson: University Press of Mississippi, 2007), 14.

32. Thomas Borstelmann, *The Cold War and the Color Line: American Race Relations in the Global Arena* (Cambridge, MA: Harvard University Press, 2001), 109; Mary L. Dudziak, *Cold War Civil Rights: Race and the Image of American Democracy* (Princeton, NJ: Princeton University Press, 2000).

33. Ronald Takaki, *Double Victory: A Multicultural History of America in World War II* (New York: Back Bay Books, 2001), 3–4, 39.

34. See also Philip A. Klinkers and Rogers M. Smith, *The Unsteady March: The Rise and Decline of Racial Equality in America* (Chicago: University of Chicago Press, 1999), 202–41; Marable, *Race, Reform, and Rebellion*, 17.

35. George Lewis, *The White South and the Red Menace: Segregationists, Anticommunism, and Massive Resistance, 1945–1965* (Gainesville: University Press of Florida, 2004), 40; Borstelmann, *Cold War*, 108.

36. Lewis, *White South*, 44–45, 69–72; David F. Schmitz, *The United States and Right-Wing Dictatorships, 1965–1989* (Cambridge: Cambridge University Press, 2006), 10; on the Civil Rights Congress, see Gerald Horne, *Communist Front? The Civil Rights Congress, 1946–1956* (Rutherford: Fairleigh Dickinson University Press, 1988).

37. Marable, *Race, Reform, and Rebellion*, 18.

38. Marable, *Race, Reform, and Rebellion*, 17–27.

39. Martin Luther King Jr. et al., *The Papers of Martin Luther King, Jr.,: Threshold of a New Decade, January 1959–December 1960* (Berkeley and Los Angeles, CA: University of California Press, 2005), 5:5; on the

impact of India's independence struggle in African American formations, see Gerald Horne, *The End of Empires: African Americans and India* (Philadelphia: Temple University Press, 2008).

40. Quoted in Westad, *Global Cold War*, 106.

41. Malcolm X, "Speech on the Founding of the OAAU," June 28, 1964. Available at ThinkingTogether.org.

42. Vijay Prashad, *The Darker Nations: A Biography of the Short-Lived Third World* (New Delhi, India: Leftword Books, 2007), 120–27.

43. On "Americanism" and "good wars," see Gary Gerstle, "In the Shadow of Vietnam: Liberal Nationalism and the Problem of War," in *Americanism: New Perspectives on the History of an Ideal*, ed. Michael Kazin and Joseph A. McCartin (Chapel Hill: University of North Carolina Press, 2006), 128–44.

44. Gabriel Kolko, *Anatomy of a War: Vietnam, the United States, and the Modern Historical Experience* (New York: The New Press, 1994), 80–82.

45. For a detailed account of the Huk rebellion, see B. Tria Kerkvliet, *The Huk Rebellion: A Study of Peasant Revolt in the Philippines* (Lanham, MD: Rowman & Littlefield, 2002).

46. Gettleman et al., eds., *Vietnam and America*, 295.

47. For a discussion of US "atomic diplomacy" in the context of the Vietnam War, see Joseph Gerson, *Empire and the Bomb: How the US Uses Nuclear Weapons to Dominate the World* (London: Pluto Press, 2007), 130–66.

48. Kolko, *Anatomy*, 83–125; Seth Jacobs, *Cold War Mandarin: Ngo Dinh Diem and the Origins of America's War in Vietnam, 1950–1963* (Lanham, MD: Rowman & Littlefield, 2006), 135–36.

49. Were it not for this orthodoxy, the US leadership may have taken the advice universally given to it, even by rivals such as Kruschev, to stay out of Vietnam. Eric Hobsbawm, *Age of Extremes: The Short Twentieth Century, 1914–1991* (London: Penguin, 1994), 244.

50. Charles E. Neu, *America's Lost War: Vietnam, 1945–1975* (Wheeling, IL: Harlan Davidson Inc., 2005), 99–101; Jonathan Neale, *A People's History of the Vietnam War* (New York: The New Press, 2004), 62–80; Krenn, *Color of Empire*, 89–92.

51. Quoted in Mike Marqusee, *Redemption Song: Muhammad Ali and the Spirit of the Sixties* (New York and London: Verso, 2005), 240.

52. Ibid., 214–15.

53. Gettleman et al., *Vietnam and America*, 297–98.

54. Quoted in Tom Wells, *The War Within: America's Battle Over Vietnam* (Lincoln, Nebraska: iUniverse, 2005), 124.

55. Neale, *Vietnam War*, 127–29; Gettleman et al., *Vietnam and America*, 299.

56. Gettleman et al., *Vietnam and America*, 299.

57. Nancy Zaroulis and Gerald Sullivan, *Who Spoke Up?: American Protest Against the War in Vietnam, 1963–1975* (New York: Doubleday, 1984), 27–32; Melvin Small, *Antiwarriors: The Vietnam War and the Battle for America's Hearts and Minds* (Lanham, Maryland: Scholarly Resources, 2002), 5–6; Neale, *Vietnam War*, 127–29.

58. Gettleman et al., *Vietnam and America*, 296–97, 304; Small, *Antiwarriors*, 32–34.

59. Gettleman et al., *Vietnam and America*, 297–8; James G. Blight and Janet M. Lang, *The Fog of War: Lessons From the Life of Robert S. McNamara* (Lanham, MD: Rowman & Littlefield, 2005), 204.

60. Small, *Antiwarriors*, 3; Gettleman et al., *Vietnam and America*, 296–304.

61. Gettleman et al., *Vietnam and America*, 300–06.

62. Ibid., 296.

63. Gettleman et al., *Vietnam and America*, 297–8; Neale, *Vietnam War*, 127–29.

64. Levy, *New Left and Labor*, 47–51.

65. Levy, *New Left and Labor*, 49–58.

66. Quoted in Tom Wells, *The War Within: America's Battle Over Vietnam* (Bloomington, IN: iUniverse, 2005), 450.

67. Joe Allen, *Vietnam: The (Last) War the U.S. Lost* (Chicago: Haymarket Books, 2008), 118.

68. It's worth observing that a great deal of the literature either ignores the SWP's role completely or is unfairly hostile and condescending to this "Trotskyite" party. Where they are acknowledged, it is usually to describe the rigidity, dogma, and sometimes destructive behavior of the party in the movement, at the expense of any fair assessment of their constructive role. For some discussion of the Cold War's impact on the Trotskyist groups, see Stanley Aronowitz, "Is It Time for a New Radical Party?," *Situations* I, no. 2 (2006); on criticisms of the SWP, unfortunately one-sided and laced with contempt, see Zaroulis and Sullivan, *Who Spoke Up?*, 215–16, 335–36; for more measured criticism, see Joe Allen, *Vietnam*, 118; Geoff Bailey, "The Rise and Fall of SDS," *International Socialist Review* 31 (September–October 2003); Small, *Antiwarriors*, 29–32, 47; for memoirs from SWP members, see Fred Halstead, *Out Now! A Participant's Account of the Movement in the US Against the Vietnam War* (Atlanta: Pathfinder, 1991); and Sheppard, *The Party*.

69. Gettleman et al., *Vietnam and America*, 300; David Cortright, *Soldiers in Revolt: GI Resistance during the Vietnam War* (Chicago: Haymarket Books, 2005), 70.

70. Gettleman et al., *Vietnam and America*, 300–06; Cortright, *Soldiers in*

Revolt, 3–27, 43–47, 167–71.

71. Arthur Schlesinger Jr., *The Bitter Heritage: Vietnam and American Democracy 1941–1966* (New York: Houghton Mifflin, 1967), 19–79, 102–07; Noam Chomsky, *"Bitter Heritage—*a Review," in *American Power and the New Mandarins* (New York: The New Press, 2002), 295–307; Robert Tomes, *Apocalypse Then: American Intellectuals and the Vietnam War* (New York: New York University Press, 1998), 9–122.

72. Kevin L. Yuill, *Richard Nixon and the Rise of Affirmative Action: The Pursuit of Racial Equality in an Era of Limits* (Lanham, MD: Rowman and Littlefield, 2006), 100; Hal Bochin, *Richard Nixon: Rhetorical Strategist* (Westport, CT: Greenwood Press, 1990), 58.

73. Dan Hind, *The Return of the Public* (New York and London: Verso, 2010), 79–82.

Chapter Five

Fred Halliday, *The Making of the Second Cold War* (New York and London: Verso, 1986), 242; quoted in Steven Rattner, "Volcker Asserts US Must Trim Living Standard," *New York Times*, October 17, 1989. Note that Volcker was not expressing a Reaganite nostrum. This was also the view of the Carter White House; Jonathan Schell, *The Fate of the Earth and the Abolition* (Palo Alto, CA: Stanford University Press, 2000), 117–18.

1. See Callinicos, *Imperialism and Global Political Economy*, 184–87.

2. David Harvey, *A Brief History of Neoliberalism* (Oxford: Oxford University Press, 2005), 8–9.

3. See Eric Lichten, *Class, Power and Austerity: The New York City Fiscal Crisis* (South Hadley, MA: Bergin & Garvey, 1986).

4. Harman, *Zombie Capitalism*, 201.

5. Harvey, *Brief History*, 27–29.

6. See Nicholas Guilhot, *The Democracy Makers: Human Rights and International Order* (New York: Columbia University Press, 2005).

7. Lawrence S. Wittner, *Confronting the Bomb: A Short History of the World Nuclear Disarmament Movement* (Palo Alto, CA: Stanford University Press, 2009), 141–42; Foglesong, *American Mission,"* 174–79.

8. Wittner, *Confronting the Bomb*, 142–43.

9. Noam Chomsky, *Turning the Tide: U.S. Intervention in Central America and the Struggle for Peace* (Boston, MA: South End Press, 1999), 177–78.

10. John Lofland, *Polite Protesters: The American Peace Movement of the 1980s* (Syracuse, NY: Syracuse University Press, 1994), 265; David Cortright, "Assessing Peace Movement Effectiveness in the 1980s," *Peace*

& Change 16, no. 1 (January 1991).

11. Wittner, *Confronting the Bomb*, 144–50; David S. Meyer, *A Winter of Discontent: The Nuclear Freeze and American Politics* (Westport, CT: Greenwood Press, 1990), 137–38; Lawrence S. Wittner, "What Activists Can Learn from the Nuclear Freeze Movement," *History News Network*, August 18, 2003; Lawrence S. Wittner, "The Nuclear Freeze and Its Impact," *Arms Control Today*, December 2010.

12. Ann Morissett Davidon, "The US Anti-Nuclear Movement," *Bulletin of the Atomic Scientists*, December 1979.

13. Wittner, *Struggle Against the Bomb*, 76–77.

14. Wittner, *Confronting the Bomb*, 152–5; Wittner, "Nuclear Freeze."

15. Robert Kleidman, *Organizing for Peace: Neutrality, the Test Ban, and the Freeze* (Syracuse, NY: Syracuse University Press, 1993), 137–38

16. Linda Pershing, *The Ribbon Around the Pentagon: Peace by Piecemakers* (Knoxville: University of Tennessee Press, 1996), 71–72; Wittner, *Struggle Against the Bomb*, 72–73.

17. Barbara Epstein, *Political Protest and Cultural Revolution: Nonviolent Direct Action in the 1970s and 1980s* (Berkeley and Los Angeles: University of California Press, 1993), 161–63.

18. Wittner, *Struggle Against the Bomb*, 76; Meyer, *Winter of Discontent*, 247–50; for an exhaustingly detailed account of the freeze campaign in Congress, see Douglas C. Waller, *Congress and the Nuclear Freeze: An Inside Look at the Politics of a Mass Movement* (Amherst: University of Massachusetts Press, 1987).

19. Wittner, *Confronting the Bomb*, 166–70; Wittner, "Nuclear Freeze."

20. Cagan, a socialist-feminist, civil rights activist, and long-standing peace activist who continues to be influential on the US left, is today a member of the Committees of Correspondence for Democracy and Socialism, a group she cofounded, which split from the CPUSA after the dissolution of the Soviet Union in 1991. For some biographical background, see Dick Cluster, *They Should Have Served That Cup of Coffee: 7 Radicals Remember the Sixties* (Boston, MA: South End Press, 1979), 225–60.

21. Christian Smith, *Resisting Reagan: The U.S. Central America Peace Movement* (Chicago: University of Chicago Press, 1996), 117–19, 175.

22. Schmitz, *The United States and Right-Wing Dictatorships*, 85–86, 134–35; George White Jr., *Holding the Line: Race, Racism, and American Foreign Policy toward Africa, 1953–1961* (Lanham, MD: Rowman and Littlefield, 2001), 91–109.

23. Borstelmann, *Cold War and the Color Line*, 250–51; Stephen Ellis and Tsepo Sechaba, *Comrades Against Apartheid: The ANC and the South African Communist Party in Exile* (Bloomington: Indiana University

Press, 1992), 90; Y. G.-M. Lulat, *United States Relations with South Africa: A Critical Overview from the Colonial Period to the Present* (New York: Peter Lang Publishing, 2008), 217–44.

24. Schmitz, *Right-Wing Dictatorships*, 96.

25. Sarah A. Soule, "The Student Divestment Movement in the United States and Tactical Diffusion: The Shantytown Protest," *Social Forces* 75, no. 3 (March 1997); Donald R. Culverson, "The Politics of the Anti-Apartheid Movement in the United States, 1969–1986," *Political Science Quarterly* 111, no. 1 (Spring 1996).

26. Sarah A. Soule, "The Diffusion of an Unsuccessful Innovation," *Annals of the American Academy of Political and Social Science* (1999); Gay W. Seidman, "Monitoring Multinationals: Lessons from the Anti-Apartheid Era," *Politics & Society* 31 (2003); Christabel Gurney, "The 1970s: The Anti-Apartheid Movement's Difficult Decade," *Journal of Southern Africa Studies* 35, no. 2 (2009); Lulat, *United States Relations*, 292–94; Francis Njubi Nesbitt, *Race for Sanctions: African Americans against Apartheid, 1946–1994* (Bloomington: Indiana University Press, 2004), 132.

27. Sylvia Hill, "Presentation: The Free South Africa Movement," Durban, South Africa, October 10–13, 2004; Ann Wilcox Seidman, *Apartheid, Militarism and the U.S. Southeast* (Trenton, NJ: Africa World Press, 1990), 69; Nesbitt, *Race for Sanctions*, 123–32; Cheryl Hudson and Gareth Davies, *Ronald Reagan and the 1980s: Perceptions, Policies, Legacies* (Hampshire, UK: Palgrave Macmillan, 2008), 124.

28. Culverson, "Politics of the Anti-Apartheid Movement"; on the constructivist argument regarding apartheid and US policy, see Audie Klotz, "Norms Reconstituting Interests: Global Racial Equality and U.S. Sanctions against South Africa," *International Organization* 49, no. 3 (Summer 1995).

29. Soule, "Diffusion."

30. Kevin Danaher, "Confronting Southern Africa Solidarity Work," *Issue: A Journal of Opinion* 18, no. 2 (Summer 1990); Lulat, *United States Relations*, 299.

31. Danaher, "Confronting Southern Africa Solidarity Work"; Hill, "Presentation."

32. Jeane J. Kirkpatrick, "Dictatorship and Double Standards," *Commentary* (November 1979), www.commentarymagazine.com/article/dictatorships-double-standards; Greg Grandin, *Empire's Workshop: Latin America, the United States and the Rise of the New Imperialism* (New York: Metropolitan Books, 2006), 100–06.

33. William I. Robinson, *Promoting Polyarchy: Globalization, US Intervention, and Hegemony* (Cambridge: Cambridge University Press, 1996),

222–23; Noam Chomsky, *The Culture of Terrorism* (London: Pluto Press, 1989), 42.

34. Héctor Perla Jr., "*Si Nicaragua Venció, El Salvador Vencerá*: Central American Agency in the Creation of the U.S.–Central American Peace and Solidarity Movement," *Latin American Research Review* 43, no. 2 (2008).

35. Sharon Erickson Nepstad, "Creating Transnational Solidarity: The Use of Narrative in the U.S.–Central America Peace Movement," *Mobilization: An International Journal* 6, no. 1 (2001): 21–36; Robert Surbrug, *Beyond Vietnam: The Politics of Protest in Massachusetts, 1974–1990* (Amherst: University of Massachusetts Press, 2009), 176–77; Smith, *Resisting Reagan*, 60–61.

36. Smith, *Resisting Reagan*, 60–70.

37. Ibid., 70–78.

38. Ibid., 60–61, 78–86.

39. For the full background on the FBI's campaign, see Ross Gelbspan, *Break-Ins, Death Threats and the FBI: Covert War Against the Central America Movement* (Boston, MA: South End Press, 1992); Bud Schulz and Ruth Schulz, *The Price of Dissent: Testimonies to Political Repression in America* (Berkeley and Los Angeles: University of California Press, 2001), 368–72; Roberto Marín Guzmán, "A Century of Palestinian Immigration into Central America: A Study of their Economic and Cultural Contributions," *International Journal of Middle East Studies* 37, no. 2 (May 2005); Political Research Associates, "The FBI Probe of CISPES," available at PublicEye.org; Ward Churchill, *The Cointelpro Papers: Documents from the FBI's Secret Wars against Dissent in the United States* (Boston, MA: South End Press, 2002), 17; Holly Sklar, *Washington's War on Nicaragua* (Boston, MA: South End Press, 1988), 353–55.

40. Gelbspan, *Break-Ins*, 209–19.

41. Ethel Brookes and Winifred Tate, "After the Wars: Cross-Border Organizing in Central America," *NACLA Report on the Americas* 32 (1999); for CISPES campaigning today, see cispes.org.

42. Department of Defense, "The Operation Desert Shield/Desert Storm Timeline," *American Forces Press Service News Articles*, August 8, 2000; Fred Halliday, *The Middle East in International Relations: Power, Politics and Ideology* (Cambridge: Cambridge University Press, 2005), 58; Marion Farouk-Sluglett and Peter Sluglett, *Iraq since 1948: From Revolution to Dictatorship* (London: IB Tauris, 2003), 284–87; Zbigniew Brzezinski, *Second Chance: Three Presidents and the Crisis of American Superpower* (New York: Perseus Books, 2007), 58–59; Noam Chomsky, *Deterring Democracy* (New York: Vintage, 1992), 190–93; A. Kitty, *Don't Believe It: How Lies Become News* (New York: Disinformation, 2005), 143–46.

43.   Richard Sobel, *The Impact of Public Opinion on US Foreign Policy Since Vietnam* (Oxford: Oxford University Press, 2001), 145–48; John Mueller, "American Opinion and the Gulf War," in *The Political Psychology of the Gulf War: Leaders, Publics and the Process of Conflict*, ed. Fred I. Greenstein and Stanley Allen Renshon (Pittsburgh: University of Pittsburgh Press, 1993), 202.

44.   Mueller, "American Opinion and the Gulf War," 209; Zinn, *People's History*, 610.

45.   Mueller, "American Opinion and the Gulf War," 203; Thomas D. Beamish, Harry Molotch, and Richard Flacks, "Who Supports the Troops? Vietnam, the Gulf War, and the Making of Collective Memory," *Social Problems* 42, no. 3 (August 1995).

46.   Robert A. Hackett and Yuezi Zhao, "Challenging a Master Narrative: Peace Protest and Opinion/Editorial: Discourse in the US Press during the Gulf War," *Discourse Society* 5 (1994); Patrick G. Coy and Lynne M. Woehrle, "Constructing Identity and Oppositional Knowledge: The Framing Practices of Peace Movement Organizations during the Persian Gulf War," *Sociological Spectrum* 16 (1996); for a detailed analysis of the media's framing strategies, see Douglas Kellner, "The 'Crisis in the Gulf' and the Mainstream Media," in *The Persian Gulf TV War* (Boulder, CO: Westview Press, 1992), available at http://gseis.ucla.edu/faculty/kellner/essays/gulfwarch2.pdf.

47.   Mark Van Ells, "No Blood for Oil: Protesting the Persian Gulf War in Madison, Wisconsin," *Journal of the Study for Peace and Conflict* (1998–1999), jspc.library.wisc.edu/issues/1998-1999/article3.html.

48.   "The Antiwar Movement: A Great Beginning," *International Socialist Review* 26 (November–December 2002).

Chapter Six

Patrick E. Tyler, "A New Power in the Streets," *New York Times*, February 17, 2003; Peter Philips, "A Report from Cairo on the International Campaign Against US Aggression on Iraq," *Counterpunch*, December 17, 2002; Mike Prysner, "Winter Soldier Testimonies," YouTube video, Iraq Veterans Against the War. Available at www.youtube.com/watch?v=4i5ZUfpxnV0 and www.youtube.com/watch?v=-iTdxBECos8&feature=related; quoted in *The Ground Truth: After the Killing Ends*, directed by Patricia Foulkrod (New York: Plum Pictures, 2006).

1.   "Excerpts from Pentagon's Plan: 'Prevent the Re-Emergence of a New Rival,'" *New York Times*, March 8, 1992.

2.   Zbigniew Brzezinski, *The Grand Chessboard: American Primacy and*

Its Geostrategic Imperatives (New York: Basic Books, 1998), 30, 39–40. Expansionist intent was also signaled by Clintonite National Security Advisor Anthony Lake, who explained the shift "from containment to enlargement" in terms of Wilsonian shibboleths of expanding the scope of "market democracies"—or, in another idiom, "capitalist democracies." Such expansion would "expand our exports and create American jobs" while improving "living conditions," and encouraging domestic liberalization. This is the dominant ideological register of neoliberal imperialism. See Anthony Lake, "From Containment to Enlargement," *DISAM Journal* (1993–94). For a left-wing critique, see Noam Chomsky, "The Clinton Vision," *Z Magazine*, December 1993.

3. Giovanni Arrighi, *Adam Smith in Beijing: Lineages of the Twenty-First Century* (New York and London: Verso, 2008), 149–51.

4. Peter Gowan, *The Global Gamble: Washington's Faustian Bid for World Dominance* (New York and London: Verso, 1999), 248–59.

5. For by far the best contemporary history of the Yugoslav breakup, see Susan Woodward, *Balkan Tragedy: Chaos and Dissolution after the Cold War* (Washington, DC: Brookings Institution Press, 1995).

6. For a detailed account of the geopolitical logic of US intervention in the former Yugoslavia, see David N. Gibbs, *First Do No Harm: Humanitarian Intervention and the Destruction of Yugoslavia* (Nashville, TN: Vanderbilt University Press, 2009); for my own argument on the nature of the Yugoslav breakup and the subsequent wars, contrasted with the intellectual and ideological responses in the United States, see Seymour, *Liberal Defence of Murder*, 190–216.

7. Quoted in Vassilis K. Fouskas, *Zones of Conflict: US Foreign Policy in the Balkans and the Greater Middle East* (London: Pluto Press, 2003), 49.

8. Bob Edwards and Sam Marullo, "Organizational Mortality in a Declining Social Movement: The Demise of Peace Movement Organizations in the End of the Cold War Era," *American Sociological Review* 60, no. 6 (December 1995).

9. See Kathy Kelly, *Other Lands Have Dreams: From Baghdad to Pekin Prison* (Petrolia, CA: Counterpunch Books/AK Press, 2005).

10. Joy Gordon, *Invisible War: The United States and the Iraq Sanctions* (Cambridge, MA: Harvard University Press, 2010), 20–38.

11. Kathy Kelly, "Raising Voices: The Children of Iraq, 1990–1999," in *Iraq Under Siege*, ed. Anthony Arnove (Boston, MA: South End Press, 2000), 146.

12. Geoffrey Leslie Simons, *The Scourging of Iraq: Sanctions, Law, and Natural Justice* (Hampshire, UK: Palgrave Macmillan, 1998), 224–25.

13. Kirsty Gathergood and Dave Rolstone, "Helping Children in Iraq,"

Lancet 356, issue 9223 (July 1, 2000).

14. "'We Will Not Pay a Penny of This Fine': Federal Judge Fines Voices in the Wilderness $20,000 for Taking Medicine to Iraq," *Counterpunch*, August 15, 2005.

15. Sharon Smith, "Building the Movement to End Sanctions," in *Iraq Under Siege*, ed. Arnove, 222–38; Rae Vogeler, "The U.S. Movement against Sanctions on Iraq," *Against the Current* 93 (July/August 2001).

16. Hans von Sponeck, *A Different Kind of War: The UN Sanctions Regime in Iraq* (New York: Berghahn Books, 2006); Scott Ritter, "The Case for Iraq's Qualitative Disarmament," *Arms Control Today*, June 2000.

17. For the whole sordid story, see Peter Hallward, *Damming the Flood: Haiti, Aristide, and the Politics of Containment* (New York and London: Verso, 2007).

18. See Jeffrey M. Ayres, "Framing Collective Action against Neoliberalism: The Case of the 'Anti-Globalization' Movement," *Journal of World Systems Research* 10, no. 1 (Winter 2004).

19. For an account of Nader's politics and his relationship to the new left that developed after Seattle, see Joel Geier, "Nader 2000: Challenging the Parties of Corporate America," *International Socialist Review* 13 (August–September 2000).

20. Alex Callinicos, "The Anticapitalist Movement after Genoa and New York," in *Implicating Empire: Globalization and Resistance in the 21st Century World Order*, ed. Stanley Aronowitz and Heather Gautney (New York: Basic Books, 2002), 134.

21. J. C. Myers, "What Is Anticapitalism?," in *The Anti-Capitalism Reader: Imagining a Geography of Opposition*, ed. Joel Schalit (New York: Akashic Books, 2002), 25–26.

22. Barbara Epstein, "Anarchism and the Anti-Globalization Movement," *Monthly Review* 53, no. 4 (September 2001).

23. For some trenchant critiques of this argument, see Gopal Balakrishnan, ed., *Debating Empire* (New York and London: Verso, 2003).

24. Alex Callinicos, "The Future of the Anticapitalist Movement," *Anticapitalism: Where Now?*, ed. Hannah Dee (London: Bookmarks, 2004), 98.

25. The Iraq Liberation Act of 1998, passed with Clinton's blessing, called for the overthrow of Saddam Hussein's government—though as yet not authorizing "the use of United States Armed Forces."

26. Gopal Balakrishnan, *Antagonistics: Capitalism and Power in an Age of War* (New York and London: Verso, 2009), 37.

27. Stephen Holmes, *The Matador's Cape: America's Reckless Response to Terror* (Cambridge: Cambridge University Press, 2007), 170.

28. See Seymour, *Liberal Defence of Murder*, for extensive background.

29. On the escalation of police brutality toward protesters, see Luis A. Fernandez, *Policing Dissent: Social Control and the Anti-Globalization Movement* (New Brunswick, NJ: Rutgers University Press, 2008).

30. Michael T. Heaney and Fabio Rojas, "Coalition Dissolution, Mobilization and Network Dynamics in the US Antiwar Movement," in *Research in Social Movements, Conflicts and Change*, ed. Patrick G. Coy (Bingley, UK: Emerald Group Publishing, 2008), 46–47.

31. T. V. Reed, "Globalization and the 21st Century US Peace Movement," in *Peace Movements and Pacifism After September 11*, ed. Shin Chiba and Thomas J. Schoenbaum (Cheltenham, UK/New York: Edward Elgar Publishing, 2008), 183.

32. Michael Albert, "Ten Q&A on Antiwar Organizing," *ZNet*, October 24, 2002.

33. Barbara Epstein, "Notes on the Antiwar Movement," *Monthly Review* 55, no. 3 (July–August 2003).

34. Ibid.

35. UFPJ is credited with organizing 150 antiwar rallies across the United States in January 2003. Ted Gottfried, *The Fight for Peace: A History of Antiwar Movements in America* (Minneapolis, MN: Twenty-First Century Books, 2005), 113.

36. "San Francisco Ends World Peace Rallies," BBC News online, February 17, 2003.

37. David Cortright, "A Peaceful Superpower: The Movement against War in Iraq," in *Peace Movements and Pacifism After September 11*, ed. Chiba and Schoenbaum, 201; David Michael Smith, "The Crisis in the U.S. Anti-War Movement—and How to Overcome It," *Journal for the Study of Peace and Conflict* (2005–2006).

38. See the websites for USLAW and CODE PINK at uslaboragainstwar.org and codepink4peace.org, respectively; Rachel V. Kutz-Flamenbaum, "Code Pink, Raging Grannies, and the Missile Dick Chicks: Feminist Performance Activism in the Contemporary Anti-War Movement," *NWSA Journal* 19, no. 1 (2007).

39. Michael T. Heaney and Fabio Rojas, "Coalition Dissolution, Mobilization and Network Dynamics in the US Antiwar Movement," in *Research in Social Movements, Conflicts and Change*, ed. Coy, 67–68; Maya Schenwar, "Counter-Recruitment Day Sweeps U.S. Colleges," *CommonDreams.org*, December 5, 2005.

40. Dahr Jamail, *The Will to Resist: Soldiers Who Refuse to Fight in Iraq and Afghanistan* (Chicago: Haymarket Books, 2009), 3.

41. See Heaney and Rojas, "Coalition Dissolution," 47. The Muslim American Society was one of those to take issue with UFPJ's stance.

Its executive director Mahdi Bray complained that UFPJ's aversion to pro-Palestine activism underlay its decision in 2005 to march separately from an antiwar rally called by ANSWER: "UFPJ called for a segregated March in DC after the A.N.S.W.E.R. Coalition made the initial call. They listed all kinds of excuses why they can't join a unity effort. The reality is that a strong peace agenda put forth by the Muslim Community is not a reality that UFPJ is willing to accept and that is most unfortunate for the Peace and Justice Movement. I was there at a unity event when UFPJ removed the Palestinian flag from the stage. That speaks volumes for the leadership of UFPJ. However, I don't believe that the UFPJ leadership's aversion to the Palestinian struggle is representative of the position of UFPJ's grass roots." See "National Muslim Leadership Rejects UFPJ 'Segregation' Approach to September 24 March on Washington," Muslim American Society, July 2005.

42. Joe Stork, "The American New Left and Palestine," *Journal of Palestine Studies* 2, no. 1 (Autumn 1972); Sunaina Maira and Magid Shihade, "Meeting Asian/Arab American Studies Thinking Race, Empire, and Zionism in the U.S.," *Journal of Asian American Studies* 9, no. 2 (June 2006); Marilyn Naimark, "American Jews and Palestine: The Impact of the Gulf War," *Middle East Report* 175, 19–32; Palestine and Israel in the New Order (March–April 1992); Charmaine Seitz, "ISM at the Crossroads: the Evolution of the International Solidarity Movement," *Journal of Palestine Studies* 32, no. 4 (Summer 2003); Josie Sandercock, *Peace under Fire: Israel/Palestine and the International Solidarity Movement* (New York and London: Verso, 2004), 17–24.

43. Snehal Shingavi, "Students Fight for Justice in Palestine," *International Socialist Review* 23 (May–June 2002); Peter Schworm, "Hampshire College Cuts Ties with Fund Invested in Israel," *Boston Globe*, February 12, 2009; see "SJP Mission Statement," USC Students for Justice in Palestine, August 29, 2006.

44. See Omar Barghouti, *Boycott Divestment Sanctions: The Global Struggle for Palestinian Rights* (Chicago: Haymarket Books, 2011), 19, 27.

45. Elizabeth Martinez, "Looking for Color in the Anti-War Movement," *Z Magazine*, November 2003; Epstein, "Notes on the Antiwar Movement"; Meredith Kolodner, "The Future of the Antiwar Movement," *International Socialist Review* 39 (January–February 2005); Smith, "Crisis in the U.S. Anti-War Movement."

46. Toussaint, *Contemporary US Peace Movement*, 122–24; Heaney and Rojas, "Coalition Dissolution," 46–70; "United For Peace and Justice Statement on Obama's Iraq Withdrawal Plan," North Carolina Peace Ac-

tion, available at http://www.ncpeaceaction.org/resources/ufpj-obama
-iraq-plan.html.

47. Toussaint, *Contemporary US Peace Movement*, 122–24; Heaney and
Rojas, "Coalition Dissolution," 46–70.

48. It is only fair to acknowledge that this is a volte-face reversal of my previous argument, wherein I charged Cockburn with "pessimism" (a cardinal sin on the left), based on "a misunderstanding of how antiwar
movements have succeeded in the past." Richard Seymour, "Resisting
the War," *Socialist Worker* (UK), November 17, 2007.

49. Alexander Cockburn, "Whatever Happened to the Antiwar Movement?," *New Left Review* 46 (July–August 2007).

50. Michael T. Heaney and Fabio Rojas, "The Partisan Dynamics of Contention: Demobilization of the Antiwar Movement in the United States,
2007–2009," *Mobilization: An International Journal* 16, no. 1 (2011).

51. For insurgent attacks, see Department of Defense, "Measuring Stability
and Security in Iraq," March 2010; on the Mahdi Army, see Richard
Seymour, "The Sadrist Revolt," *MR Zine*, June 4, 2008; also see Patrick
Cockburn, *Muqtada al-Sadr and the Fall of Iraq* (London: Faber &
Faber, 2008).

Epilogue

1. In a series of announcements in May 1940, he announced that the United
States would develop a two-ocean navy, a large standing army, and a mil-
itary-industrial base capable of producing sixty thousand aircraft per
annum. Figures given in Adam Tooze, "Could Hitler Have Won?," talk
given at the Marxism 2004 conference, Institute of Education, London.

2. See Regin Schmidt, *Red Scare: FBI and the Origins of Anticommunism
in the United States, 1919–1943* (Copenhagen, Denmark: Museum Tusculanum Press, 2000), 346–47.

3. For some background on this subject, see Seymour, *Liberal Defence of
Murder*, 250–60.

4. Some of this section is adapted from my essay "Imperialism and Revolution in the Middle East," *Socialist Review*, May 2011.

5. See Charles Levinson, Margaret Coker, and Jay Solomon, "How Cairo,
U.S. Were Blindsided by Revolution," *Wall Street Journal*, February 2,
2011.

6. Dan Murphy, "Joe Biden Says Egypt's Mubarak No Dictator, He
Shouldn't Step Down...," *Christian Science Monitor*, January 27, 2011;
Andrew Sparrow, "Blair Says Leak of Palestine Papers 'Destabilising'
for Peace Process," *Guardian*, January 28, 2011.

7. Laura Rozen, "Polls Show American Public Not Sold on Libya Intervention," *Envoy*, March 18, 2011.

8. See David Boaz, "What Ever Happened to the Antiwar Movement?" *Britannica Blog*, March 21, 2011.

9. On the controversy surrounding ANSWER's antiwar activism, see Clay Claiborne, "No Libyans Allowed at ANSWER Libya Forum," *Daily Kos*, June 23, 2011; Michael Fiorentino and Jeremy Tully, "A Disservice to the Antiwar Movement," *SocialistWorker.org*, July 12, 2011; and ANSWER's defense, "ANSWER LA Responds to Attack on Eyewitness Libya Forum," ANSWER Coalition, June 24, 2011.

10. See UFPJ, "End War on Libya," press release, March 25, 2011.

11. See Juan Cole, "An Open Letter to the Left on Libya," *Informed Comment*, March 27, 2011.

12. On the intervention in Haiti, see Hallward, *Damming the Flood*.

13. Gilbert Achcar, "Libyan Developments," *ZNet*, March 19, 2011; Gilbert Achcar, "Libya: A Legitimate and Necessary Debate from an Anti-imperialist Perspective," *ZNet*, March 25, 2011; Gilbert Achcar, "NATO's 'Conspiracy' against the Libyan Revolution," *Jadaliyya*, August 16, 2011. For what it's worth, the weakness of Achcar's position seems to me to fall significantly on his analysis of the motivations for US involvement. In declaring a clear US interest in toppling Gaddafi and preventing human rights abuses, he subscribes to a bizarrely reductionist, inverted "war for oil" argument. This argument is fatally weakened by the apparent lack of evidence for the coming massacre that would allegedly have compelled the United States to apply an oil embargo. It is also undermined by the fact that an oil embargo was nonetheless imposed. And it is further weakened by the fact that it doesn't acknowledge that US state planners were if anything even more divided over Libya than over Iraq, and that the decision to intervene thus couldn't reflect such a determinate, unambiguous "interest." As a result, Achcar later interprets the lack of aggression in NATO's bombing campaign as a deliberate effort to protect the Gaddafi regime until the rebel leadership is fully under control. In fact, the rebel leadership has rarely seemed to be anything but under control. Achcar avoids the possibility that the United States was actually being *cautious* for a variety of reasons: because the commitment of more forces may ultimately lead to a ground war that the defense establishment doesn't want; because there are leading elements both within the US and within the NATO coalition who were skeptical of the war to begin with; because imperial state-building projects appear, post-Iraq, to be very expensive ventures, susceptible to catastrophic failure, and it simply made more sense to try and leverage Gaddafi out of the existing

state that will remain intact; and because the likely bloodshed resulting from escalation may undermine any remaining political support for the war. In the end, far from undermining the opposition advance, the strategy of deliberately low-intensity bombing was one of the factors resulting in its success. Understanding US motives for involvement in terms of a hastily concocted attempt to intervene in the Middle East revolutionary process *on the side of the forces of conservatism* would have rendered NATO's subsequent conduct predictable.

14. Patrick Cockburn, "Amnesty Questions Claim that Gaddafi Ordered Rape as Weapon of War," *Independent*, June 24, 2011; "Libya: Renewed Rocket Attacks Target Civilians in Misratah," *Amnesty.org*, June 24, 2011; Alan J. Kuperman, "False Pretense for War in Libya?," *Boston Globe*, April 14, 2011.

15. Kim Sengupta, "Libyan Rebels Have Conceded Ground since Bombing Began," *Independent*, July 27, 2011.

16. See Patrick Cockburn, "Why the West Is Committed to the Murderous Rebels in Libya," *Independent*, July 31, 2011; Chris Stephen, "Libyan Rebel Leader Sacks Entire Cabinet," *Guardian*, August 9, 2011.

17. Sam Dagher, "Libya City Torn by Tribal Feud," *Wall Street Journal*, June 21, 2011; Luis Sinco, "Journalists Visit Prisoners Held by Rebels in Libya," *Los Angeles Times*, March 23, 2011; Berthold Eder, "Es fand eine regelrechte Jagd auf Migranten statt," *Der Standard*, July 6, 2011.

18. For detailed background, see Richard Seymour, "Libya's Spectacular Revolution Has Been Disgraced by Racism," *Guardian*, August 30, 2011. On ethnic cleansing, see David Enders, 'Empty Village Raises Concerns about Fate of Black Libyans," *McClatchy*, September 13, 2011.

19. See Sheila Carapico, "No Exit: Yemen's Existential Crisis," *Middle East Report Online*, May 3, 2011. On negotiations with the Syrian opposition, see Jay Solomon and Nour Malas, "Syria Opposition Seeks No-Fly Zone," *Wall Street Journal*, September 29, 2011.

20. "Dissidents in Syria Reject Foreign Intervention: Kilo," Agence France-Presse, September 30, 2011; the Local Coordination Committees have put their statement in English on Facebook. See "Statement to the Syrian People," Facebook, August 29, 2011.

Acknowledgments

I am indebted to numerous people for their help in the drafting of this manuscript. First of all, thanks to Ashley Smith for giving me the conception for this book. He also provided abundant references and original materials while I was writing it and reviewed the early drafts with copious suggestions. Thanks also to Anthony Arnove and John McDonald, who were both very supportive of the project in a practical and moral sense. The team at Haymarket has been wonderful. Julie Fain was tireless and patient, even though I pushed deadlines well into their afterlife. And Dao Tran offered the most exacting and careful advice on my use of American English, as well as prompting much-needed clarifications of my arguments. Finally, thanks and love to my partner Marie, who assisted in the research and to whom this book is dedicated.

Index

E

East Timor, 179
Egypt, 196, 204–5, 206
Einstein, Albert, 93
Eisenhower, Dwight D., 111–12, 148
El Salvador, 156–62 passim
Empire (Hardt and Negri), 182
Encounter, 132
Eperjesi, John, 42
Epstein, Barbara, 186
European Nuclear Disarmament
    (END), 147
Ewing, Scott, 188

F

Fagen, David, 51
Faribundo Martí National Liberation
    Front (FMLN), 160
Farouk, 205
FBI, xxii, 85, 160–62
Fellowship of Reconciliation (FOR),
    156, 165
Ferguson Niall, x
Fisher, Harry, 90
Florida, 6, 13, 24
FMLN. *See* Faribundo Martí Na-
    tional Liberation Front (FMLN)
FNLA. *See* National Front for the
    Liberation of Angola (FNLA)
FOR. *See* Fellowship of Reconcilia-
    tion (FOR)
Foreign Affairs, 132
Foreign Agents Registration Act,
    108, 160
Forsberg, Randall, 143, 144, 146
Fort Dearborn, 11
Foster, William Z., 106
France, 2, 5, 106; Indochina and,
    114, 120, 121
Franco, Francisco, 88–89, 93

Franklin, Benjamin, 4
Free South Africa Movement, 153
Free Trade Area of the Americas
    (FTAA), 180
Frelinghuysen, Theodore, 21
French and Indian War. *See* Seven-
    Year War
Friedman, Milton, 137
Frisbie, George, 46–47
Funston, Frederick, 51

G

Gaddafi, Muammar, 206–15 passim,
    251–52n13
Gaddafi, Saif al-Islam, 208
Gallagher, John, 37
Gandhi, Mohandas, 118
Garrett, Garet, 109
Garrison, William Lloyd, 19, 32, 49
Gates, Robert, 194
Gathergood, Kirsty, 178
George, Henry, 80
Georgia, 17, 20–21, 22, 122
Georgia (country), 195–96
Gergen, David, 146–47
Germany, xxi–xxii, 91; Haiti and, 75;
    Spanish Civil War and, 88–89;
    World War I and, 79, 82, 112,
    113. *See also* Anti-Comintern
    Pact; Hitler-Stalin Pact; Molotov-
    Ribbentrop Pact; West Germany
Ghana, 115
Ghoza, Hafiz, 209
Giddings, Joshua, 30
Glaspie, April, 163
Gleason, Thomas, 128
Goldsmith, Kristopher, 188
Goldwater, Barry, 128
Gompers, Samuel, 39, 40, 49, 53–54,
    68, 72, 82
Goodell, William, 31

About Haymarket Books

Haymarket Books is a nonprofit, progressive book distributor and publisher, a project of the Center for Economic Research and Social Change. We believe that activists need to take ideas, history, and politics into the many struggles for social justice today. Learning the lessons of past victories, as well as defeats, can arm a new generation of fighters for a better world. As Karl Marx said, "The philosophers have merely interpreted the world; the point, however, is to change it."

We take inspiration and courage from our namesakes, the Haymarket Martyrs, who gave their lives fighting for a better world. Their 1886 struggle for the eight-hour day reminds workers around the world that ordinary people can organize and struggle for their own liberation.

Visit us online at www.haymarketbooks.org.

Also from Haymarket Books

The Forging of the American Empire
Sidney Lens

Vietnam: The (Last) War the U.S. Lost
Joe Allen

The Democrats: A Critical History
Lance Selfa

The American Way of War: How Bush's Wars Became Obama's
Tom Engelhardt

North Star: A Memoir
Peter Camejo

Subterranean Fire: A History of Working-Class Radicalism in the United States
Sharon Smith

Winter Soldiers: An Oral History of Vietnam Veterans Against the War
Richard Stacewitz

About the Author

Richard Seymour is a socialist and writer, raised in Northern Ireland and living in London. He is the author of *The Liberal Defence of Murder* and *The Meaning of David Cameron*, and his work is published regularly in the *Guardian*. Seymour is currently researching a PhD dissertation at the London School of Economics.